A NEW CONCEPT OF DEVELOPMENT

A New Concept of Development
Development BASIC TENETS

François Perroux

CROOM HELM
London & Canberra

UNESCO
Paris

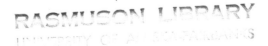

© 1983 Unesco

First published 1983 by the United Nations Educational, Scientific and Cultural Organization,
7 Place de Fontenoy, 75700 Paris, France
and
Croom Helm Ltd, Provident House, Burrell Row,
Beckenham, Kent BR3 1AT, United Kingdom

British Library Cataloguing in Publication Data

Perroux, François
   A new concept of development.
   1. Development psychology
   I. Title
   155   BF713
ISBN 0-7099-2040-7 (Croom Helm)
ISBN 92-3-102057-9 (Unesco)

Printed and bound in Great Britain
by Billing and Sons Ltd, Worcester.

CONTENTS

FOREWORD: DEVELOPMENT – TO WHAT END?

M.A. Sinaceur

Philosophy and Development Theory

Philosophy? Development? How are they connected? What traditional links are there between them? Diverse considerations point to the existence of some basic link. Firstly, it has been recognized since Plato's time that thought proceeds from contradiction, and the notion of development brings out the major paradox of our era: the desire for progress and mistrust of its consequences. Secondly, the approach to the whole question of development is, at once, the key to an understanding of the present and the real and, conversely, reflects in positive, critical terms a demand which must be regarded as springing from a rational view of the present, giving us a glimmer of light in the gloomy prospect facing mankind as the century draws to a close, or representing the first-fruits of a pattern for the future which will shape our potential to fit our designs.

What of the philosopher himself? What rôle can he play today? Simply that of a man who, despite the risks, in a field where actions and ideas are exposed to the extreme limit of egoism and ideology, seeks to demonstrate the illuminating value of intellectual effort. Analysing the ideas and theories propounded by the economic approach is an integral part of his elucidatory work, and in particular of the philosophical task. The latter's purpose and questioning aim not so much to impose a formula of the truth as to clarify the meaning and direction of research, which, like 'all knowledge and all ignorance', is especially prone 'to take opportunist paths'. Not that it is a matter merely of criticizing the biased orientations of research on development: also and above all eternal vigilance is needed, for the development universally desired and advocated cannot alter the fact that 'tyranny always has a happy beginning'.

No one is better qualified to say this than François Perroux, for whom the economic approach is not simply a matter of standing up to the test of reality but seeks to uphold the logic of truth in both the epistemic and the practical sphere, both as discursive truth and as

1

ethical truth. As truth unqualified, we should say, even if we were to
abandon the attempt to define truth (which is more than a symbol or
convenient convention), admitting – to illustrate the difficulty – that
Saint Augustine's comment about time applies also to truth: we
know that it is when no one asks us but not when we try to explain it!
What is involved is something much more than calculated truth,
truth-as-validity, or the rehabiliation of some particular system of
values: we must aim at action that is constantly inspired by
meditation on the meaning of action and the meaning of
knowledge, leading to thought that is both meditative and practical,
paying as much attention to our refusals and resistances as to the
analysing of our doctrines and our theories. Thought in this context
is in harmony with action in its highest significance. It strengthens us
in our insecurities; it is a bright ray of hope; it is essential for the
pursuit of that ideal of maximum results at minimum cost without
which economics can neither exist nor be imagined; it bolsters our
aspirations. It rescues them from the very real concatenation of
dangers which, when statically assessed, leads us to confuse the
crabbed old age of worn-out civilizations with the future fate of
civilization itself. To say, as the poet might have done, that the
promises of enlightenment may one day turn out to be 'a vain fancy
refuted by the shadows' is merely to say that enlightenment is not
vouchsafed to all. Development has not taken place: it represents a
dramatic growth of awareness, a promise, a matter of survival
indeed; intellectually, however, it is still only dimly perceived.

A Term with Many Meanings

Let us consider whether the term itself is to blame, at least in part,
for this obscurity. 'Development' means both the act of developing
and the resultant state. The ambiguity, however, is compounded by
another, more fundamental, ambiguity rooted in the vitalistic
images and even in the very substance of the history and science of
life, where it invariably implies a statement on the essence of
becoming, of change and of evolution.

Before taking on economic significance and political and
polemical functions, which can be seen in the constantly reiterated
distinction between development and growth, in the apologia of
development and in criticism of the 'myth' of development, the
'religion' of development, the 'illusions' of development, etc., the

term suffers from the original sin of having been born from the encounter of two realities: everyday reality, with its cohort of familiar images conjured up by the idea of anything that grows, and scientific reality, with the succession of changes, crises and corrections peculiar to it. And this history weighs all the more heavily on the notion because its evolution, in the context of the social sciences, has stabilized neither its meaning nor the strict positivity demanded for a scientific concept.

For this reason, without postulating a causal connection between the notions of growth, development and progress, and without assuming a logical connection in the transition from biological to economic and social knowledge, it is worth while to draw attention to the significant stages in the line of enquiry that is steadfastly set on breaking the tenuous links between the images of reality and the description of facts. This can teach us, firstly, something about relativity: development has been taken to mean growth, and growth – in the early biologists' discussions on the relationship between generation and development – was contrasted with the notion of development, and hence with the definition of 'generation', as being merely 'increase in size'! Secondly, something about modernity that is perhaps as far-reaching in its implications as was the law of falling bodies within its sphere of application; since Harvey, development has been the operative concept of the theory disseminated by his *Exercitationes de generatione animalium* (1651), the theory that overturned the principle adopted by Aristotle of the classification of living creatures according to their method of generation and put in its place the principle of *ex ovo omnia* – a principle that treated as identical things differentiated by Aristotle, undermined the foundations of the theory of spontaneous generation and opened the way to epigenesis, omnigenesis and a theory of life based exclusively on knowledge of life. And lastly, something about the relationship between science and ideology, in the elaboration – as complex as it is exemplary – of the nineteenth-century evolutionism that has permanently impregnated the concepts of economics, sociology , psychology and the philosophy of history. It is true, of course, that the new concepts in embryology introduced by Von Baer (1828), from whom Darwin and Spencer took their ideas, played their part in the erection of biological theory and social philosophy, and legitimized the terms 'development' and 'evolution': evolution – because of the importance of the problem of natural selection in the life process;

development – because of the spread of the ideas on progress of Comte, Spencer and their followers. First, Auguste Comte, who held that progress is development and that it is biology that gives history its fundamental laws; 'the term *development*, by its nature, has the inestimable advantage of directly determining wherein the true *perfecting* of mankind necessarily consists . . .'. (The italics are mine.) There is no idea of history being a human undertaking: it is nothing more than a law of nature. Hence development introduces and justifies the use of organic metaphors in representing human evolution as proceeding without crises, interruptions and innovations. Next, Spencer. Between Comte and Spencer, Darwin had introduced drama into life, with its essential reference to death; hence the different connotations preferred by Spencer at the end of the nineteenth century. The embryological model was succeeded by the epigenetic model, all evolution being regarded as proceeding from the simple to the complex, whether it be the evolution of the cosmos, of life, of man and his productions or of society and its forms. This increasing complexity, however, is the result of the organism's interaction with agents different from itself. All evolution is epigenetic, entailing structural modification and transition from homogeneity to heterogeneity and hence both growth and development. Admittedly, Spencer – unlike Marx in another version of the same model – adopted only the epigenetic aspect of Darwin's thesis concerning the struggle for life, as was to be expected both for reasons of tradition and because it enabled him to reconcile his synthesis with the requirements of political individualism and economic liberalism. The final result, then, was what has been called a vast engineering project, a specifically Spencerian project, based on totally unified knowledge. And the object of that project was to institute the various forms of cultural and social engineering that would fulfil on a world scale the promises of a specific model of human experience.

An Ideological Notion

We are therefore dealing with much more than the arbitrary extension of given concepts to domains in which their use is left ill-defined and poorly controlled because it is under-regulated. Under cover of an anti-theological view of things, there has grown up an anti-teleological view. What is more, it is a line of thought that challenges ends but without criticizing its own means or questioning its standards, the latter being assumed but not explicitly stated or seen as such. It is also a line of thought that has compromised research in the social sciences by giving dominating powers the pretext of civilizing intentions with which to salve their consciences.

Turning to the present, the context changes but the ambiguity remains. Hence those modes of discourse in which fact is confused with value, the idolatry of origins with fascination with the future, and nostalgia for pre-development with confidence in the spread of progress. Has it not been said that development is the West reproducing itself, and that the world could develop differently? Such an utterance crystallizes deeper questioning, the anxiety generated by a critical future. The critical aspect there is no doubt a symptom of the fact that a conflict situation is sanctioned and even legitimized by the recognition that development can never be defined in a universally satisfactory way, i.e. for all countries, all experiences and all requirements. Nor is it enough to say that development should be carried out differently, that it should take various paths. What then should determine this diversity within diversity? A form of development? Which one? What makes it 'a form of . . .' and of what development is it a form? If the paths so far followed seem impracticable, the paths ahead also seem impenetrable. We oscillate between a model that has lost its virtue and charm and an idea that has yet to demonstrate its effectiveness. This is in plain language what is usually referred to as 'the crisis'. For to paraphrase a famous remark, the problem of human destiny is nowadays expressed in terms of development: and the joint effort for the development of all takes on such urgency and dimensions that it is confused with survival and peace. The peace in question is world peace, hampered by the accumulation of wealth and productive and organizational innovation at specially favoured points; or redistributive peace in the sense that the economic system that causes conflicts reproduces them, in today's complex world, in the deepest strata of society, which are also the most vulnerable.

This cannot be regarded as a localized problem, short of proving that there are political and social microsystems capable of being understood without reference to the global, and hence international, environment; or else that resistance to the breaking-down process, which subordinates all development to the reproduction of an identical model, seems efficient; or again that the movement which opposes the integration process, the cause of the worst disparities, and the internationalization for the benefit of the world productive system, has finally succeeded in preventing all human societies being absorbed by the modern economic machine, with its financial resources, its technology and its markets. Failing such proof, the striking thing is the evidence of development gone astray; the export of staple produce, import substitution, industrial exports. The result is the crisis of development, which is a real crisis, and then crisis ideology and the crisis of theory. What we then have – since we have arrived at the stage of a general formulation – is certainly a universal problem. It can be summed up in a word: the causal connection between growth and development is unsound, and the idea that growth leads to development even more so, bearing in mind that what lies behind this is not words but 800 million victims of abject poverty! But the universality of the problem also remains to be demonstrated. The language of challenges helps to do this. But is it not too dramatic, too partial, too unilateral? François Perroux suspected as much 20 years ago! The rehearsal of the challenges is always linked to the following question: 'How can we change the societies and cultures *we* meet so as to make them suitable for *our* kind of industrialization?' or worthy of a growth enriched by the injection of doses of generosity. As though the fact of being a society different from the *prevailing* model were an obstacle to development, the cause and reason of the 'crisis', and this theory of poverty did not also mask the poverty of the theory. All in all, what we are concerned with is not so much a universal crisis as an appearance of universality associated with the nature of the international scene.

Nevertheless, It Points to Universality

The crisis is therefore worldwide. But in a new sense. For this is not a critical moment in a continuing process, but the breakdown of that process. On the one hand we have integration, internationalization and universalization; and on the other problems which lead inevitably to individualization, the emergence of the regions and demands for identity. Opposing movements are not opposite parts of one and the same movement. They are indicative of potential universality, not because their arena is the same world, or because the underdevelopment of some and the overdevelopment of others are complementary aspects of 'misdevelopment'; but also and above all because the required solution must be the proper development of all – in other words a political and cultural blueprint worthy of a world in which mankind would only have to undertake the tasks it can properly carry out because they correspond to problems it can effectively state and solve. This, of course, is only a subjective view of the crisis, extrapolated to its limits from the standpoint of its undesirable aspects: employment crisis, crisis of the towns, oil crisis and the end of affluence, or else a worsening of general destitution and the pauperization of the majority in the world. All in all, though cynicism teaches that even death is viable, if the human rights to work and dignity still have any meaning, the world of conflicts in which we live is not a viable world. Granted. Whether we reject *homo consumens* or can no long meet his needs, the challenges are the same. That which we reject and can no longer provide leads us on to criticize the models of education, the ideas of science and culture and the ends of politics. Here young people's spontaneous thinking about emancipation, human rights and peace links up with the nations decolonization movements and the anxieties of contemporary thinkers. Movement links up with movement; and the crisis is seen to be a crisis in the order of things and in the process it engenders and controls. A challenge to its legitimacy too, and all the more painful in that the prevailing universality is challenged and discredited by the universality which identity prompts us to demand. A crisis of modernity, too. The promises and speeches which for long portrayed history as a unifying process have now revealed the reality; and it is an economy and a technology which have seized upon the goods of the defeated and now threaten to seize the one good left to them, viz. their souls. The image of progress is tarnished: poverty and violence give it the lie. But it is still prevalent, for the idea of a balanced, differentiated growth comparable to organic growth (and comparable, moreover, to the growth of a biological organism shaped by the process of natural selection[1] . . . as though the state of the world were the product of natural history) is still stressed. As though the process of integration-disintegration ruled out any positive constructive intention to provide a secure basis for development or to set up a new world movement which, like the computers of the future, would think not so much in series as in parallel. Like the 'multiple history' to come, it would take the form of co-ordinated chronologies, rather than the homogeneous mode of history to which other histories, despising the multiplicity of social and historical eras and the diversity of cultures that converge in tomorrow's universality, are subordinated.

A Sociologically-based Approach

We are indebted to the epistemological sensitivity of François Perroux, determined to conceptualize that which organicist metaphor sought to conceal, for something which neither Neoclassicism nor Keynesianism gave us.

His effort runs in several directions.

The first step is to place growth, development, progress and social progressiveness in the context where their meaning can be made clear: that of science-oriented economics 'considered' as a science. Not that all metaphors are to be rejected, but there are some metaphors which mask and obstruct thought; others are more heuristic. In this attempt at rethinking, it is a question not of understanding scientific method but of getting it to move forward. The aim is more subtle: to find a middle way between ideas unrelated to facts and facts unsupported by ideas. For if we are to enter the field of economics, it is because it can be the scene of enlightened decisions and actions – and enlightened by knowledge. Economics is also a mode of action which has become the object of scientific investigation and continual critical analysis.

Admittedly the increasing naivety of economists, as of pretty well all social scientists, has been deplored. Some have suggested subjecting them to sociological study: the sociology of the social sciences and sociologists. Recourse to logic has even been recommended. And this is important: taken literally, this recommendation cannot be put into practice without carrying out a specific programme of formalization, justification and elucidation of observable facts, aligning and matching expression with experience. That which causes or explains economic and social change must be covered by this conceptual flexibility which is more significant than etymology, more operative than semantics and more efficient than pure philosophy, and which aims at an intelligent grasp of economic phenomena. Analysis therefore focuses on the field of real forces where active units confront one another: the individual or collective subjects of the economy.

Its characteristic: the omnipresence of power. Its specific features: relations between unequal partners, and dissymmetries.

Observation is then photography, a close intepretation of series of data that history illuminates but does not explain. That history should count for something is in itself a again! It rounds off an analysis which the reader will clearly understand on reading François Perroux' book. It adds a temporal dimension to growth in the usual dimensions; for economic reality, even when reduced to the measurements that describe it, remains a datum in real 'space-time', space that is limited and time that runs out. It culminates in the analysis of the structural changes, types of organization and lines of force through which social advances pass. Growth, an indicator of size, takes on significance from the development which surrounds it, while remaining distinct from it, and as it advances, shows its effectiveness. Economics is no longer, in this case, a science of the relationships between things, but a praxis of competitive complicities and co-operative conflicts, as different from the components of the homogeneous market regulated by the price mechanism as it is from the struggles for prestige and the fight to the death illustrated by the dialectic of master and slave. François Perroux thus postulates as the principle of *science-oriented economics* a fundamental axiom: life, the combination of forces that resist death.

Convergence of Science and Values

It follows that science here coincides not only with common sense but with perspicacity: the peoples' realization, as François Perroux says, 'that they had been duped into passively accepting ideas, formalizations and strategies which not only had not been arrived at on the basis of their own experience, but had been furnished them by the West' and thrust upon them to serve the purposes of the wealth-owning powers alone. He was accordingly interested in the central theme of the meeting that Unesco organized in Quito (Ecuador) from 27 to 31 August 1979 on the idea of overall, endogenous and integrated development; of these three concepts, endogeneity is probably the most difficult: signifying the mobilization of nations' domestic resources, it means primarily taking into account the system of cultural values deserving respect, and not merely the system of values that are calculable. It means confronting the secret, hidden truth, that development is impossible without the participation of all those for whom it is

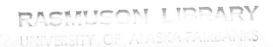

meaningful, and that it cannot take place if it goes against their interest, representing deprivation under the cover of dubious promises. It consists in achievement, fulfilment and liberation. It is not a topic for academic debate between pessimists and optimists: no one can dismiss as unrealistic the effort to use knowledge and action to launch a movement that is more conducive to the achievement of human aspirations and more attuned to scientific requirements.

Development for All People and for the Whole Person

Development, then, may be seen as the focus of a tension leading to the creation of knowledge and value, which it is Unesco's duty to foster and to advantage.

It must do this through philosophical reflection, which is useful in more than one respect: development does not result from spontaneous evolution, it is not the outcome of a consensus on the common interest, it cannot be reduced to the realization of models devised by experts, and it goes beyond a straightforward moral injunction to satisfy human needs. Although some of these factors contribute to its advancement, it must necessarily be the fruit of resolute endeavour, in which the constraints of reality and the constraints of truth converge.

For all social scientists, but especially for economists, this must be a requirement specifically depending on the self-awareness of a body of knowledge that is capable of looking again at its own foundations, linking up with other bodies of knowledge and assessing the relativity of its basic tenets and the impact of the powers to which it is exposed by reason of its naivety. The effort of critical reassessment helps us discern the conditions governing cognition, and reminds us that reality itself cannot escape from the hold of truth and that a rigorous approach is indispensable. And if it be asserted that the old philosophy of development is associated with historical conditions and circumstances that have changed, then we may reply that it is an exhilarating intellectual undertaking to think out the conditions governing the historical possibility of the new development. Our present reality demands it. Philosophy needs only to remind us that this new development is something other than an extrinsic imperative depending on circumstances: it is the idea of the context of new meanings that will make freedom tangible. Ths is the idea that François Perroux has constantly set before us and that will, if we address our efforts to it, lead us forward into a new world.

28 October 1981

The opinions expressed in this book are the responsibility of the author alone and do not necessarily represent the views of Unesco.

Notes

1. See the text quoted in Maurice Byé – G. Destanne de Bernis – *Relations économiques internationales*, J, 4th ed., p. 1020.

PREFACE

The redistribution of world power since the last war has produced a chain reaction which called for a review of traditional ways of thinking about economics, society and relationships between nations. Doctrines out of Europe are criticized and rejected by the underprivileged peoples, who can now bring out into the open the resistance they long nursed in resentment and silent protest. With the upsurge of emergent nations and common peoples no longer willing to be forgotten, trends of thought are appearing under the impetus of wide-ranging and irreversible aspirations.

They take on form and meaning in the quest for a *new international economic order* and a *new development*. It is the latter that Unesco suggested I should write about by way of follow-up to a recent meeting of experts in Quito (Ecuador).[1]

I did not object, though well aware of the responsibility that fell on me and of the intimidating task of writing an introduction to the philosophy of development. Since for 30 or so years[2] I have been engaged in describing and analysing development, I hope I will not be accused of idle presumption: my aim is to make a modest contribution to the efforts of the many capable teams at work throughout the world. It may be that every conscientious economist owes it to them to search his conscience, together with them, about what he has done, and to bear witness to what his chosen discipline is capable of.

My personal conviction is that emphasis on development presages radical changes in the field of economics and in the analytical tools used therein. The point is that development has to do with man as subject and agent, and with human societies and their aims and obviously evolving objectives. Once the idea of development had been accepted, a series of new developments could be expected, conditioned by successive variations in human values and the way they have historically been translated into deeds and action.

The call for a different kind of development[3] comes at a time when world development strategies have not had the results expected of them. While the first Development Decade was positive, the second did not achieve its aims: neither a 6 per cent growth rate, nor the amount of official aid (1 per cent of the gross national product of the developed countries for total aid, ·7 per cent for official aid), nor efficient co-ordination of action.

The *new* development sets out to be 'global', 'integrated' and 'endogenous'. Each of these terms has several meanings, and combining them does not give a univocal meaning. Moreover, the disparity of interests involved gives rise to contradictory interpretations.

It is as well to pinpoint these difficulties from the outside before determining them analytically.

Global describes a view of all the dimensions of a human whole and the disparity of aspects that must be accepted in their interrelationships, over and above specific analyses. The term is of course applied to entities of different sizes and structures, such as a nation, a group of nations or the whole world.

Endogenous, in normal mathematical parlance, refers to the variables that make up the selected system of equations, as opposed to the exogenous variables which represent data and may be subjected to different logical processing. In the vocabulary of international organizations, however, the adjective is used to denote a nation's internal strengths and resources and their rational exploitation and use.

As for *integrated*, the polysemy of the word is obvious. If a number of nations are integrated, they are grouped together in a more coherent whole. More generally, the term 'integration' denotes the grouping together of units or factors to form a single whole. Integrated development may therefore mean either the integration of a number of regions or increased cohesion between sectors, regions and social classes. The two meanings are mutually compatible when appropriately analysed.

It is important to realize at the outset that each of the terms may be interpreted by different interests on the basis of economic doctrines which start from different premises and hence lead to different recommendations. Rational and historical trickery in international negotiations produces opposing interpretations, which vested interests then apply to generalizations. Thus global development draws criticism from econometricians accustomed to their own indicators of growth, decline in growth and rate of growth; they are tempted to say that development does not offer the same rewards when indicated by many indicators. As for the advocates of development, some will rather stress its external conditions, others its internal conditions in a given group. In the context of basic needs, some will fear an attempt to bring back underdeveloment by means of gifts; others that rejecting a legitimate extension of the 'gift' economy will mean not giving every human being the wherewithal for his or her subsistence. They will denounce acquiescence – on practical grounds or out of loyalty to a mistaken interpretation of liberalism – in the destruction of potential physical and intellectual energies. Likewise urging frugality on peoples at the minimum subsistence level will strike some as a commonsensical approach, and others as questionable advice to give to peoples whose level of ambition is the driving force of development.

Objective analysis clears up many of these misunderstandings. This clarification is necessary, because the very future of the new development philosophy is at stake.

During the 1950s research concentrated on the growth of gross national product. The special attention given to growth arose out of the conjunction of national accounting systems, long-term statistical studies and static representations of balanced growth.

The new analytical approach has for some 30 years sharply differentiated observable, formalizable and roughly quantifiable features such as *growth*, *development*, *advances* and *progress*. It made its breakthrough only when the underprivileged peoples realized that they had been duped into passively accepting ideas, formalizations and strategies which not only had not been arrived at on the basis of their own experience, but had been furnished them by the West in order to serve its own interests.

The consequences of this realization are slowly gaining ground. Innovation always arouses strong resistance. When after two centuries of political and commercial hegemony intellectual innovation upsets the very definite interests underlying the often ill-defined terms 'market economy' and 'capitalism', resistance is exceptionally strong and widespread. Overt or clandestine, straightforward or hypocritical, it arises at all levels; it stems from the powerful coalitions of governments and ruling classes, and of practitioners and people timid enough to sacrifice truth to a trouble-free career or social approval.

The development of the whole man and of all men is a goal that should be unanimously accepted by politicians, economists and research workers, now that some of the cruder tricks have been exposed by contemporary history at the price of bloody violence aroused by specifically institutional violence.

The first generation of classical English economists quite rightly took the whole world and all mankind as their field of study. They led people astray by ascribing to industry the ability to bring about universal peace, and to market expansion the capacity to allocate resources in accordance with the requirements of 'economic efficiency' and 'feasible' justice.

The mass of the people want to live, but have not the means; what they need is a radical review of the presuppositions and consequences of the legacy of the classical English economists and their disloyal son Neo-classicism.

Growth in wealth, as recorded by incomplete and misleading accounting systems, is becoming less and less convincing. It may or *may not* be the result or means of development of people and actual or potential resources. Vast reserves of untapped human energy call for interpretations that will exploit and use them. This is the inner meaning of the new development, which though not an export product for rich Westerners, concerns them just as much as it does the underprivileged peoples.

New forms of development among the rich are essential for the better development of the most underprivileged. A twofold effort with a common goal may help to correct the most flagrant ills in the world economy. A visible reorganization of production and trade calls for a renewal of doctrines and analytical tools. Authentic cultures, in which human groups have during a long history sought to record their philosophy of life, are invited to participate in this civilizing task.

Seen in this light, the new development becomes in the context of the new international economic order a collective effort, whose conception and implementation entail rethinking the foundations of economic thought.[4] Economics is usually defined as the 'science' of the allocation of scarce goods. The abstraction of scarcity stems from the fact that there are more possible uses than goods, or in other roughly equivalent words that needs exceed the goods available. Reductionism applied to this inequality has the effect of equating utility with the importance attached to a good, and need with desire to buy, thus turning both into supposedly neutral concepts. Here we see the sort of 'purification' to which V. Pareto has accustomed us: it replaces the individual by the balance between quantities of goods and sums of money, i.e. concerns itself with the supposedly isolatable result of the exchange rather than with the *shaping* of the decision that lead up to it. Motivation is likewise interpreted as the search for a *net 'profit'* in merchandise or money.

All that this pure economics needs for its existence is the market and its (supposedly homogeneous) space in which supposedly similar and equal persons are active. The hierarchical organization inherent in all societies is taken as read and assumed to have no influence in trading exchanges. The result is that scarcity, the fundamental concept of the whole construct, is defined as the balance either between a given supply of goods and the demand for possible uses or between ability to pay and desire to buy. The 'neutrality' of these mental operations masks the fact the physiological needs, natural impulses and intellectual and ethical aspirations are put on the same footing. This, by the inner logic of the system, implies reference to a utility which, embracing all types of motivation and all types of valuation, means that they need only be identified to become real or which, symbolizing commonplace materialism, takes no account of human behaviour or history.

The consequence of this position is failure to differentiate between the types of scarcity that everyday experience and systematic observation suggest ought to be distinguished. The individual's awareness of scarcity when directly confronted with nature has never led to the theoretical reactions expected of an individual sentenced to isolation (Robinson Crusoe); people have gathered together to cope with natural scarcities, thereby transforming them into social scarcities, that is to say, scarcities involving inequality among individuals. In advanced societies, it will therefore be important to identify the scarcities occasioned by institutions which assign individuals their roles and, by so doing, define the scope of their socially possible actions. The scarcity revealed by the market is not independent of the roles that society assigns to those involved in it, and more particularly, to the wage-earner and the executive who decides how the means of production are to be used. The efforts made to bring about a relaxation of the constraints attaching to the social distribution of roles affects the forms and working of markets.[5]

This initial analysis of scarcity as an abstraction in conventional economics suggests the need to question the *maximization within limiting conditions* which is the standard or paradigm of rational economics. For decision-making purposes, a computer selects the combination of means and ends which seems the best, i.e. the one which, subject to the specific constraints of the operation, offers the best result at the least cost. The procedure is obvious and there is no special difficulty about translating it into algebraic and numerical terms, *provided* that the level of abstraction is such that the question of *who* maximizes, *what* is maximized and what *secondary effects* accompany the maximization is not considered.

This can be illustrated by an example. A major company establishes a branch in a developing country. It maximizes the expected profit in terms of value within the limiting conditions of production, transport and distribution costs. But does it take into account the pollution caused, the damage done to local communities, and cultural breakdown? Obviously not; that is not the object of the operation, and if there are clauses in a schedule evaluating such items, they are a matter for top-level negotiations.

In an obviously different context, the same questions arise in the case of a major company and its natural and social environment in a developed country. From the logical standpoint, private maximization can be shown to be generally defensible only in a context of public, collective maximization. The latter, however, is not yet subject to strict, clearly defined and readily applicable rules.

If any such attempt were made, it would tend to maximize the vague entity known as 'welfare', inferred from market-dependent values, prices and quantities, which does not have the virtue of generating equality among the individuals concerned, who are unequal in terms of resources and information. Maximization within limiting conditions and the combination of such maximizations give rise to a standard whose applications, when fully operational, are subject to strong reservations.

From the standpoint to theory, maximizations are static and exclude the time factor. The reason is obvious: time brings with it novelty and risk and, notwithstanding some progress, is only very patchily incorporated in probabilistic models.

The most sophisticated economic calculations assist in decision-making but are not decisive. If they are intended to assist in political decision-making, they are not only extremely complex, but of a different order from the decision itself, which is taken on the basis of values that cannot be reduced to quantities and costs, such as the security and freedom of a people, for example. The limitations of quantitative expression – without which, as some say, there would be no economic phenomenon – therefore need to be specified. If economics is to be defined in terms of observable reality, we shall have to look beyond such institutions as the market and, moreover, shall have to make do with a rather hazy demarcation line.[6]

Economics is the adjustment of human relations for the good of the individual and in the common interest, through the use of rare goods that can to some extent be socially quantified and accounted for.

This definition, be it noted, places the emphasis on the relationships between people and groups of people, not on the relationships between people and wealth.

Recent economic thinking is very laboriously and incompletely ridding itself of the utilitarian individualism which prevailed when it came into being and which has degenerated into a crude hedonism and materialism very different from their originals. The 'philosophy' underlying modern economics reflects a sort of trading mentality which breaks down the sense of fellowship among people and, concomitantly, the values specifically regarded as human by all philosophies and all religions.

It is in this that the clash between traditional societies and the practical 'economism' of the so-called developed societies becomes understandable.

Notes

1. Meeting of Experts on 'Research on the Idea of Integrated Development', Quito, Ecuador, 27–31 August 1979.
2. F. Perroux, 'De l'avarice des nations à une économie du genre humain', address to the Dijon *Semaine sociale*, 1952.
3. Unesco. *Medium-Term Plan (1977–1982). Thinking Ahead (Unesco and the Challenges of Today and Tomorrow)*, Paris, Unesco, 1977. *Suicide or Survival? (The Challenge of the Year 2000)*, Collective work, Paris, Unesco, 1977.
M'B ow, A.M. (Director-General of Unesco). *Moving towards Change (Some thoughts on the new international economic order)*, Paris, Unesco, 1976. *From Concertation to Consensus (Unesco and the solidarity of nations)*, Paris, Unesco, 1979.
Hammarskjøld, Dag. *Report* prepared for the seventh special session of the United Nations General Assembly, 1975.
4. Koopmans, Tjallin C. 'Economics among the sciences,' *AER*, March 1979. Lichnerowicz, A., Gadoffre, G., Perroux, F. Séminaires pluri-disciplinaires du Collège de France, in: Pierre Delattre (ed.), *Recherches interdisciplinaires*, Paris, Maloine, 1977. *Fundamenta scientiae*, Vol. 1, No. 2, 1980. Oxford, Pergamon Press.
5. Perroux, François. 'Activité économique et science économique', *La sociologie et les sciences de la société*, CEPI, 1975.
6. 'The fragility of what are known as the social sciences may be due to this: that they deal in impressions (whence the setbacks and the *taxonomic difficulties* of economics), which immediately changes the concept of science.' Barthes, Roland. Inaugural Lecture, Collège de France, Chair of Literary Semiology, 7 January 1977 (booklet).

ABBREVIATIONS

Reports, bulletins and publications of international organizations

UN	United Nations
ILO	International Labour Organization
Unesco	United Nations Educational, Scientific and Cultural Organization
OECD	Organization for Economic Co-operation and Development
EEC	European Economic Community
IMF	International Monetary Fund
WB	World Bank
BIS	Bank for International Settlements
FAO	Organization of the United Nations for Food and Agriculture

Journals

AER	*American Economic Review*
CISMEA	*Cahiers de l'ISEA,* now *Cahiers de l'ISMEA*
EDCC	*Economic Development and Cultural Change,* University of Chicago Press
EA	*Economie Appliquée* (archives de l'ISMEA) Institut de Sciences Mathématiques et Economiques Appliquées, 11 rue Pierre et Marie Curie (Institut Henri Poincaré) – 75005 Paris
ES	*Economies et Sociétés* (Cahiers de l'ISMEA), same address as EA
MED	*Mondes en Développement,* trilinqual review (French, English, Spanish), same address as EA. Director: F. Perroux. Editor: F. Denoël.
CJN	*Croissance des Jeunes Nations,* Director: G. Blardone, Paris
CBPP	*Conjoncture* – Bulletin economique mensuel of the Banque de Paris et des Pays-Bas, Paris
COO	*Coopératives,* Revue des Etudes Coopératives, Paris
CRI	*Critica* (La Nuova Critica, Editor: Valerio Tonini), Rome

DOC   *Documentation, Problèmes économiques*, La Documentation Française, Paris

FA   *Foreign Affairs, America and World*, Baltimore, Md.

JPE   *Journal of Political Economy*

JR   *Jaune et Rouge (Le)*, Amicale des anciens élèves de l'Ecole Polytechniques, Paris, special issue, Le Tiers-Monde, February 1979

TR   *Trimestre* (El Trimestre Economico, Mexico City)

TM   *Tiers-Monde*, IEDES, Paris, Presses Universitaires de France

WD   *World in Development*, London, Pergamon Press

P.S. The contentions advanced in the following pages are based, so far as possible, on some of the author's recent works: the reader will appreciate that the discussion here is intentionally concise.

1 CONCEPTS AND INDICATORS

A New Approach to the Problems

The aim of scientifically-minded economics is to draw up a coherent and universally valid body of relations capable of being applied to a category of phenomena defined as economic. Among these, special importance is attached to the phenomena of *evolution*, which means changes that are interlinked, as opposed to a 'random' succession of events and structures occurring in irreversible and historical time.

When considering the evolution of an economy within a society, growth may be viewed in terms either of scale or of complexity.

The same distinction may be drawn in the case of a living organism, a plant, an animal or a human being, the concept of development being clearly the most informative both for analytical and for practical purposes. We shall see that this is equally true of an economic analysis, provided that a new and more searching approach is adopted. Hitherto, the attention and studies of researchers have concentrated on the question of growth, owing to a tendency towards conventional and arbitrary reductionism which has been repudiated by the newest approach and its constituent concepts and formalizations.

1. All human relationships are composite, being made up of contention and co-operation, of conflict and mutual assistance.[1] The same is true of the interaction between different and unequal agents in any given operation. The agents differ in biological, mental and social terms: they have neither the same income, nor the same background, nor the same position in the social hierarchy. The idea of equality *vis-à-vis* the market is highly ambiguous and has been formulated with purely vindicatory intentions: it would be valid only in the impossible event that the agents were atomistic entities of equal and infinitesimal dimensions, bereft of all power to influence a price which they had to accept passively and by which they were determined.

The ambiguity and ambivalence of the *conflict–co-operation* relationship between groups organized on the basis of kinship, locality and activity are equally evident and well established by methodical observation and reflection. An individual belonging to such a group may derive from it either strength or weakness: it may either enhance or diminish his personal coefficient and his particular rating as regards resources and information-gathering capabilities.

2. This state of conflict-ridden co-operation may pass unnoticed (and may be undesired) by those concerned; thus the type of dynamic competition subject to certain conditions which rewards 'the fittest' and 'eliminates the less fit' is a struggle that is always kept under control: the conflictual activities of all agents taken together rebound, subject to certain conditions, to the community's advantage. The situation might be compared to an effective model of voluntary co-operation if the rules of the game were known, accepted and observed by everybody or if, alternatively, an omniscient and all-powerful umpire could intervene immediately and at no expense to correct faults. Needless to say, these conditions are never fulfilled.

In all systems of monopolistic competition, the element of conflict is quite obvious; under certain known conditions, the outcome of the conflict may, in the area of economic dynamics, prove beneficial to society.

3. Adopting a broader view, we see that, in any society, competitive dealings between individuals are carried on thanks to an infrastructure which is of a collective nature as regards the resources used to build it and the services it renders. Moreover, competitive dealings are conducted according to certain rules and within the framework of an organization. The market, which is the network linking presumably independent economic units and agents by means of flows and prices, stems from this organization and functions thanks to its existence; it can only be described and understood by reference to the *pre-market situation* – the factors having conditioned and shaped it in a specific way – and the *post-market situation* – the consequences it entails and its impact on the life of society. W. Röpke was entirely justified in looking *beyond* the question of supply and demand – and his attitude was exemplary since he was a professed liberal.

4. In a market system functioning purely and simply according to the rule of solvency, anyone unable to pay could not survive. But this severity is always alleviated in contemporary societies by forms of support requiring no direct counterpart from the beneficiaries (gifts, grants) and by various levies (taxation). Commercial

transactions are therefore conducted within a framework of social transfers and fiscal transfers and this framework determines their conditions, their scale and their impact. In this respect, every observable economy is a composite one.[2] The content and consequences of market transactions cannot be correctly appraised by simply balancing goods sold against goods bought, having calculated their value in terms of price.

Economic competition within complex modern systems exists in symbiosis with competition between nations and between social groups. Those who have obstinately attempted to homogenize the economic and social world with a view to controlling its development by applying simple or sophisticated mathematical formulae have failed, principally because that world is intrinsically heterogeneous.

It is made up of many elements: individuals, *structured* sub-groups, sub-groups of economic activities described as 'industries', regions, nations and 'groups of nations'.

5. The concept of structure[3] is abhorred by economists who view the economy as a homogeneous species within which molecules move about under the action of prices. Yet it is necessary, for any realistic investigation or reasoned policy, to view the economy as a combination of proportions and relationships existing at a given moment or over a short period, and to bear in mind that, during the long period of irreversible time, certain variables described as structural as opposed to functional variables register changes that are slower, less frequent and less far-reaching than the latter. The existence, on the one hand, of capital that is fixed because of its physical structure and inevitable indivisibilities and, on the other hand, of organizations that are hierarchy-conscious and have a propensity to inertia – these two characteristics being generally combined – indicates that no present-day economy can be said to display more than a very limited degree of malleability under the impact of prices or exogenous changes.

From the concept of structure may be derived:

the concept of *structural preference* – the preferences expressed by population groups and/or those who speak on their behalf; and that of *structural ascendancy*, as exercised by one structure over another during medium-term and long-term periods, from firm to firm, from industry to industry, from region to region and from nation to nation.

Social structures – and structures of social groups – are shaped by social roles and the rules governing life in society.
6. Each structure is organized and the structures are interlinked by decision-makers whose decisions, which are scarcely ever perfectly and continuously compatible with each other, give rise to 'intersections', in other words to conflicts.

It is therefore inevitable that in every society there should exist a Power, which can be seen to be performing its various functions in such a way as to make conflicts between opposing parties turn to the advantage of the population as a whole.

The study of all aspects of power, and more particularly the aspect that has just been mentioned, is one of the weakest points of the type of neo-classical analysis that is very widespread today. Nevertheless, it must be actively pursued along new lines if we are to grasp the full meaning of under-development and development.
7. Among the structured parts or sub-groups of a whole that is itself structured, development is brought about dialectically, through dynamic conflicts between structured groups – actions and reactions which, in contrast to the laws of 'pure' dialectics, do not lead to the *destruction* of one sub-group by another but, under conditions of dynamic inequality, to the transformation of both into a new structure, this being the outcome of the clash between two original structures. Such a *modus operandi*, which can be applied to economic structures and social structures in innumerable ways, seems, when it is put to the test, to be of crucial importance for the description and interpretation of development.

In the foregoing paragraphs we have reviewed, very briefly, a trend of research and a number of concepts that have been discussed at length in previous works. This recapitulation was a necessary introduction to the analysis presented below.

Growth

By growth[4] we mean the increase in the size of a unit, usually a country, expressed in terms of its gross national product (the total of goods and services produced within a given period, allowing for depreciation) in relation to the number of inhabitants. Whereas the word 'expansion' is used when we are considering a short period, 'growth' concerns a long period (the time required, for instance, to carry out more than four five-year plans).

This notion of a lasting increase in size is useful but *vague*; it owes its success to its relative simplicity and to the relative, largely illusory, ease with which it can be expressed by a figure. States have often announced their economic policy objectives in terms of growth rates compared with those of other states for the same period, which is convenient but may give rise to appalling confusion.

Thanks to the worldwide statistical studies carried out by Simon Kuznets, we are now aware of the shortcomings of quantitative measurements of growth. They are due to the statistical material itself and to national accounting procedures. Despite the abundance of statistics, no specialist can deny the inadequacy of our information regarding the data which are available, today and in respect of the past, in the essential fields of production and distribution.

The questions that cannot be answered are precisely the ones raised for the purposes of the most recent analysis because they are calculated to shed light on the evolution of developing countries. This is not surprising because the statistics were compiled with completely different ends in view from those of the study of growth: they *hinder* descriptive and analytical investigation and would have had to be completely overhauled – a slow and costly task – to make them really manageable and significant.

We are still very poorly equipped for a *rigorous* and *quantitative* evaluation of Research-and-Development and of its impact, through innovation and dissemination, on education and vocational training, on pollution and other nuisances and on the connections between qualitative changes in population groups and growth rates.

Growth is rightly considered to be concomitant with all structural changes: there is no such thing as homothetic growth or growth that is evenly distributed in space. But changes in proportions and in relationships between parts within the whole are brought to light by summary breakdowns concerning the 'branches' or 'sectors' of production, and are only embryonic in respect of regions, so that assumptions regarding the pull exercised by one sub-group on another can only be checked in a very indirect way. When a first-class statistician establishes a parallel between the growth of the GNP and that of major aggregates – investment, consumption, savings, etc. – there is good reason to doubt whether what he is doing amounts to more than taking the first step towards a causal analysis, despite the title of his well-known book.

Efforts to satisfy the need for fully developed analytical studies come up against the shortcomings of national accounts and their statistical treatment. For instance, the Cobb-Douglas production function ($P = T^a K^{1-a}$), which links the quantities of two factors assumed to be homogeneous (labour, capital) under conditions of constant returns, is open to criticism because, besides having serious intrinsic weaknesses, it leaves out of account some 40 to 60 per cent of the GNP pertaining to developed countries; this unexplored part, which should not be confused with the notion of technological progress, embraces, theoretically, the best time-phased allocation of resources, the best quality factors of production, the learning of agents and the varied forms of innovation.

In order to attempt to evaluate the impact of one sector (I) on another (II) in this field, we need to use two functions, for instance, the logarithmic expression:

$$P_1 = aT_1 + bK_1 + R_1 \tag{1}$$

$$P_{11} = F(cT_{11} + dK_{11} + R_{11}) \tag{2}$$

from which we might *assume*, as the starting-point for a causal analysis, that:

$$R_{11} = f(R_1) \tag{3}$$

or some other expression illustrating the productivity induced by I in II. We have as yet no detailed formula or statistical test for this type of link, although its existence and importance are revealed by observation and experience.

Nothing in the practice of compiling statistical records and breakdowns would prevent us from drawing a distinction, within the 'national' product, between the sub-group of activities which escapes national control and that which depends on decisions made by the national authorities. Not everything said to be 'national' comes under the control of the 'nationals' of a country and, nowadays the expansion of direct investments, transnational corporations and transfers of technology with its specialized personnel sometimes magnifies the difference enormously, whether we are concerned with the relations between developed countries and developing countries or with those established between two developed countries of unequal size and power. This is one of the most important features of international trade which escapes evaluation for lack of relevant data.

The leading expert in the field, Simon Kuznets, has had the honesty to write that research into economic growth has resulted in a set of rough preliminary findings, both empirical and analytical, and that we have covered only a small part of the road leading to an adequate evaluation and analysis of economic growth and structures. Many years ago, at one of the discussions organized on the occasion of the bicentennial celebration of Columbia University, Simon Kuznets, replying to this writer's insistence on the need for a sectoral study and an inquiry into the centres or poles of development, said that he sympathized with that view but felt that it was desirable to start by undertaking global research. This goes to show that the two approaches are not contradictory.

On the basis of data concerning GNP growth, economists have drawn up models of macroeconomic growth (E. Domar, R.F. Harrod, R. Solow, J.R. Hicks), all of which describe, in static terms, and by reference to an output curve, a savings curve and an investment curve, the point at which balanced growth will occur, which is at the intersection of the savings curve and the investment curve. This equilibrium is considered to be stable, although the model has not clearly demonstrated the spontaneous inevitability of correcting a state of disequilibrium by means of a change in the rate of interest or by flow readjustment and has not, of course, taken into account the 'complications' introduced by the sectoral analysis and the structuration of savings and investment.

A sectoral analysis (a structuration) of income would also make growth more intelligible by relating it to the agents, their expectations and their inequality as regards access to information. It would be conducive to a more significant breakdown in models where it is shown only in the form of major macroeconomic aggregates.

It is noteworthy that the very concept of growth, as defined, utilized in theoretical studies and formalized over the past 30 years, proves, on analysis, to be a totally inadequate basis on which to build on economic policy to be applied to or by developing countries. The aspect of economic phenomena that this concept selects and highlights for model-building reasons is quite irrelevant, if isolated from the other aspects, to the task of defining a strategy even for the rich countries, let alone the poor countries.

Growth *for what purpose*, with what end in view? Under what *conditions* is growth beneficial? Growth for *whom*? For only some members of the international community or for *all*? How can our answers to these questions have any relevance if we are dealing with aggregates that are assumed to be homogeneous for model-building reasons?

Questions such as these are at the root of the demands being made by developing countries, but it must be clearly understood that they have to be faced by anyone concerned with operational models and practical policy.

They are questions that introduce into the world of objects and things the human being, the individual, the actor, nor just the producer or consumer, who is the slave of the market and obliged to accept the prevailing price system, but real individuals and their groups who are capable of altering their environment by deliberately planning and organizing activities to that end. It is common knowledge nowadays that the growth of the aggregate product may have an *impoverishing* effect if, for example, it results in the destruction or deterioration of natural resources. We know that this growth rate takes no account of the possibility of harming or destroying people because it is indifferent to everything that might be described in figurative terms as the depreciation of human capital. But we are still reluctant to admit that current growth theories and analyses, whatever their merits, have been developed by economists who have ignored, even excluded, the actor and his activity.

From this point of view, a growth mechanism can be regarded as the counterpart of the Walras-Pareto mechanism of general equilibrium, as will be shown below.

The aggregate gross (national) product[5] is by no means a quantity of purely analytical significance; it is an empirical and statistical aggregate representing the total volume of goods of a national economy over a given period. The prices of the various items are added up and the total volume cannot be quantified in any other way. But this is not a rigorous method of measurement because in all cases, and more particularly in the case of the developing countries, price structures vary widely in different branches, sectors and regions. The sum total obtained by adding up items that have ceased to be strictly addable and, consequently, the growth rate of the whole are thus merely rough estimates representing at best, the *first stage* of an analysis. The aggregate and the growth of the aggregate are in themselves concepts whose vagueness is not dispelled by the reference to the number of parties concerned or the size of the population, that is to say, by the figure given for the *per capita* product (income).

V. Pareto, in his *pure* and *static* economic theory, uses indifference curves to establish a quantitative relationship between two kinds of goods (or between one good and money); it then seems unnecessary to begin by making a direct reference to the individual, the human being: this is replaced by the *result* of a comparison between two items of merchandise (two things with or without a price attached) and by their possible equilibrium. The validity of this procedure cannot be tested empirically in any environment.

It becomes ridiculous when applied to the developing countries; it implies that the relationship between goods or between goods and money does away with the need, at the stage of making 'a first approximation', to include man in the field of analysis.

Yet it is on the basis of a similar procedure that statements have been made about growth or *per capita* growth in Bangladesh just as in the Federal Republic of Germany, in the United Republic of Tanzania just as in France, etc.

It must be understood that we are not concerned at this stage with the difficulty of making statistical comparisons between countries. On a more fundamental plane, we are questioning the concept itself and suggesting that its content is inherently unsuitable; the aggregate described as the total output of merchandise (or of goods considered as merchandise) in a given economy is irrelevant when the market *does not yet exist* or when the constituent parts of the market do not all come into play in a habitual and regular way. The recourse to shadow prices can only be, by definition, a temporary expedient.

The aggregate product is one *block* which the statistician sets in relation to other *blocks* – aggregate investment, aggregate consumption – and which enables a mechanism of growth, and of so-called self-sustained growth, to be visualized and constructed.

It uses the equations applied in national accounting: Product (Income) = Consumption + Investment; Product (Income) = Consumption + Savings and, in an *equilibrium situation*, Investment = or ≡ Savings.

From this are derived the following equations which have now become commonplace: the growth rate of the Product (Income) (g_1) is equal to the growth rate of the population (h) *plus* the growth rate of productivity (pr); or: that growth rate (g_2) is equal to the growth rate of Savings (assumed to be equal to Investment) (e) divided by the inverse coefficient of capital (K); or: that growth rate (g_3) is equal to the growth rate of labour (T) and of capital (K) in specified proportions plus a coefficient expressing the effect of improvements in technology and organization (r).

Such is the basis of the algebraic expression of all models of *balanced growth* which are produced when national accounting aggregates are combined with an idea of equilibrium reduced to the equality between characteristic sub-aggregates.

At all events, suffice it to note for the time being that investment is usually regarded as the motive sub-aggregate, whether it be considered on its own or equated with savings. Investment and not the investor, the agent making an investment. Similarly: savings and not the saver; wages and not the wage-earner. The sub-groups, the blocks, are adjusted in relation to each other to produce instant equilibrium; they are assumed to be mutually compatible and equal at a point known as the point of equilibrium. *Short of* this point savings are larger than investment and *beyond* it investment is larger than savings. In itself, and simply by reason of the variables which it has selected, this representation can tell us nothing about the attitudes of the agents, nor about their aspirations and their ability to react to a given situation: the stability of the equilibrium is achieved by a mechanical process set in motion when two quantities are found to be unequal.

In developing countries the consequences of acquiescing in the existence of this mechanism on the assumption that it will have beneficial effects would be even more serious than in advanced capitalist systems. The developing countries show us, as if through a magnifying glass, that, instead of assembling a mechanism or imposing a blueprint for equilibrium on their present or future situation, we should endeavour to improve the population's productive and innovative capacity in order to bring about a lasting rise in its standard of living.

Development

Development presupposes dealings between people in the form of exchanges of goods and services and of information and symbols.

In the economic context, it is grasped at three levels:

A. The linking up of the parts within a whole. The parts are organized sub-groups: branches, industries, regions, enterprises. Each sub-group has its relative importance and its place in specific networks of prices and flows, of transfers of material goods, or of goods whose significance and value do not bear a strictly identifiable relation to the material infrastructure. These networks are based on a material and intellectual system of communications for which the community has usually had to pay.

B. The direct or indirect action and interaction of the various sectors, this being none other than the dialectic of structures as defined earlier. In the language of systems analysis we say that action and feedback need to be regulated. The reorganization of the parts or of the whole is brought about during this process. It is important to note that there is no question here of blocks (of variables) encountering other blocks and of assuming them to be capable of modifying each other and changing the whole, without saying why nor how.

It is the agents, the active decision-makers, who initiate the operations, it being understood that those operations do not necessarily fulfil the originators' intentions, and may often prove to be even at variance with those intentions. Economic structures are thus bound up with the mental structures and social structures of groups in organized society: the former and the latter interact.

C. In evolutionary structures, all forms of human resources stand some chance of gaining in effectiveness and in quality. As the economic and social machine becomes more powerful and more complex, it yields a wider and more sophisticated range of economic and intellectual products. In order to obtain them, more capable and more skilled agents are required. Conversely, users and customers become more demanding in regard both to quantity and to quality. As a result individuals are propelled forward by the machine and the machine is propelled forward by individuals in a cumulative process.

We have just referred to mere *chance*. Indeed, it is always possible that this propulsion process may be concentrated and focussed exclusively upon one part of the population and that (we have not so far formed any value judgement) the most abundant and sophisticated products are those which threaten the very survival of human beings or have the effect of weakening their physical and mental powers.

A contrario proof of the accuracy of the foregoing description is found in the developing countries. They display the following features in varying degrees:[7]

A. Defects in the linking up of the parts within the whole. Transport networks are inadequate or concentrated in such a way as to serve only certain regions and communities. Markets are localized and encourage the formation of non-communicating groups. The particularism of closed societies, tribes, ethnic groups stands in the way of peaceful exchanges; language differences are a further barrier. Even if an innovatory investment project or a leading enterprise is established in one of the many isolated parts of the national territory, the benefits of the multiplying effect and the complementarity of the new activities do not reach other parts. The seaboard economy looks abroad and does not communicate with the hinterland. Enclaved economies are juxtaposed without being interconnected.

B. Contacts between such economies and developed countries can only be established on an unequal footing and their one-sidedness can be corrected only gradually and at the cost of great efforts. The less developed economies are dominated by the others; their structures are exposed to the danger of being taken over and, in certain fields at least, there is a tendency for the conditions governing the exchange of goods, services and information to be fixed unilaterally.

C. Wastage of human resources. The physiological effects of poverty will eventually raise the mortality rate to such a high level that a large proportion of newcomers will die before they become thinking and productive men and women. Biological and mental inferiority will always be the lot of a fraction or even the majority of the population. Multi-dimensional human resources have no chance of being fully employed, and still less of being fully developed.

Fundamentally, therefore, as will be seen in more detail further on, any development policy consists in:

(1) promoting the *dynamic factors in development*, which are simply the dynamic factors in human life, since they amount to the natural demographic trends and the quality of the population, the capacity for technical progress – invention and innovation – and the renovation of institutions, whether they be organizing institutions such as the family and the production unit or standardizing institutions such as property laws, market

controls or distribution systems;
(2) providing the material facilities and information services required in order to organize the *propagation* of economically beneficial effects.

These views and their implications were clearly and un-ambiguously expounded by the French schools some 30 years ago. It is encouraging to see them substantially accepted by international organizations such as the United Nations and Unesco and to find them set out in major international documents.

In the report entitled, 'Reshaping international order', we find an explicit statement on the distinction between growth and development, between harmonized growth and more or less spontaneously balanced growth. Structures, inequalities and forms of domination in international trade are analysed. Power phenomena are taken into account and no less attention is given to the disjointed nature of economies and the inadequate coverage of the *coûts de l'homme* (costs of a truly human life for all). Human resources are extolled as the best of all resources. Is there reason to hope that the proponents of the official economics are about to adopt these concepts, which they have long resisted as 'deviant' and dangerous?

Moreover, an interesting *Interfutures Report* prepared for the Organization for Economic Co-operation and Development (OECD) bears witness to a trend in the same direction, which is all the more significant inasmuch as the purpose of the document is an economic one. 'The market', it says, 'is an excellent resource-allocation mechanism but some of its theoretical stipulations are inadequately met in reality.' It functions badly if it is interfered with by 'dominating positions' and policies 'changing the relative costs of various goods and services'. The market in no way guarantees 'a distribution of incomes judged acceptable within nations or between nations'. Hence the need for dialogue on the possibility of sharing added value or productivity gains and to organize appropriate forms of discussion on the question of *gains from trade*.

What is more, cultural values 'play a fundamental role in economic growth', which is nothing but a means. Cultural values are at the root of the motivations which curb or accelerate growth and determine the legitimacy of growth as a target.

It is not just '*economism*' which is annihilated by a movement generated by various schools of thought; criticism is also levelled at the narrow economy which is the result of substituting *market mechanisms* for the decisions and activities of agents.

Taking development into consideration means calling attention to the danger of growth without development. This danger obviously exists in developing countries when economic activity is concentrated around branches of foreign firms or major public works and does not have nationwide effects. Even in developed countries we see that, as growth progresses, the benefits of development are being unevenly distributed in geographical terms, because relatively 'empty' regions still exist, and in social terms, because 'pockets of poverty' have not disappeared.

These are only the outward signs of growth without development; we gain a deeper insight into their significance when we consider their repercussions insofar as the multidimensional energy of the agents is concerned.

As for development without growth, this is concisely expressed, in the abstract, by the superficial and pernicious slogan which met with some success in Europe a few years ago, namely, 'zero growth'. The simplistic line of reasoning on this subject may be summed up more or less as follows: if growth stopped once a certain level had been reached, it would be possible and desirable to change the product and income distribution pattern. In a country where growth had continued until it amounted, at a particular period, to 3 per cent, it would be possible to improve the overall product/income distribution pattern without achieving any further growth. Going into more detail, we may add that this improvement will be thought of as an increase in the share of wages in the national income while sectoral wages remain at their existing level, or as an increase in the share of wages in the national income accompanied by changes in sectoral wages, or, other things being equal, as a relative increase in social transfers. It is recognized that none of these strategies is practicable and desirable unless it is certain not to entail any decline in resources or *real* incomes, in other words, unless the general price index remains at a given level.

This argument does not bear scrutiny.

An increase in the relative share of wages in the national income entails a proportionate decrease in the share of profits, and hence in the share of investments inasmuch as the latter, understood in the broad sense, are financed by total profits and are planned on the strength of anticipated profits. Accordingly, the previous rate of growth will probably not be sustained. Nor is there much hope of being able to keep sectoral wages at their existing level: sectoral productivities would only be maintained if certain wages were higher than the corresponding productivities at the time of the change and if an enlightened strategy succeeded in redistributing wages in such a way as to bring them all closer to their respective productivities – which is already too much to hope for – and without inducing the henceforth less well-off categories to resist a worsening of their lot by comparison with that of the others.

As for a relative increase in social transfers occurring without any other change, this has an inflationary effect under the usual conditions.

We must also lay stress on a point of decisive importance in the industrialized countries. These countries evolve thanks to successive reorganizations of their investments on lines considered to be profitable. The investments link up from one period to another and the increases in investments in the different sectors are interdependent. To abide by a rate of growth reached at t_0 would be to forget that the investments in progress at that date were made at t_{-1}, t_{-2}, etc. on the assumption that the product would subsequently increase and that the components would change correspondingly. The policy criticized here would nullify the most soundly based forecasts and would lead to losses with a multiplier effect. The structural adjustment of a dynamic economy is brought about mainly by means of the *fresh* labour and capital resources identified, period by period, during the process of growth.

Only badly balanced and wasteful development would be compatible with zero growth. The slogan was merely the reflection of some economists' perplexity when they were faced with mounting social demands: it went out of fashion almost as quickly as it came in. It deserved the brief comments which we have made in order to show that, whereas growth without development is an observable phenomenon, development without growth has never been more – luckily! – than an idle hypothesis. A redistribution of resources unaccompanied by the growth of the product would entail cumulative losses and these would have the effect of lowering the rate of growth which had been achieved.

Let us now analyse an essential feature of the development process, understanding it to be the interaction of the agents over a period of irreversible time. The development process as such is full of novelty. Change affects every agent, relationships between agents, production and exchange mechanisms and relations between these mechanisms and their users.

The model of a stationary circuit,[8] according to which goods and currency follow exactly the same paths from one period to another is, like general equilibrium, a pure hypothesis. It becomes plausible only because it throws light on objects, on things, without giving close attention to people. As soon as a change is *dated*, the agents alter, their perception of their past experience, their memory and their approach to their projects, are no longer the same. An individual assumed to remain unchanged by the passage of time is an abstract idea, which is still further removed from reality than the idea of objects being unaffected by wear and obsolescence. Irreversible time brings with it innovations: when these are prejudicial to the agent or disappoint him, they compel or stimulate him to make an effort at least to adapt himself, or to invent some strategy for transforming his environment accordingly. On a small or large scale according to the complexity of the economy and the capacity of individuals holding different positions in the social hierarchy, new trends give rise to changes which, in the economic sphere, the theorists of equilibrium and the stationary state have tried to ignore, since they have always been incapable of integrating them fully into the oversimplified models they have formalized and presented in mathematical terms.

In the economies of societies open to observation, the relative positions of the agents in the hierarchies of wealth, culture and politics change with the passage of long periods of time. Hence the conflict – co-operation relationships between social groups, the demands, protests, alliances and coalitions which we can observe, leaving aside all value judgements, in every society and which are shown by normative criteria to be fruitful, relatively neutral or harmful from the point of view of the population as a whole.

Innumerable observations and studies of all types of community have established that social conflicts are never motivated by material interests alone. They are coloured or determined by individuals who are fighting for their identity, their dignity, the esteem of their community, society's respect for their occupation. In the industrialized nations, since such individuals have some experience of the ways in which society functions, they try to bend the rules of the social game in their favour.

Even an economic analysis has to do with individuals as intellectual and moral entities, and we can say, for the sake of brevity and without referring for the moment to any philosophical train of thought, that it is concerned with people, who aspire to satisfy much more than their basic needs. In verbal or non-verbal communication systems people express their reactions to one another through imitation, mimetic support or opposition, conversations and other forms of dialogue between individuals and groups. Words have a meaning and an impact; they designate objects and actions, giving them an emotional colouring; consciously or unconsciously, they convey a biased idea of what they express. An economy is immersed in a cultural environment in which everyone conforms to the rules, customs and behaviour patterns of his own group without being entirely determined by them. Each individual, being motivated by the pursuit of aims which are given relatively well ordered priorities by relatively well defined values, makes his contributions to economic and social developments, but also resists them by voicing objections and taking obstructive action. This is the dialectical process of the development of a group and the personal development of an individual, which, as history has shown, never comes to an end.

Advances, Progress and the Progressive Society[9]

The dialectic of structures operates under conditions of inequality between regions, groups of economic activities and social categories. This is so because of the inequality between decision-makers and agents equipped with differing skills and resources and no less because of the variety of propulsion effects and the environments in which they occur.

Economic spaces and social spaces are not homogeneous and there is no indication that they are tending to become so. Consequently we can give no historical example of evenly distributed growth or development.

This is true of developed countries and, under specific conditions, of developing countries too. At first, feudal regimes go together with marked inequalities in land ownership, accumulated assets and standards of education; there is a wide social gap between the elite and the ignorant and oppressed masses.

When units of capitalist enterprise establish themselves, they take every advantage of their superiority over the other elements of the system. As they develop, they draw the richest and most powerful individuals into their sphere of interest and influence, detaching them from their own people by offering profitable deals and a Western style of life.

Inequality of development leads to inequality of results, that is to say, to inequality of advances.

In a given system – for example, an economic system – advances will take the form of an increase and an improvement in the real income earned by social sub-groups. An advance of this kind, having been made in a direction deemed desirable by those concerned, should always be evaluated by qualified and impartial observers on the basis of a *wide variety* of economic, social and cultural indicators. Since advances cannot be and never are made in parallel and separate directions, but are always interdependent, it is the way in which they are combined within an evolutionary structure that is decisive. Assuming that the highest degree of equality is not, in itself, a sufficiently precise definition, we should say that progress consists in a general extension of advances made in different categories within a structure where an optimum state of inequality is tending to become established as the result of its economic and social effects.

Since there is no market without a society and without an organization, the transition from economic advances to economic progress presupposes the existence of conditions of security and freedom, training and education, which fall into the political and social sphere. The changes involved will be accepted all the more readily inasmuch as their intended effects are likely to command general support. The general extension of economic advances should ideally go hand in hand with a growing awareness of their meaning.

Here we should point out, without stating a paradox, that progress, considered as a set of objectives and achievements, is a task. In the nineteenth-century, with the enthusiasm aroused by science, technology and basic education, people held the view that progress was a 'fortunate necessity' and a self-sustaining and cumulative process. Experience has proven the opposite: progress depends on never-flagging inventiveness, exacting and attentive supervision, and perseverance. Just as there is no self-sustained growth, there is no self-sustained progress.

Furthermore, no economic system or political regime can claim to have the exclusive right to the promotion or progress or prove that progress is guaranteed by its own laws. The fact is that progress is not brought about by the operation of mechanisms; it occurs in the course of the activities, counter-activities and conflicting evaluations conducted by human agents. Neither capitalism nor socialism, however modified and corrected, can bring progress to the developing countries; the only hope of doing so lies in the efforts made by enlightened pragmatists to provide indigenous peoples with institutions of their own.

Progress is bound up with the *progressive society*. The Western model currently on offer may contain some elements suitable for strongly *corrective* and *creative* imitation by elite groups and individuals in the developing countries. In any event, the decisions as to its acceptance and remodelling, as well as the results, are entirely in their own hands.

The progressive society tends to eliminate the costs consequent upon the violence and destruction inflicted upon material and human resources. It even tends to reduce to a minimum the cost of constraints accepted by those concerned. In the economic field, this is hardly open to question. But what of social relations? In the developing countries, hierarchical and authoritarian regimes are grappling, both in the traditional societies and in the youthful democracies, with exceptional difficulties caused by longstanding malpractices and aggravated by the clash between indigenous and imported cultures. When the contradictions are deep-seated and can be overcome only very gradually, the return to normality is a slow process. Self-discipline and a society held together simply by spontaneously generated forces of cohesion, are models for which no parallel can be found in any large human community.

In order to move smoothly from traditional hierarchies via transitional ones towards new hierarchies in a developing country which is carrying out internal reforms so as to enter the world trade cycle, it is necessary to make an honest and painstaking effort to develop the traditional cultural values in new directions. It certainly seems that the need to set new standards and find fresh means of updating the old values without distorting them is the crucial problem of development and that the degree to which this is achieved is the touchstone of its complete and lasting success.

Insofar as the model of the progressive society can be assimilated and reworked by indigenous cultures on the initiative of the developing countries themselves, it offers them opportunities for creative interpretation provided that three demands are met:

(a) over a *long* period, it must raise the standards of individuals and groups as regards living conditions, culture and the forging of a political will (condition for social advancement);

(b) at *all* times it must slant the specifically economic and social structures in the direction of the optimum general structure for promoting the full personal development of the individual members of the community (condition for good structuration);

(c) once the two preceding conditions are fulfilled, it must encourage the *dissemination* of the benefits of innovation and investment, scientific knowledge and artistic creativity as rapidly as possible throughout the entire population.

This seems to be the appropriate point at which to recapitulate the main findings of the preceding pages in Table 1.1, which shows how the realization that personal development cannot be reduced to the formulae of economic development becomes a motive force in national development.

Indicators

We have renounced facile reductionism and have identified the components of development, their manifold interrelationships and the complexity of their influence on man in the course of irreversible time.

Development is quantified by means of statistical records and indicators: it should be borne in mind that an indicator is, in itself, neither a statement of an objective nor an adequate and ready-to-use instrument of evaluation.

The services rendered by indicators and their limitations become apparent if we study their fairly long history and its results, which are far from satisfactory.

Indicators Developed 'Around' Growth[10]

It is significant that the construction, examination and use of statistical indicators relating to growth have followed a curve leading from a single figure to an organized abundance of quantitative references.

The Original Indicator: the Real Per Capita Product. At the beginning, the indicator was the real total product (income) per

Table 1.1

Areas	Typical form	Diachronic sequence	Criterion
	Growth	Increase in scale	Rise in average income
Economic development	Development	Dialectic of structures	Optimum structure
Quantification and costing	Advances	Benefits for participants	Increase in benefits for participants
	Progress	General extension of benefits	Coherence
Personal development values	Aspirations and conceptions	Activation and application of values	Hierarchy and coherence of values

head of the population. Its shortcomings were revealed when it was applied in practice.

The deflation of the numerator could only be quite accurate if it was *homogeneous*, that is to say, if it faithfully reflected the prices of the goods and services included in the numerator, and if it was properly weighted, that is to say, taking into account the proportion of specific quantities in aggregate production and aggregate consumption.

To these construction difficulties are added those connected with the significance of the indicator. It is concerned with production and consumption. Aggregate consumption and net investment are shown in the numerator. Net investment – leaving aside the tricky problem of calculating depreciation – comprises the increase in the means of production and the net balance on external account. Furthermore, it designates the net increase in the resources used to augment the final product during a period extending from the time of setting up additional means of production to the point at which a final product is obtained. The actual investment figure includes annual investments which, *ex post facto*, and after contraction and liquidation, will prove unwarranted; the elimination of cyclical fluctuation would be impeded by uncertainty concerning the duration of the cycle.

The *structure* of the economy under consideration must never be forgotten. In developing countries with a dualist (pluralist) structure, foreign investment is automatically included in the growth of the real product.

Moreover, this growth reflects purely cyclical improvements in foreign trade relations, so that it would seem necessary to adjust it by taking productive capacity and long-term production into account.

It should be added that since the indicator is an average figure, it disregards the pattern of distribution of incomes and its modification with the passage of time. Average growth tells us nothing about the breakdown between profits and wages or between different sectors or regions. Adjustments made on the basis of a sequence of the concentration areas of Lorenz curves would merely indicate, when the statistics were available, the rate of increase or decline inequality.

Living Standards and Supply Balances. In order to obtain more information regarding the effects of growth on the population, attention has been focussed on data pertaining to consumption, living standards or aggregate supply balances.

The composite idea of the *standard of living* may be broken down into three elements:

> *the 'content' of life*: the goods and services, specified according to their nature and proportions, which are used by an individual or a group during a given period (breakdown of household budgets);
>
> *the norms set for the 'content' of life*: the collection of goods considered by individuals or groups to be due to them under normal circumstances or the collection of goods that an expert considers to be a minimum, maximum or decent target under certain specified conditions;
>
> *the standard of life*: in the strict sense of the term, which denotes the point reached on a scale of 'contents' of life or target 'contents' of life which has been established by the people concerned or by a competent observer.

These distinctions refer us to *structures* which are often too intricate for our statistical means of analysis and their long-term content: they introduce us to the facts of the development process, that is to say, to the relations between objects (products) and human beings.

The same may be said of aggregate supply balances, which are arrived at by an entirely different method.

They are established (Combined Food Board of the United Kingdom, 1943) by listing aggregate quantities of foodstuffs converted into energy (calories). There is no objection in principle to extending the procedure to other basic elements that can be measured in terms of physical units. In this way, a body of unbiased data is built up, which is more informative than data obtained from the market and can be used as the starting-point for an economic analysis.

Productivity. Similar remarks may be made concerning the scope and limitations of statistical indicators of productivity, which are still far removed from the economic concept of productivity.

Establishing a relation between a tangible product and the amount of labour directly employed in order to obtain it – for example, establishing the number of metric tons of coal extracted by a shift worker in a given unit of time – can only be meaningful if there is an implicit reference to an economic and social environment delineated with rigour and accuracy. This condition must be fulfilled in all countries, but more particularly in the developing countries, where the inequality between the power of entrepreneurs and that of wage-earners is quite flagrant.

On the other hand, to calculate productivity by dividing the sum of values added by the number of working hours spent directly on production is simply to broach the analysis of the conditions in which profits (and wages) are formed. A rise in productivity in terms of value shown by statistics may be due to a monopolistic policy or to a strategy which accepts unemployment, since the latter does not entail a proportionate decline in value added.

All these indicators are based on breakdowns of variables, they draw attention to aggregate variables resolved into components, the proportions of which can only be interpreted by a strictly economic analysis; this alone can show how the statistical survey relates to human beings: it becomes intelligible when placed in the context of the economic structure and the social structure of an organic whole.

Structural Indicators. The well-known division into primary, secondary and tertiary sectors, which was first used by Colin Clark and was taken up by his imitators and commentators, has been widely accepted because of its convenience: it will remain unreliable, however, so long as the content of each of the sectors has not been carefully defined (and broken down), and it is rather opaque because the link-up between the three sectors has never been made inelligible or tested as a law of development.

As far as the developing countries are concerned, the dominant factor throughout their economic history has been their industrialization by foreigners. It is they who choose where to make direct investments and establish their enterprises, being guided by the likelihood of making good profits. In the early stages, neither the whole of the host country's natural resources nor the whole of its population is affected. Subsequently, the setting-up of a transport and communications infrastructure depends either on the availability of foreign capital or on governmental decisions. Vocational and general education systems are also determined by the government's policy. Development is therefore *exogenous* with respect to market operations and, likewise, *external* because it depends on the decisions of economic and financial enterprises and groups based outside the host country. Acting according to their own interests and with private profit-making ends in view, they will sometimes invest (in Latin America or the Middle East) in mining or energy-producing industries and sometimes create relatively labour-intensive manufacturing industries using sophisticated machinery, as they have done in the Republic of Korea, where they have equipped textile and electronics plants.

The developments initiated and promoted in the host country depend on the relationship between the negotiating powers, the gradual enrichment of the developing country and its political will.

In order to assess the *overall* development of a country, it is necessary to resort to significant groupings of *appropriate indicators* (national income, distribution of the national income, employment indicator, working conditions and hours), taking care to compile accurate data concerning groups of variables that are often overlooked: costs in terms of constraints, the creativity of social elites.

This survey of the statistical indicators, which were originally elaborated for the purpose of understanding growth, has extended far beyond the quantitative question of size: our attention has been unavoidably drawn to factors that can only be interpreted when clarified by the idea of development.

'Social' Indicators[11]

The distinction between the 'economic' and the 'social' is based on the assumption that a clear dividing line can be drawn between economic and social factors.

As a matter of fact, the historical tendency in Western societies has been towards such a separation; the reason why is worth investigating.

Traditional societies in Europe (and elsewhere) were based on a principle of solidarity among members of the extended family and on intermediary bodies which purported to do their best to provide some measure of security for their members; this claim, however, should not be accepted uncritically. Modern business, on the other hand, has gradually detached itself from its original family and handicrafts background. The result has been the depersonalization of economic relations, extolled in the name of efficiency by apologists for contemporary systems, particularly in nations which have founded their prosperity and power on the mythology of enrichment and the accumulation of material goods. The trend in favour of the nuclear family and the relaxation of family discipline and ties have promoted and accelerated these changes, which are all heading in one unmistakable direction.

Those who plead the cause of the market economy on the grounds that it is capable of creating surplus products and income whose beneficial effects eventually spread throughout society, have been slow and reluctant to realize that the rule of solvency, if strictly applied, works ruthlessly against children, old people, the sick and anyone handicapped by a physical or mental disability. The 'consumption' of human beings during the process of accumulating things and capital in all its forms, cast a tragic shadow over the beginnings of industrial capitalism and, as people became better informed about the actual workings of society, this factor made it impossible to conceal the increasingly flagrant contradiction between social welfare standards proclaimed by states and their violation in practice. For this reason, it became necessary, in all Western countries, if only to make the system bearable, to reconstruct security and solidarity networks at national level in the form of welfare and social security schemes and social transfers in general.

Whether this development was imposed by rebellion or prompted by religion and morality (including state 'morality') does not alter in any way the conflict – still unresolved today – between the *principle of solvency* and the *principle of solidarity*. Accordingly, the distinction between the 'economic' and the 'social' has been taken as a pretext by theorists who have interpreted it in the narrowest sense with the support of powerful interests, for working a sort of collective confidence trick. Ignoring supposedly subtle distinctions, they hold the cursory view that social transfers are 'expenses', consisting of social security contributions, which add to the economic costs of production and distribution. The wage-earners and the underprivileged population groups have striven, for their part, to defend social security contributions as such on the grounds that they are an essential element in a sound evaluation of the level of workers' earnings; the wage has come to be regarded as a job allowance and not as the counterpart of what labour has produced; militancy for its own sake has become more common with the growing tendency to bring politics into trade union and strike action.

We are not concerned here with the major indisputable facts that have transformed the so-called allocation of resources and the hypothetical distribution of income by the 'verdict' of the market into a contractual economy supervised by the public authorities, in which organized groups of employers and employees confront one another. Earnings are now discussed by the representatives of negotiating powers and have therefore ceased to be directly related to the productivity of the recipients, whose share of the rewards were formerly presumed to be determined solely by the 'neutral' workings of the market. The shift seems beyond dispute, particularly since the market is distorted, as compared with the abstract and implicitly vindicatory model, by horizontal and vertical oligopolies and by omnipresent monopolistic competition. Anything that is not a reward for productivity – which is usually difficult to measure in both theoretical and statistical terms – is looked at askance by liberal purists, the natural allies of the profit-making system.

The distinction between the economic and the social lies at the heart of the working and even the structure of the market economy. What is at stake is the physical and personal integrity of the worker and of all those whose inferior status denies them a share in the total national product and income.

The seriousness of the situation is concealed by the intellectually lazy habit of repeating, purely as a matter of routine, the distinction which has been established once and for all between the economic and the social. Depending on the current power relations and the prevailing circumstances, the distinction varies in content and has accordingly different effects. In a period of contraction – except in extreme cases – labour demands become more pressing at the very time when production costs should be tightly controlled in order to encourage recovery. To these difficulties are added the manoeuvres of political parties.

In all cases, abstract models of distribution prove to be of very little help. Too few people realize that theoretical economies, whatever its tendency, ceases to be armed with a criterion and standard of distribution, in a situation of general equilibrium, as soon as ideal competitive conditions cannot be fulfilled. In fact, these are not merely unrealistic, but quite impossible; they are concerned with similar and equal molecules moving about as dictated by the price of products and the price of services; they describe the remuneration of abstract *factors*, but not at all the remuneration of *actors*, of agents.

In the economic conditions prevailing in the West since the Second World War, the theoretical, analytical and philosophical 'vacuum' to which we have just drawn attention has been transposed from the social classes within a state to the nations and emergent nations within the world economy. The developed nations, equipped with powerful industries and driven by social conflict, are engaged in a dialogue of the deaf with the newly independent countries who are forging their nationhood in the midst of difficulties caused by radical cultural changes and their inequality in the technological and economic fields.

The developing countries are clearly subject to especially acute internal tensions, aggravated by their awareness that they are the stakes in a worldwide struggle. The Western 'social' model is inapplicable to them, because it was shaped by a different stage of development, and the type of society which produced it has very little in common with the traditional societies which it apparently expects to improve.

Most of the developing countries, as such, are looking for a way to form a political alliance that would enable them to present a united front within the international organizations. Apart from their purely political divergencies, their cohesion is undermined by their very unequal capacity for absorbing the techniques of capitalism and particularly for assimilating those habits of Western thinking that they consider desirable for themselves. In the richest of these countries, receptivity is increased through the medium of their upper classes, but these are cut off from their own people and try very clumsily and inadequately, by applying the methods of political coercion dear to authoritarian systems, to make up for their inability to distribute the benefits of economic surpluses throughout the population. Revolutionary violence destroys local resources and its advocates prove to be just as incapable of changing the conditions governing the indigenous economy's relations with external forces and the international power structure.

Guidelines for the allocation of real resources and the international distribution of income and products are therefore urgently required.

Since this function cannot be assumed by the markets, which operate very imperfectly and are, moreover, manipulated by monopolies of all kinds, it is necessary to rely on organizations that are capable of working for common good, setting this above private interests. It has been said over and over again that there is still no world state. Much less emphasis has been placed on the fact that national states, which might at least agree to draw up joint strategies, cannot find guidance in the conventional theory of inter-*national* trade. Contrary to what this epithet suggests, foreign trade is not understood as being trade among nations, but as a commercial exchange of products and services that are scarce in varying degrees and depend directly on relative supplies of factors of production (labour, capital, natural resources) subject to the law of world market prices. A picture of provisions of homogeneous factors combined by a production function comprising constant returns does not describe nations but excludes everything that determines them specifically: external economies and states; *inter-government* trade ignores private commercial transactions, the evolutionary structures of the nation as a whole are not taken into account and any action by the public authorities is automatically suspect, their presence being regarded in all cases as a regrettable interference in the decisions taken by private enterprise. In other words, the only bodies that might assume the responsibility for changing the rules of the game in favour of the community of peoples are kept outside the field of study and analysis.

There can be no doubt that the world market is manipulated by large monopolies and powerful financial groups, which are reminiscent, on a different scale, of the 'tacit combination of masters' so farsightedly denounced by Adam Smith, but the only hypothesis considered worthy of attention by reasoned economics is that of perfect competition between small private units of comparable size and without the means of circumventing the price system.

It is therefore no cause for surprise that, in international life, the distinction between the economic and the extra-economic is used to restrict, as far as possible, social transfers made out of a sense of solidarity between the industrialized countries and the less developed countries. This way of disposing of the matter is even less justifiable in the current state of relations among nations than in relations between the different parts of one nation.

In the light of the foregoing analysis, it is easier to understand the conflicts concealed by the apparently self-evident distinction between the 'social' and the 'economic'. These are:

(1) The conflict between the demand for greater social security which is voiced by the wage-earners and underprivileged groups in the industrialized countries, and the elementary demand for the

bare necessities of life which is made by people starving to death throughout the world. Neither the rich nor the not-so-rich in the industrialized nations are willing to lower their standard of living for the benefit of distant and little-known countries. Only the state, which is 'overlooked' in the theory of foreign trade, might be able, through education or various forms of pressure, to correct this 'indifference' to reality; to do so, it would have to rise above the demands of its electorate.

(2) The latent conflict between the richest and the most disadvantaged of the developing countries, the former being caught up in the capitalist system and the latter remaining outside its networks.

(3) The conflict, within one developing country, between social categories, some of which are rapidly getting rich while the others are still struggling to emerge from a state of stagnation or regression. The 'social' outlook, which challenges institutions and structures, impresses upon everyone the need for a radical revision of the standard idea of what is 'economic', whose narrowness serves, more or less consciously, the special interests of classes and nations. This is one of the most profoundly significant aspects of the current crisis, which is a crisis of society.

Against this background, let us now attempt to evaluate the services which can be rendered by social indicators and to define their limitations. The plethora of social indicators existing in any given nation and at the level of the international community has so far produced only very poor results. This is particularly striking in view of the very high quality and skill of researchers working in this field.

Within one country, for example France – which can serve as an illustration of what can be said in many similar cases – social indicators represent a compromise with the commodity economy system, whose inner logic is not affected. The proper allocation of resources is supposed to be ensured, as a general rule, by the decentralized economy and by market forces. The preferences of the participants are put on the same footing, but the demands of disadvantaged groups belie this distorting view; the need to make minor adjustments will therefore be acknowledged and the content and results of these changes will be listed with the help of appropriately selected indicators.

The object of those demands is a blurred and confused entity known as welfare, which, upon closer examination, will be seen to be derived from the quantities of goods currently exchanged at prices determined by the aforementioned market whose workings ought to be rectified. Economists who are statisticians and are not satisfied by this definition expend much ingenuity on devising subtle combinations of criteria relating to the idea of 'happiness', which remains elusive in spite of all their efforts. Before compiling any quantitative list, we must point out that the reality itself, on which we are about to focus attention, slips from the grasp of observers and analysts. This reservation is applicable regardless of the choice of indicators and their combinations, as the reader will realize after thinking for a moment about the contents of Table 1.2, which provides us with a framework within which to rough out a classification and preliminary interpretation of the social indicators used in Western nations. They vary according to their structure, with Sweden at one extreme as an example of socialized capitalism or capitalist socialism and the United Kingdom at the other extreme, for there a liberal or moderate attempt at socialism has come up against the difficulties arising from the need to export and to reorganize industry, while between the two the Federal Republic of Germany has had long experience of social capitalism and social liberalism owing to the favourable conditions created by its

Table 1.2: Classification of Social Indicators

According to content
- social and demographic accounts
- social statistics
    - according to fields: housing, health, research
    - according to social groups: old people, 'youth', immigrants
    - according to scope:
        overall (national) programming
        sectoral programming

According to use
- descriptive
- normative
    = purposes of objective
    = explanation of constraints

According to methods of inclusion
- complementary accounts
- planning-programming-budgeting system
- social report
- social balance sheet

powerful industry and the moderation of its trade unions. All this goes to show that the social atmosphere of a nation *qualifies* all the phenomena to which indicators draw attention, and that as the influence of the qualification process pervades the whole of society it is a challenge to quantification operations with their combinations and weightings.

It will be remembered that a great effort has been made at the international level since the publication of the *United Nations Reports* (1954, 1963) and the Compendiums of Social Statistics (1963–68).

The Handbook of International Trade and Development Statistics (1979) includes the following tables:

Basic indicators (growth of population and of gross domestic product, global data and structures, growth in agricultural and industrial production, levels and growth rates of production, employment and labour productivity in the major branches of industry, energy consumption by regions and branches);

Economic and social indicators (vital statistics, economically active population, public expenditure on health, tourism, domestic mail traffic).

There is an obvious lack of coherence in this collection of figures. Public expenditure by category is presented alongside indicators relating to underprivileged sections of the population.

When a compendium covers poverty, unemployment and inequality, it is dealing with difficult ideas and the abundance of figures cannot dispel the reader's uncertainty about the reality that has to be appraised. If the methods of conducting analyses had improved at the same rate as the techniques for collecting numerical data, there would be grounds for optimism; this is definitely not the case.

An indicator gives a false impression of axiological neutrality. Yet the facts to which it refers are social realities whose content is normative in any organized society. If we see that this is so, we must admit that, apart from norms that an observer might wish to highlight by virtue of a value judgement, whether explicit or not, all indicators are normative because of their subject even before they become so because of the way in which they are handled. Social indicators attest to the fact that if normal living conditions do not exist in a given community, no satisfactory substitute will be created by the spontaneous workings of the market and of capitalism. Besides being plain common sense, this finding implies a rejection of the outmoded notion of natural economic laws and an indictment of 'ineluctable economic necessities'.

No specialist would dream of making out a case for a single indicator or the juxtaposition of several indicators. The fact remains, however, that the relations between several indicators, in all countries and more particularly in the developing countries, are very far from clear.

Certain theories on this question have become almost classics.

The growth of the *per capita* gross national product does not necessarily entail a proportionate decline in symptoms generally regarded as revealing obstacles to development.

Poverty, which has been widely studied in rich and poor countries alike, is the subject of administrative evaluations that can be used to establish thresholds for its definition. Poverty is to be found even in countries with the highest real *per capita* income. Can we say then that these 'pockets of poverty', as opposed to the vast poverty-stricken areas of the past, are gradually being eliminated by the dynamism of the economy of the contemporary world? Any such claim would imply, without proof, that our modern economy is prevented by its very momentum from creating new zones of poverty. It would also imply a failure to recognize that an increase in wealth generates relative poverty inasmuch as some strata of the population feel frustrated in a society where the strata above them are getting richer. There is no point in dwelling on the moral aspect of the value judgements expressed by people when talking about their neediness, their comfortable circumstances or their affluence. The subjective aims of personal development cannot be reduced to quantitative terms; an individual's comparison between the chances of escaping from poverty and the burdens of wealth is always coloured by his awareness of his own identity.

In the case of unemployment, it is not easy to forget the carelessness with which percentages have been proposed as a means of identifying the so-called 'hard core'. Furthermore, whenever structural adjustments are required, the same growth rate for the aggregate product is accompanied, according to circumstances, by different unemploymnt rates. Although the opposite is sometimes said for reasons of convenience, an increase in the rate of growth of the gross national product does not automatically reduce the rate of unemployment. Moreover, the personal and moral factor surfaces again when a distinction has to be drawn between a worker seeking employment and one who decides, after comparing the unemployment benefit with the standard wage, that it is not worth making the effort to find work.

As regards inequality, the question calls for a more searching inquiry than it is usually thought to warrant. The reduction of inequalities is a provisional objective: it is useful in a transitional period, but its proponents will have to prove that it is relevant to the state of affairs towards which we are moving. Can such a state be regarded as desirable if it is characterized by the equality of rewards and functions? There is every reason to feel doubtful. Inequality as regards functions and social status can be observed in all societies throughout history and it is not incompatible with equality before the law; it is grounded in inequality of skills, capabilities and training; it is bound up with the social hierarchy in its most fertile and enduring aspects. As for the hierarchy of salaries and wages, it may reasonably reflect specialization and the cost of vocational training. In societies riddled with militancy for its own sake, there is an insidious risk of confusing the egalitarian ideal with the principle of equality in terms of the dignity and worth of human beings.

With regard to education, there is a wide gap between the information supplied by indicators and the hoped-for social impact. An education system is intended to produce members of a particular kind of society. The most tolerant of societies cannot avoid meeting this requirement, which raises the whole issue of the conflicts between private education and public education. In the case of the former, the barriers to admission are raised by the cost; in the case of the latter, the conflicts are concerned with the freedom for teachers and students to choose the values which always underlie the transmission of knowledge. Whether we consider the adaptation of teaching to the education system or the degree to which the teaching meets the wishes of parents and children, we find that both problems belong to quite a different order of ideas from what indicators can tell us, however varied and detailed they may be. The transmission of basic knowledge (reading, writing and arithmetic) cannot significantly be measured merely by the degree to which a stock of 'raw material' of information and skills has been acquired, but by the minimum use to which it can be put by the learner on his own account and for the purposes of his trade.

In the eyes of a government or a party, whether it says so or not, an education system is always a human space to be conquered and organized in order to serve political ends. For this additional reason, it cannot be appraised by referring simply to an enrolment rate. Personal development resists any attempts to mould the individual learner in a way that is foreign to the aspirations of his innnermost being.

We shall now turn to highly synthetic social indicators such as life expectancy at birth or at a given age. These are concerned with the basic condition for the enjoyment of all goods and services and indicate the capacity or potential for economic and social development. They tell us nothing, of course, about the quality of life from the standpoint of society, nor from that of an individual. Furthermore, at a strictly economic level, we are still groping our way towards a serious study of labour, its output and earnings and the ways in which it is used during the life cycle and according to social categories. Consequently we are also at the tentative beginnings of an analysis of what individuals or groups of individuals contribute to the community and what they cost the community.

Because the criticisms of indicators relating to hygiene and health are so well known, we shall confine ourselves to recalling that the very idea of health is grasped in very different ways and with very different results depending on which of two opposed aims is regarded as the more important: one is to reduce to the minimum the number and virulence of physical and mental diseases and disturbances, and the other is to promote the full development of human energy without harming the individuals by drawing too heavily on his personal reserves.

In any attempt to suggest an overall evaluation of the so-called 'social' indicators, two comments may usefully provide the inquirer with food for thought.

In the first place, a social indicator is situated at the point at which the multidimensional objectives of a community intersect with the multidimensional projects of an individual ready and eager to enjoy a personal life. The resulting complexity defies all combinations and weightings, however ingenious. The challenge is even greater when societies have moved away from a common life-style and have become or are becoming pluralist, whether by choice or by necessity.

In the second place, throughout the history of human development, communities and individuals have been immersed in qualitative values. They give to verbal allusions and to symbols, whether intentionally or unintentionally conveyed, a significance which underlies or transcends what can be communicated by words. Economists and sociologists, who count, weight, calculate averages and combine them, are tempted to concentrate on things, on material objects. This leads nowhere, since neither men nor societies are things.

The tension existing between the external signs of economic development, with its paltry obsession with acquiring wealth and accumulating capital, and the plans for living made by individuals and their communities may be regarded, in the light of experience, as a mainspring and motive force of the least inhuman of the observable societies.

The reader will probably have noticed that the concept of development which we have personally proposed here adds further difficulties to the task of defining even the most rough-and-ready indicators.

The economic dialectics between sectors that are in the course of changing their structure and giving rise to new structures, are based on the propulsion effect.

Dialectics, paradialogues and, in the best cases, real dialogues between individuals and social groups also need to be stimulated by propulsion effects, but of a different kind.

The periods into which time is divided for the first and second of the above-mentioned dialectics are not superposable. The pace at which an economy becomes more complex and efficient is not the same as the pace of the mysterious progression of ideas or the transmission of values.

Irreversible time, if rightly understood, frees us from the simplistic theories of the apologists for static systems which destroy the agent. This is only the step towards gaining an understanding – essential though almost beyond our grasp – of what we longingly and regretfully refer to as *historical* time.

Notes

1. Perroux, François. *Pouvoir et économie*, 2nd ed, Paris, Dunod, 1974.

2. Perroux, François. *Economie et société – Contrainte, échange et don*, 1st ed, Paris, Presses Universitaires de France, 1960. 'The Gift: its Economic Meaning in Contemporary Capitalism', *Diogenes* (Paris, Unesco), No. 6, April 1954, pp. 3–26.

3. Perroux, François. 'Sur la notion de structure économique'. Preface to: M.

Byais, *Formation du capital et reconstruction française*, Centre d'Etudes Economiques, 1952. Structures économiques. *CISMEA*, M Series, No. 6, December 1959. *Oekonomische Strukturen. Der moderne Strukturbegriff*. Darmstadt, Wissenschaftliche Buchgesellschaft, 1973. 'Structuralisme, modèles économiques, structures économiques', *EA* No. 3, Vol. 24, May 1971.
    4. Kuznets, Simon. *National income and its composition, Modern economic growth*. 1966. *Economic growth of nations*. 1971. *Economic Growth and Structure*, W.W. Norton, 1965. Perroux, François. 'Matériaux pour une théorie de la croissance', *CISMEA*, June–July 1978. 'La croissance harmonisée selon Colin Clarke', *Banque*, 1949. 'La croissance, le Développement les progrès, le Progrès', *Grand Larousse*, 1970. Myrdal, Gunnar. *Against the Stream: Critical essays on Economics*, London, Macmillan, 1974.
    5. Perroux, Fran çois (with Uri, P. and Marczewski, Jean). *Le revenu national, son calcul et sa signification*, Paris, Presses Universitaires de France, 1947. *Les comptes de la nation*, Paris, Presses Universitaires de France, 1949.
    6. There are extensive treatises, the titles of which include the word 'development', which in fact attempt to adapt the static theories of growth to the problems of development. Higgins, Benjamin. *Economic Development*, revised edition, New York, NY, W.W. Norton, 1968. Perroux, François. 'Qu'est-ce que le développement?' *Les Etudes*, January 1961. *L'économie du XXe siècle*, 3rd ed Paris, Presses Universitaires de France, 1969. Gannage, Elias. *Economie du développement*, Paris, Presses Universitaires de France, 1962.
    7. Perroux, François. 'Trois outils d'analyse pour l'étude du sous-développement: économie désarticulée, coûts de l'homme, développement induit', *CISMEA*, F Series, No. 1, 1955. Reprinted in *CISMEA*, June–July 1978. Tinbergen, Jan (Co-ordinator). *Reshaping the International Order*, New York, 1976. *Tiers-Monde et Mondes industrialisés*, Paris, D.C., 1978 (papers prepared for the Dag Hammarskjold project). Lesourne, J. (Co-ordinator). *Interfutures Report*, 1979 (prepared for the OECD). Giersch, Herbert (ed.). *Reshaping the World Economic Order*, Symposium, Institut für Weltwirtschaft an der Universität Kiel, 1976.
    8. Perroux, François. *La pensée économique de Joseph Schumpeter, Les dynamiques du capitalisme*, Geneva, Droz, 1965.
    9. Perroux, François. 'Théorie générale du progrès économique', *CISMEA*, Vols. 1 and 2. *La distinction entre les progrès économiques et l'idée d'économie progressive*, symposium in honour of Prof. C. Gini of the Rome Institute of Statistics, 1957. 'L'idée de progrès devant la science économique contemporaine', *Encyclopédie française*, Vol. IX: L'univers économique et social, Larousse, 1960.
    10. For all bibliographical references concerning this section of Chapter 1, cf. Perroux, François. 'Théorie gérérale du progrès économique' (*op. cit.*), Vol. 1.
    11. *Measuring development* (Special issue on development indicators), Vol. VIII, No. 3, April 1972. In particular: Baster, Nancy, 'Development indicators. An introduction', McGranaham, Donald, 'Development indicators and development models', p. 91 *et seq*. Drewnowski, Jan, 'Social indicators and welfare measurement. Remarks on methodology'. Lorenzi, Jean-Hervé, Pastre, Olivier, Toledano, Joëlle. *La crise du XXe siècle*, Paris, Economica, 1980.

2 THEORETICAL FORMULATION

There have really been very few studies, to say the least, directed to the systematic investigation of how far economic theory as it is commonly taught in the West is compatible with the conditions characteristic of the developing countries. This is no accident.

The most widely-held general economic theory over the past century has been built up on the experience of the developed countries, in response to clandestine pressure from their ruling classes, by England-speaking authors writing for England, whose prosperity depends on external trade and on finance. This general theory, in many respects implicitly normative, serves the interests of the country in which it originated both by its premises and by its construction; if applied uncritically in the developing countries, it would be detrimental to them since the 'market' to which they would in fact be subjected is one in which they participate against a background of deep-rooted, universal and lasting inequality.

Furthermore, comparatively few established economists are acquainted with the actual situation in the developing countries. By and large, they are narrowly concerned with their own social experience and the economic and financial workings of their own countries, and tend to relegate development to a very subordinate position, appended to the theory and analyses of Western capitalism and its monetary and financial mechanisms.

They deprive themselves, and us, of what the developing countries can teach us, of the broadening of horizons needed if any progress is to be made towards a more general theory than the one to which we are accustomed. The word 'general' is improperly used in such expressions as interdependent general equilibrium or 'The General Theory of Employment, Interest and Money' in the title of that famous work.

In both cases, contrary to what is suggested, they are not general by *very* special theories, applicable only to the Western countries and in circumstances which, when given some thought, can be seen to be extremely restrictive.

I shall show that the so-called 'general' theories so widely held today are of very little help when it comes to interpreting the pattern of events in the developing countries and guiding their economic policies, and that they need to be radically revised.

I shall then go on to describe the main features of the current movement to revise those theories.

For the purposes of comparison, an assessment of some attitudes towards development will be needed.

These considerations will serve as an introduction to a discussion of the motive forces and dynamics of development.

Only after this condensed but precise introduction will it be possible to raise meaningful questions about the place of the new economic thinking in the current progress of science. In this respect, I feel that the *relative* decline of classical mechanics and the advance of thermodynamics cannot be indefinitely ignored by the fanatical partisans of market mechanisms.

If we assume that what are known as the human sciences cannot be evolved without reference to some concept of Man, whether this be stated explicitly or carefully concealed, it will then remain to discover some correlations between the forms of general economic theory prevalent today and the philosophical positions they imply or with which they are compatible.

The Neo-classical Theory of Interdependent General Equilibrium

No would-be coherent economic theory can dispense with consideration of the economic system as a whole, its separate components and its functioning. This is what a theory of general equilibrium sets out to do.

Despite appearances, the continuity of English thinking is incontrovertible. Alfred Marshall (*Principles of Economics*, 1890) placed emphasis on *partial* equilibrium analysis, which, had it been allowed to go beyond a narrow conception of market forces, should have led on to an analysis of structured sectors and the relationships between them. This did not happen, and as a result the *general* theory of equilibrium remained substantially the same from the time of S. Jevons to L. Walras (1874) and V. Pareto (1906), who enlarged upon it, and is to be found again in J.R. Hicks's statics and metastatics.

Nobody has forgotten the Keynesian 'revolution' and the ensuing 'counter-revolutions' – impressive-sounding words which give an exaggerated and even distorted idea of the changes they describe so dramatically. In his celebrated work *The General Theory of Employment, Interest and Money*, and in his own comments on it, John Maynard Keynes broke radically with the theory of general equilibrium advocated by A. Cecil Pigou, who described it in terms of micro-, meso- and macroeconomics. But Pigou's rebellious disciple failed to give us any detailed account of the relationships between micro-, meso- and macroquantities and left us in doubt about the price systems compatible with his macroeconomics. It must be said that his treatment of the relationships between macroeconomic flows would have lost nothing and would indeed have gained a great deal from such elucidation. Quite clearly, the area to which Keynes's recipes could be applied would have been much less vague in regard to the developing countries, and the danger of his prescriptions would have been directly revealed.

After J.M. Keynes, general equilibrium continued as before to be the main diet served up to the students who were ultimately to become the top executives of the major private or public business enterprises, and who would eventually be called upon to interpret the economies of their own societies and possibly those of distant lands. Wherever they might be, students of economics would always, before gaining any first-hand experience, be provided with a matrix for analysing economic activity anywhere in the world.

The spread of this teaching in the West was to entail serious consequences, for the theory of general equilibrium based on the mechanics of market forces was repeated *ad nauseam* and expressed in terms of simple mathematics which gave it an aura of prestige in the eyes of the general public. Thus consecrated, it became, by sheer force of habit and emulation, a sort of cornerstone of theory, wrongly made out to be unshakeable. When put to the test, the premises and substance of the system lose all credibility; great cracks appear in the fabric of the building that was supposed to be so securely established.

Walras' and Pareto's theory of equilibrium[1] is based on small units (individuals and firms) subject to a price over which they have absolutely no control; the price gives them all the information they need and they consequently have to make the necessary adjustments by altering the quantities they produced. Optimum full employment of resources is brought about by establishing individual equilibria in which supply equals demand, thus providing a general equilibrium price. Money becomes simply coins and notes, or just another commodity which makes economic calculations and exchange possible at any point in an abstract, homogeneous space.

Such a theory, which goes against observation and experience, presupposing as it does that small units (or firms) are totally independent of one another, has been advanced as a 'pure' theory because of its reference to the equilibrium of Lagrange's classical mechanics (1788) and because of its system of equations. These are:

1. Equations for the *behaviour* of the small units, each one maximizing the result of the use of its resources by ensuring equal marginal productivity of the productive factors and ensuring that the marginal utilities of the goods traded are proportionate to their prices.
2. Equations for *linkage*: the equilibrium price ensures that all supply equals all demand. In other words, it links up the employment of all goods and all services.
3. Equations for *balance*: equilibrium allows of neither a surplus nor a deficit (underemployment of resources).

Taken in the stationary, timeless state, this system means that the optimum of individual units coincides with the optimum of the whole: the optima are co-determined mathematically in conditioning of perfect competition. Ingeniously constructed, it does away with all *activity* by any human *agent*; the decision-maker could be replaced by a robot which records the price and can accordingly make the necessary adjustments in the use of the quantities available.

Although *this* particular, so-called general, equilibrium is now challenged by seasoned economists from all over the world, it is still a model that is commonly taught, reformulated in various mathematical styles, but left intact as regards its basic structure. And *that* very structure is essentially misleading for the crucial reason that it assumes that things and goods are ordered by allegedly neutral market forces instead of allowing for human activity, for people's ability to change and to change their material and human environment.

It can easily be seen in any country, and particularly in the case of the developing countries, with their marked amplification, that this outline provides no sound basis for description, interpretation or action, for the following reasons:

A. It is a notable example of 'prefabrication', claiming as it does to resolve in advance, simultaneously and in static conditions, the questions of the *existence*, *uniqueness*, optimality and *stability* of equilibrium.

B. It presupposes perfect competition between *like units*, between identical items in such numbers that none has the power to influence prices or to influence any of its counterparts.

C. Each of these macro-units is *passive*, simply adapting quantity to price, always in a context of perfect competition.

D. The model is *instantaneous*, being constructed at a given instant; moreover it is *timeless* in that the small component units have neither memory of the past nor plan for the future.

E. The model excludes *structures* and *structured sub-sets* (industries, regions, social groups).

F. It has never succeeded in proposing an identical theory for application to *both* international exchanges *and* domestic exchanges. This is not surprising, since the nation is a structure and an organization and hence beyond the scope of a model which rules out any structure or organization.

G. With this model, it has never been possible to relate the equilibrium of the micro-units *analytically* with the aggregates of national accounting. These aggregates are supposed to represent the sum of goods in terms of value but the prices applied are not homogeneous because of the combination of different forms of competition, monopolies and oligopolies. Furthermore, the transition from the general equilibrium of micro-units to the general equilibrium of macro-units has never been strictly analysed.

H. The model provides no explanation for the relationships between *historical forces* (background) and *economic dynamics* (functioning).

I. The model is not operational in the very precise sense that it does not allow of *calculating* the quantities it defines; nor of determining an equilibrium position on the basis of statistical data and curves.

Progress cannot be made by concentrating attention on *disequilibrium* positions (*leaving the concept of equilibrium unchanged*) but only by accepting a *different* concept of general interdependence and of the ordering of the components that constitute the whole.

A comparison between this model and the *conditions* which, to a greater or lesser extent, are *common to all the developing countries* shows that it is utterly inapplicable to them and that the obsessions to which it gives rise are indeed extremely dangerous. In a developing country, the economic spaces involved are heterogeneous (in contrast to B, E and G above); and a sound strategy for developing countries calls for changes in the historical forces operating (in contrast to H), implies restructuring (in contrast to E, F) extends over a period of time which is irreversible (in contrast to D) and presupposes a shift in power relations (in contrast to B).

Any well-informed reader will have no difficulty in enlarging upon these incompatibilities, with concrete examples to illustrate them.

In short, the model depicts a pure market situation with perfect competition, using mechanical analogies; it is diametrically opposed to the conditions common to the developing countries, which can emerge from the limitations of their status only through the combined *efforts* of their elites and peoples to change their immediate and more remote environment. If the developing countries really tried to understand the standard theory of equilibrium, they would learn that it may be attempted, without significant success, to form a mechanical representation of how things move in a homogeneous environment instead of recognizing the combination of activities in the essentially heterogeneous human environment in which life and history follow their course.

J.M. Keynes's Macroeconomic Equilibrium

The General Theory of Employment, Interest and Money (1936)[2] was written not long after the depression (1929–33) which affected the United Kingdom so severely. Alive to the difficulties besetting his country, with its declining hegemony and outdated structures, J.M. Keynes understood the problems of an economy based on free markets and the power of capital, and spoke of the 'decay of capitalism'. But in respect neither of the British economy nor of other economies did he fundamentally and explicitly consider structures, historical forces and structural inequalities.

His *diagnosis* was directly conditioned by his chosen field of observation: the economy of those countries in which there was a capital market, a money market and business enterprises backed by a sophisticated financial and banking system.

The *cure*, or set of remedies he proposed, matched his diagnosis. Experience has shown that it is of doubtful effectiveness in the case of the developed countries; even more clearly, it is neither relevant nor practicable in the case of the developing countries.

According to Keynes, the market economy works spontaneously at a level below that of full employment. For given production functions, the level of global income depends on investment and on the (marginal) propensity to consume or, in other words, on investment and the multiplier (the opposite of the propensity to save).

The propensity to consume is less than 1 and it does not rise in proportion to an increase in income; a proportion of that income is not spent on consumption and is regarded as being excluded from consumer spending. Additional investment will be necessary to compensate for that deficiency.

So long as full employment has not been achieved, the additional money supply brings about a surplus in the real national product by mobilizing idle economic resources (unemployed labour, unused productive capacity); it is a form of productive inflation.

The trouble is the insufficiency of effective demand, of consumer spending and of investment; the remedy is to increase expenditure on consumption, or to increase investment by lowering the interest rate or through public investment.

A large number of post-Keynesian writers have enlarged upon the model and produced their own interpretations of it, some departing from orthodox free enterprise and capitalist thinking (Joan Robinson, M. Kalecki) and others standing by it (Leijonhufvud). The theories of 'balanced growth' advocated by R.F. Harrod, E. Domar and J.R. Hicks and later by R. Solow and again J.R. Hicks in his alternative interpretation, stemmed from the Keynesian model.

Some of the contributions attributable to these revised versions are undeniable. The basic features of the Keynesian model are, however, tenable only in a very special case, in an historical situation similar to that of the United Kingdom around the 1930s and even then not without distinct reservations.

The point we are dealing with here is quite specific: can the Keynesian model provide the basis for a development policy? Does it describe the obstacles to development and the economic handicaps of the developing countries? Can it help in selecting the means of remedying them? The answer to all these questions is, more certainly, *no*.

Without going again into the detailed demonstrations given elsewhere, let us compare in Table 2.1 the conditions for the success of the Keynesian model with the situation to be observed in the developing countries, singling out, of course, only the most striking points.

Table 2.1

Conditions for the success of the Keynesian model	Situation to be observed in the developing countries
a. The money supply circulates in an environment through which its effects *spread* rapidly and widely	The effects of the money supply are very unevenly and incompletely spread (localized unabsorbed inflation)
b. It is assumed that, by raising or lowering the interest rate, idle capital can be mobilized (pseudo-savings (hoardings) in advanced capitalist economies)	No 'national' capital or money market. Traditional hoarding rural dwellers in pre-capitalist economies
c. Mobilization of idle resources (workers *already trained*, potential of an *already existing* production apparatus)	'Idle' resources in developing countries are only potential; the workers have to be trained and the production apparatus built up
d. Leakages, i.e. breaks in the multiplier effect are: – paying off of previous debts – refraining from spending altogether – an increase in imports	Such leakages in the developing countries are attributable to structural factors: – accumulated and enduring debt – pre-capitalist-type saving – financing of *essential* imports (e.g. food)
e. Positive elasticity of supply in relation to increased money supply	Inelasticity of supply for structural reasons, e.g. preponderance of agricultural production
f. 'Involuntary' unemployment (a somewhat obscure expression denoting underemployment as a result of insufficient overall demand). No serious bottlenecks	Structural unemployment: – disguised unemployment as a result of overpopulation – lack of basic equipment and *trained* labour
g. An export surplus ($\bar{X} > \bar{M}$) has roughly the same effects as an investment	The *structural* deficit of the balance of trade and payments necessitates imports. An import surplus ($\bar{M} > \bar{X}$) over any period stimulates the capital equipment of the developing country

The contrasts emerging from this comparison are supported by historical evidence; very briefly and summarily the comparison illustrates the fundamental inapplicability of the Keynesian model to the situation of the developing countries.

Among other consequences, the Keynesian *balanced-growth* models are not applicable to the developing countries. Their growth patterns can be seen even more clearly than those of the developed countries to be a concatenation of *'bearable disequilibria'* leading, on certain conditions, to the formation of economies capable of ensuring subsistence and an improved standard of living for the population concerned and of fitting into the networks of international competition.

The Keynesian model was constructed *from the standpoint* of the developed countries and *for* them, at a time when the balance of power was tipped against the developing countries. Any reference the latter make to it today is for very different reasons and in an entirely different context from those originally prevailing. The use of aggregates in national accounting (national product, consumption expenditure, investment) is a convenient way of classifying the components of any policy, but their inclusion in development schemes or plans has very little to do with the sort of subtle *government by money* recommended by Keynes, in the interests of his own country, to intelligent bankers and businessmen whom he hoped to emancipate by relaxing the constraints of orthodox liberal economic doctrine.

The level of development necessitates drawing a distinction between the sphere of imported capitalism and that of the indigenous economies, and treating each appropriately. Unless there is a policy for communication between the two, and a no less watchful control over the effects of the former on the latter, the developing country's interests will be turned outwards and its economy will not serve those of its population as a whole.

To take the argument even further, it is absolutely necessary to adopt a strategy that will take in the various sectors of *all* the branches of industry and the various sectors of *all* the branches of agriculture. A mesoeconomic system of this kind is left out of account by Keynesian macroeconomics and would throw it into serious disarray.

It is not difficult to see how appealing the doctrine of productive inflation may seem to the government of a developing country. As a general rule, a money surplus is welcomed by countries with a deficit and a burden of debt, whose whole production apparatus has yet to be built up. It must be made quite clear, however, that an additional money supply does not have any intrinsic effect as regards the training of people, the building of factories or the direction of efforts towards the production of the most essential goods and towards exports appropriate to a particular or foreseeable situation on the international market.

What is needed is a policy, difficult and complex though it may be, formulated in consultation with foreign countries and effectively guided by a plan. No such policy is provided for either explicitly or implicitly in what Keynes has to say and can certainly not be inferred from it. It would be quite a serious mistake for a developing country to believe that its only choice lies between Neo-classicism and Keynesianism; it will need to exercise its own invention and to adopt a course of action tailored to its own needs.

The General 'Equilibrium' of 'Active' Units

The mathematical equalities of macroeconomics were not what was needed to improve the traditional equilibrium theory. A growing number of competent, well–informed economists are departing from them and giving their reasons for doing so. They have been impelled to do so by the forms of monopoly and the oligopolies which are steadily encroaching, before our very eyes, on the sphere of private or semi-private economy. In an oligopoly, each decision-maker is aware of the other and any decision he makes involves predicting the decisions of the other parties. If the result is found to be in the interests of all the business concerns involved, it will be a typical case of conflict–co-operation, of struggle–synergy.

It is surely clear that any deviation from the pattern of perfect competition brings in the influence of human *activity*, the ability of individuals to direct their energy, and more particularly their expansive power, to bringing about change in their material and human environment?

To accept this – and experience shows that we must – means committing ourselves to the building up of a new theory of interdependence and global equilibrating action (i.e. action to bring about a state of equilibrium).[3]

Such a theory involves rejection of the idea of considering individuals to be annihilated, reduced to nothing, and treated as mere price-recorders, setting off automatic reactions; it cannot accept the notion of their being brought into equilibrium by external mechanisms in which they have no part to play; it distinguishes clearly between the actions and reactions of subjects capable of perception and intention, and the displacement of immutable objects moved by 'natural' forces in homogeneous space.

New treatments of the general theory are now available, describing it in a revised form in terms of present-day mathematics, starting with the *agents* or *'actors'* and active units.

The Agent and His Activity

Each individual is considered, in economic as in other matters, to be endowed with energy as a human being, whereby he can locally – i.e. in a specified area – modify his material environment and affect the other human actors surrounding him.

This energy productive of change, usually directed to expansion, depends on certain variables (personal coefficient, cultural background, social status), the study of which falls theoretically within the purview of other branches of the human sciences. If, however, we failed to consider the influence of the environment on the agent, and vice versa, as falling within our own field of study, it would be completely cut off from communication with those other branches which are most vital to it as soon as we embark on action.

The Actor

The actor or agent is an organization or an individual living in society and taking decisions, i.e. reconciling the variable means at his disposal and the variable aims he hopes to achieve, on the basis of his information and capabilities, and drawing on his memory in planning for the future.

The actor is not, therefore, the robot slavishly subject to the price system of the 'like unit', by definition identical with any other, visualized in the mechanical system of general equilibrium. Every actor is different from any other. Moreover, for any series of given operations over any given period of time, the actors are not equal. The result of their exchanges, in the most general sense, is due to the encounter of *action* and *counter-action*, and not to the halting of the movement of immutable objects controlled by the anonymous, allegedly natural forces of price-setting.

The energy put forth by the actor is applied to his *unit*, that is to say, to the goods and services directly available to him and organized by him. This area over which his power of decision is exercised – or, more succinctly, his area of decision – may, for instance, be his production unit (his enterprise or firm), which has a particular size and structure and occupies a particular place (i.e. has co-ordinates) in the whole complex considered. Through that unit, the actor can modify his environment by means of operations which delimit his operation areas (clientele, investment, information). They can be classified according to the logic of set theory and constructed as vector spaces, which can be deformed subject to the usual rules of elementary topology.

The unit on and through which the individual or corporate decision-maker exerts his energy is either a simple unit (an enterprise) or a complex unit (an enterprise and its subcontractors, a major unit and the units with which it combines to form an economic or financial group). The structure of the *complex unit*, or *macro-unit*, consists in the fact that a major, controlling unit determines the values of some of the variables of the subordinate units.

The economic spaces represented by business operations, clientele, investment and information can be applied to a geographical area. This is advantageous in two respects:

- showing a national economy to consist of differentiated economic spaces, and
- furnishing a representation which leads on immediately to the analysis of direct investment and transnational corporations within a nation.

Within a given period, the actor's exertion of his energy is either interrupted because his goal has been attained, or *temporarily* checked because of some obstacle or opposition from an opponent.

Aggregate energy will be taken to be energy productive of change resulting from the combination of the energies of all the actors and all the units over which they have power of decision.

Global Equilibrating Action by Active Units

Global equilibrating action by active units in a whole economic complex is characterized by the temporary exhaustion of the net energy productive of change in the complex (where ϕ symbolizes energy and ϕ_c the system's energy, we find $d\phi_c \simeq 0$).

This global equilibration differs *radically* from the general equilibrium of micro-units all equally and uniformly subject to the price norm and consequently compelled to accept the necessity of equal prices and costs, i.e. equilibrium, and as a result *co-satisfied* when such equalization is achieved, each unit deriving the maximum economic advantage compatible with maximum economic advantage for the whole.

An economy, however, is conceivable only in terms of a rank-ordered distribution of social *roles* and *inequality* in the size and the relative power of the units composing it.

Any economic complex must therefore be considered to be composed of the Great and the Small, the Strong and the Weak, with the co-satisfaction achieved by the Great at their level imposing limitations, in the mathematical sense, on the co-satisfaction of the Small. Equality of supply and demand at a given point in time, at an equilibrium price, does not in itself tell us anything about the agents, the levels of their aspirations or their acceptance of the situation described.

Oligopolies and oligopolistic groups, for example, having exhausted their energy productive of change, may make do with a more or less lasting equilibrium which imposes its own conditions and its own limitations on the small and medium-sized units. These will enter into competition with one another, subject to those conditions and limitations, without being able for some time to ease them.

The rule that supply will equal demand at a given price will not apply in the same form at all levels of competition, and the satisfaction of the Great at their level may be concomitant with the non-satisfaction of the Small. The former find it temporarily advantageous to suspend the struggle, as between partners of comparable size and power, while the latter have not sufficient energy productive of change, until they join forces, to alter the conditions imposed on them.

In more concrete terms, the oligopolies supplying intermediate products in a vertical line determine their prices together: the buyers of those intermediate products cannot for some time take action to modify the prices to their own advantage until they can make their combined influence felt. Or again, the big banking groups may establish a level of interest that satisfies them, to which their smaller partners have to submit; or major importers may determine satisfactory trading prices among themselves while the middle men and ultimate consumers will have to wait some time before they can challenge them.

As we can see, this is simply the generalized and detailed application of the distinction between *price-makers*, those who make or help to make prices, and *price-receivers*, those who are subjected to the prices made by others. This generalization is based on the assumption that unequal structures prevail over a period of time.

The general equilibrium of Walras and Pareto denotes the halting of the movement of objects, displaced by the forces of the price system, which act upon imaginary, unreal individuals reduced to the rank of small identical units.

Global equilibration, on the other hand, describes the result of the combined energy productive of change and activity of different, unequal actors, in other words a *situation in which equilibrium is secured* at several levels by the actions and counter-actions of units of unequal size, structure and power.

At first sight, global equilibration is not inevitably accompanied either by uniform, general co-satisfaction, or by optimalization, determined by the uniform, universal co-satisfaction of all units.

Global equilibration allows for structural inequalities and the combination of the various forms of monopoly. Since it refers to the activities of unequal agents or actors, it prompts analysis of the equalization of supply and demand at the *different* levels of trade within any one nation and between nations, and encourages enquiry into what it means each time, with the help of specific models.

This does away with the obsession with equilibrium that is supposed to be achieved mechanically, at least over a long period of time. The system is seen instead as a succession of disequilibria rendered bearable by the organization of the social groups and by variable doses of regulation intentionally injected by the public authorities.

The ensuing growth and development may be *harmonized* through the conflicts and synergies among organized social groups, and by co-ordination and arbitration on the part of public bodies, so long as they are *active* and *informed*. Growth and development are not automatically balanced by compensation and adjustment mechanisms; these do have a stabilizing effect in market economies which, through a social learning process, have acquired the appropriate reactions, but they are never enough on their own to ensure progress towards optimal equilibrium and uniform co-satisfaction.

Once the actor and the activity of individuals and groups are brought back into the revised theory of economic activity, a rigorous, operational approach to evolving development policies can be initiated. It is as far removed from historicism and institutionalism as it is from the market economy equilibrium, put forward as a pure theory based on quite *impossible* conditions and using the borrowed mathematics of Lagrangian mechanics.

Some Attitudes Towards Development

Since a discipline faced with new and pressing circumstances determined by experience cannot be completely reformed all at once, nor even in the quarter-century that has elapsed since the Second World War, the measure of confusion that still prevails in development theories and doctrines is understandable.

Key directions, marked out by writers who may be considered representative, are, however, now emerging.

The original English classics have not been superseded: they have been brought up to date by their neo-classical disciples, armed with text-book geometries and sometimes sophisticated mathematics. The reasons, of course, are not wholly intellectual: they had the merit of discovering and spelling out the problems of the *market*, and the greatest Western powers are by no means ready to forego them.

Secondly, since the outburst of empirical research has not yet been matched by a body of new theory to help it classify, interpret and digest the set of new facts, the temptation to fall back on a somewhat 'reasoned' history tends to carry the day, to some extent justifiably in view of the shortcomings of theory at a time when certain historians are pleased to present history as the science of sciences.

Lastly, Karl Marx, more often quoted and distorted than actually read, still holds a paramount role. Not the Marx who wrote the early works, nor even the one who wrote *Capital*, but rather the Marx who paved the way for V.I. Lenin's essentially political action. Leninist Marxism foments rebellion against all social injustices and, while it inspires no scientific treatises, is at least used as a highly-valued point of reference by a section of the intelligentsia, who realize that market economics need to be fundamentally rethought, but are seeking in vain for an alternative doctrine.

A necessarily brief account of each of these three currents of thought will be useful to provide the co-ordinates for our proposed interpretation.

The Legacy of the Classical Economists[4]

In a book published in 1955 under the title of *The Theory of Economic Growth*, Arthur W. Lewis shows implicitly that he does not renounce the legacy of the English classical economists. There are many reasons for regarding this work as a significant piece of evidence.

Lewis sets out his method at considerable length, emphasizing that he intends to keep strictly to a clearly marked out field. He defines growth as the increase of *per capita* output. The task of defining output and its cost he leaves to the 'theorists' of national income, and that of acquainting us with the inherent difficulties of using a general price index to statisticians. He states forcefully that he will deal directly neither with distribution nor with consumption, nor again with the debates about *welfare* or the satisfaction and *happiness* of those concerned. Only at the end of the book does he devote an appendix to the question 'Is economic growth desirable?'. His study, as he insistently repeats, concerns not the utility of output but only its growth.

As the human frame of reference he takes the *nation-group*, in the simplest possible meaning of a group of which a population census has been established and which keeps statistics on external trade.

His book will thus be concerned with *growth* and nothing but growth: should the words *development* or *progress* happen to flow from his pen, it will be only *for the sake of variety*.

With such a carefully chosen and circumscribed point of departure, the reader runs little risk of going astray – or in other words, of accepting an enlargement of the concepts or a change in the kinds of connections between the realities they denote. Without the least polemical intent, it might be argued that Lewis *narrows* down Adam Smith's field of view, since the latter, in *An Inquiry into the Nature and Causes of the Wealth of Nations*, gives us a broad and fruitful idea of national income, its formation and its development.

Varying his own statements rather than *relating* them to those of

others, Lewis seems to be convinced that the essential features of
human nature are immutable and that descriptions and
recommendations of universal validity can therefore be put
forward.

Growth, in his view, has proximate causes and mediate and
human causes. The former are *the effort to economize*, the increase
of *knowledge* and its applications, and the build-up of capital or
other resources per head. The mediate causes derive from
institutions and beliefs.

On this basis, the entire book is constructed in response to the
two problems of the *consistency* of institutions with growth and the
evolution of economic and social realities in their relationship with
growth – on the clear understanding that the laws governing
economic and social trends can neither be predicted nor even
identified. The chief thing to grasp is that: 'Different societies have
enough in common for it to be possible to deduce *some general rules
of human behaviour*'. Using those rules, we can tell how change will
occur, if it occurs; what we cannot foresee is what change will occur.
'If institutions are liberalized, human effort will increase, and more
knowledge and more capital will be applied in production'.

The entire work rests upon deductive analyses illustrated by
frequent reference to practical experience, the two being
juxtaposed rather than built up into a framework for theoretical
models.

The impression that emerges is one of an economist who
sincerely wishes to go beyond the hackneyed formulae of the
Manchester school but who thinks, all in all, that they are based on
human nature and that they alone have yielded positive results in
the past. The outcome is a balanced exposition of the 'advantages
and disadvantages' or 'pros and cons' of an attitude or institution.

The questions and answers are so interwoven with each other
that the fundamental options cannot be identified. Is the principle
of *nothing for nothing*, for example, compatible with the survival of
non-productive individuals or at least with their 'normal'
subsistence in locally prevailing circumstances? To such a direct and
uncompromising question, there appear to be only two replies.

Either it is *impossible*, in any given situation, to save human lives
– in which case this impossibility should be submitted to rigorous
scrutiny to see whether it stems from the institutions or from
insuperable natural conditions; or else the *strictly operating*
mercantile economy is the *only* rational and practicable form of

economy – in which case its merits should induce us to overlook its defects and to consign its derelicts to oblivion.

No advanced society has accepted these 'impossibilities' for itself. Moreover, from the purely *economic* standpoint, in terms of the use of all present and *potential* resources, such a line of argument would not hold water.

Lewis himself defines his book as a *map* and, with unimpeachable caution, he seems thereby to have said all that there is to be said about it. A map affords guidance – and that is not to be scorned: a theoretical or practical economist must choose his route. He may be forgiven for hesitating, despite or perhaps because of the conscientious drawing of the map, over the direction given him. Could everything depend solely on specific cases? If so, there is no point in theorizing.

Chapter VII, the last before the Appendix on the desirability of growth, gives an example of choice. In a discussion of *Government*, it contrasts – albeit without an exact matching of the terms – nine categories of Government action and nine alternatives that open the door to stagnation (see Table 2.2).

Table 2.2

Functions of government	*Ways in which government brings about stagnation*
1. Maintaining public services	1. Failing to maintain order
2. Influencing attitudes	2. Plundering the citizens
3. Shaping economic institutions	3. Promoting class exploitation
4. Influencing the use of resources	4. Impeding foreign intercourse
5. Influencing the distribution of income	5. Neglecting public services
6. Controlling the quantity of money	6. Excessive *laisser-faire*
7. Controlling fluctuations	7. Excessive control
8. Ensuring full employment	8. Excessive spending
9. Influencing the level of investment	9. Embarking upon costly wars

It cannot be doubted that the author has tabulated actual cases: he has had wide experience and possesses first-hand knowledge of the developing countries. Who, moreover, would dream of denying that these recommendations are based on the soundest common sense? None the less, many will feel that it takes far more than this to construct a *theory* of Government, regardless of the economic environment.

How remote is this book published in 1955 from the unanimous demands of the developing countries 21 years later! What is wanted today is not a subtle application of classical doctrine, but a thorough, overall restructuring of economic relations in the widest and freest meaning of the term.

While the exponents of the classical theory may invoke long experience of the enrichment of *some* classes in some *nations*, the developing countries can point to centuries of suffering, worsened rather than substantially relieved during the balmy days of Western prosperity. We need not go beyond this simple reminder, merely emphasizing that it appears not untimely in present world circumstances. Taking our cue from the author himself in his liking for reasoned balance, we shall call, as a complement to his work, for some kind of system, however sketchy, to help us to master, provisionally and as a first approximation, the uncertainties of the collections of empirical data bound together by the golden thread of classical doctrine.

We still have to consider the simple development model that Lewis deduces from the virtually 'unlimited' labour 'supply' to be found in a large number of developing countries. Such countries are seen as comprising two sectors: the one a traditional or subsistence sector (T), and the other capitalist (C). The capitalist sector is motivated by the pursuit of profits as the sole source of investment, while the T sector produces labour at relatively low wages.

The whole complex is driven by anticipated profit and maintained by the profit made, which supplies the needs of productive investment (C sector). Because of the initial difference and inequality between the two sectors, the overall product and employment may grow without leading to any marked increase in real wages (T sector). Only gradually does the bulk of the labour force come to realize its relative situation and aspire to raise its living standard. Moreover, within fairly narrow limits, that living standard, thanks to the capitalist sector (C sector) may be rather higher than that which the workers of the traditional or T sector would have enjoyed without it.

The formation of capitalist profit hence rests on a certain lag on the part of the indigenous labour force. (This is somewhat reminiscent – although the circumstances are clearly very different – of the monetary illusion in J.M. Keynes's early model, in which progress towards full employment went hand in hand with a certain *reduction* in real wages.) Lewis's model provides quite a sound description of colonial development of the exact kind that the developing countries now reject and against which they are marshalling their forces all over the world.

The rate of profit, which is the motive force of the two-sector economy, may be reduced by an increase in the cost of the workers' food, either because the latter improve their bargaining position or because food has to be imported. In either case, the lowering of the rate of profit leads to a lowering of the rate of capital accumulation. As capital and its accumulation are the motive forces of 'development', the latter loses momentum. Obviously, the upward trend in wages may be slowed if the productivity of labour in agriculture rises. But that is ultimately in the gift of the capitalists, not the population or its representatives. In this model, capitalists and entrepreneurs may decide to establish a modern farming industry in some areas – in which case they will secure a relatively high output from one part of agriculture, from which the indigenous farmers will not necessarily benefit.

The working of the model depends on a *structural* imbalance which there is no question of eliminating. On the contrary, the C sector may – and this possibility is explicitly envisaged – absorb the whole of the developing country's economy. In which case, Lewis notes with equanimity: 'An economy enters upon the second stage of development and classical economics ceases to apply. We are in the world of neo-classical economics'.

After this, it is almost superfluous to point out that Lewis seems to think that capital and capitalists are the masters of development. As he would have it, the alternative is simply between being a classical or a neo-classical economist, depending on the time. This position has the merit of bringing out the radical difference between the analysis of development 'centred' on man and an analysis of growth from the standpoint of capitalist strategy and based on gradually 'delegated' enrichment.

While not fully satisfactory, the historical attitude may possibly prove a little less disappointing.

Reasoned History[5]

Joseph Schumpeter's term '*reasoned* history' has enjoyed little success, since it has irritated specialists in two camps. One side feels that, unless the social sciences are to die out, their job is to discover laws rather than to reason about history; while the other side is convinced that history is now the queen of disciplines and has no need of 'reasoning' prior to research geared to specific questions that are clearly defined and as far as possible quantified.

Both forms of rejection stem largely from misunderstandings. Few historians would agree to be mere narrators; it is, moreover, well known that narration itself cannot do without concepts, ideas and implicit models of human behaviour, to say nothing of hypotheses suggested by personal experience and thrown up by the subconscious. How many competent and well-informed economists can pride themselves on possessing means of quantitative regulation that do not depend on a *constant* reference to structures, those structures that cannot be achieved without a knowledge and an interpretation of history?

The main factor that is overlooked, however, is that, in putting forward his somewhat unpopular expression, J. Schumpeter, unrivalled for his scholarship in the field of historical and modern economics, was setting an example of modesty and expressing a measure of the nostalgia shared by all who have undertaken to evaluate the 'scientific' nature of our discipline.

Moreover, the contribution of a somewhat 'reasoned' economic history is in no way to be despised, so long as anyone embarking upon this difficult exercise designates his objective very clearly, explains his choice of instruments, and does not put forward his own preferred hypothesis as the only possible and productive one.

In his two-volume work on *Business Cycles*, Schumpeter gives us a history of capitalism from the point of view of short cycles (Kitchin, Juglar) and long, or hundred-year, cycles; he thereby makes a great contribution to the theories of cycles since, as we all know, no comprehensive theory of these phenomena has yet been devised.

On a very different level and with a very different end in view, Walt W. Rostow, a professional historian, has written a stimulating book based on the course he gave in Cambridge in 1958 on one aspect of growth. Its title, *The stages of economic growth – A non-communist manifesto* (Cambridge University Press, 1960), goes further than its content, and is flawed by a measure of ambiguity. However, the author's intention of 'bringing modern economic theory to bear on economic history' is undoubtedly timely, and the object of his enquiry is carefully delimited.

With the exception of the applications (from page 73 onwards), the first five chapters concentrate on the concept of 'take-off', the stage marked by an economy's first major growth which, in the case of the world's principal nations, followed that which England experienced in the late eighteenth century. The book's purpose is not to provide a theoretical analysis of development in terms of explicit operative forces – population, innovation or rules of the game – but to furnish rough-and-ready benchmarks for successive, broadly described stages of growth.

This composite product of Rostow's thought and historical knowledge may help the economist to work out his own interpretations. The subject studied is *growth* in a narrow sense, there being no direct discussion of its relationship with distribution and no explicit description of the dialectics of development. It will, however, be noted that the study of *leading sectors* leads on to evolutive structures and patterns, although the logical analytical consequences thereof are not developed in this book.

In contrast to the economic systems (*Wirtschaftssysteme*) and types of organization (*Wirtschaftsorganisationen*) of the German schools, Rostow sets out to distinguish and to date the stages of growth, which he reduces to five.

(1) *The traditional society*. This uses techniques derived from pre-Newtonian physics; agriculture provides the bulk of total output; political power remains relatively decentralized.

(2) *The establishment of the preconditions for take-off*. Techniques derived from modern or post-Newtonian science are adopted and become widespread. Economic overlords become aware of diminishing returns and set out to obviate them. A cumulative growth process sets in, symbolized by reference to compound interest calculation. Often these changes will be clearly due, in a given country, to an upheaval brought about by an impulse imported from abroad.

(3) *Take-off*. Growth becomes a usual condition and is viewed as 'normal'. The cumulative process is strengthened, backed up by new social attitudes and appropriate institutions; total investment and savings climb to between 5 and 10 per cent of total income.

(4) *The drive to maturity*. Output now grows more quickly than the population. Investment and savings amount to 10 to 20 per cent of total output. *Social overhead capital* is developed. New

industries spring up in the place of old ones – one of the signs that the economy has become capable of absorbing modern technology.

(5) *The age of high mass-consumption.* The growth of the population and the complex organization of its activities based on skilled labour require the support of an extensive bureaucratic apparatus. Now fully developed, the economy at this stage is faced with the choice between a *welfare state* policy, a power policy, and a policy of horizontal, vertical and qualitative development of consumption.

This presentation is clearly underpinned by an extensive and thoughtful knowledge of economic history, enabling Rostow to put forward a chronological table for the take-off of 14 countries. For example, the dates 1780–1800 are given for England, 1825–60 for France and 1850–60 for the United States of America. Until detailed studies have been made, there is little to be gained by questioning the exact dates and duration of take-off. In the case of France, J. Marczewski seems to have established that no clear period of take-off emerges from the available statistics, and a first examination of the long records of total output between the end of the wars of the First Empire and 1900 gives a picture of successive industrial 'thrusts' resulting from groups of industries, rather than one of a take-off leading to the succession of stages described by Rostow.

These comments do not affect the central interest of the study, any more than they concern the problem we are discussing here: that of development and, more specifically, development as visualized by the developing countries around the world.

Development as we understand it is a dialectic among sectors. Rostow goes some of the way towards this conception, but not all the way. He very accurately discerns that there are parts making up the economic whole and attributes a particular role to the *leading sectors*, thus going beyond the globalism of the macroeconomic models, and *implicitly* acknowledging propulsion effects: perhaps his historian's approach absolved him from going any further.

Taking the same standpoint, it appears legitimate for an historically-minded economist to analyse the types of propulsion, the conditions under which they operate and their impacts; the resulting schemes or models are a logical sequel to the American historian's research.

It may seem more relevant to suggest some legitimate doubt about the fruitfulness of applying the narrow concept of growth to the interpretation of world development. It will, of course, be argued that this is only the first step and that the concept may later give way to the identification and analysis of the phenomena of development. With all due respect, this argument seems somewhat unconvincing. A choice between the narrow definition of growth and development is a fundamental option that commits every aspect of the inquiry: the initial viewpoint, the formation of the underlying hypotheses, the conceptualization and the formal expression. Either it is considered that the chief thing is a dialectic among structures, or it is assumed that the central phenomenon is the growth of total output, and that it is enough to relate this to general causes *without describing how those causes are interrelated* in even the simplest of models. Science and technology, the habits of the people, institutions and so on – all the factors considered by Rostow in the work we are discussing – are *juxtaposed* rather than *combined*.

Moreover, what is Rostow's fundamental view of development? A universally encountered kind of change that will inevitably, sooner or later, affect every country. The secret of the advance towards affluence is the 'first stage', the take-off, the hallmark of which is a cumulative process, appropriate institutions and a given level of investment and savings.

Structures are not wholly neglected. They are not, however, given a decisive role, and macroeconomic coefficients tell us virtually nothing about the distribution of economic results among the various groups and the population at large.

In the cases of Turkey, Argentina and Mexico, according to the table mentioned above, take-off started shortly before 1940. Should it hence be assumed that since then the succession of stages has started? And above all, regardless of whether or not that process is obvious, can the shortcomings of development centred on the fate of populations, regions and social classes be minimized until such time as the later stages of growth set in?

The worldwide demand for development, and more specifically for the new form of development, poses compelling and pressing questions: does growth 'spontaneously' call forth the optimum industrial structure and does it of itself distribute output and total income in such a way as to satisfy the needs of the *entire* population? Or, at the very least, is there any clear and incontrovertible evidence that the developing countries are moving in that direction?

There is every reason for scepticism here, inasmuch as the system that undergoes the successive stages, evidence of whose take-off is sought in the greatest variety of countries, is guided by anticipated private profit and supplied with savings and investment through the profits achieved. The experience of the developing countries and regions seems so far to allow of drawing one provisional conclusion: that reliance on the successive stages of one and the same system – the capitalist market economy – is unlikely to distribute innovation, investment and their fruits to the benefit of the population at large. This end must be sought rather by organizing and co-ordinating the structural and social dialectics among unequal and unequally active groups. Is this not another way of saying that development must be analysed, and that such an analysis leads to a policy and strategies of *co-ordinated* development?

Karl Marx and his Followers[6]

I would remind the reader, who may justifiably have read this section heading with alarm and scepticism, that my purpose is limited to setting my conception of the development process in the context of the currents of contemporary thinking on this topic.

There can be no doubt that Marx has inspired a considerable number of exegetists, a few of them studying his published works themselves but most of them working on the commentaries that interpret, rewrite and popularize those works. There is thus a degree of degradation of Marx's thought, a loss of accuracy in comparison with his original positions – which is the fate of all doctrines sufficiently fertile to endure. This is a cogent reason for examining this specialized area attentively. A more general reason is that the new form of development reflects a demand that is multidimensional as regards its objectives and its methods. Those taking part in it want a *complete* restructuring, political and economic alike, of the networks of relations between the developing countries and the industrialized countries. Is this a mistake or, on the contrary, does it reflect a very true intuition that in many respects Marxism and Leninism provide neither an interpretative framework nor a programme of action for this point in world history?

Karl Marx and his immediate disciples, Friedrich Engels and

their exegetists up to the First World War, were anything but clear in their thinking as regards the undeveloped countries of their day. Their prime field of observation and the chief historical subject-matter of their thinking were the early industrial capitalism of England and the forms it first took on the continent of Europe. Only lesser works, short studies or articles, dealt with India and China. These *backward countries* were not to our knowledge subjected by them to searching analysis. In their eyes, colonialism, no matter how cruel, started them off on the path of development: if they wished to go further, they must go through the capitalist phase.

The fact that Marx's influence still lingers on compels us to question anew the content of *Capital* for the purpose of interpreting development in the second half of the twentieth century. This enterprise is difficult in itself, and is exposed to a crossfire of criticism from all sides. It is none the less essential, no matter how risky, if only to apprehend and define for our own guidance terms that Marxists use to mean so many different things – a situation explicable by the richness of Marx's thought, his doubts and alternatives, and more especially by the fact that his work remained unfinished.

Marx's social thinking is backed by a philosophy of the liberation of those who are socially and economically disadvantaged, oppressed and exploited in the industrialized countries. Served by enormous work and unfailing courage, this aspiration commands respect. Marx wrote nothing that was not inspired by this initial standpoint in which compassionate feeling for mankind's boundless suffering is combined with reason which, refusing to despair, seeks after an effective form of action to lighten the burden of that suffering. If that effort goes no further than that of Hegel's 'beautiful soul', it can achieve nothing, as centuries of experience have shown. It is therefore assumed that, among material realities, an inexorable dialectic is the sole true motive power of liberation.

What kind of dialectic? Not the kind that we have defined on our own account, in which, in our view, the action and counteraction among parts or sectors change their structure without destroying them, and in which the resulting structure is visibly a compound of the previous structures in different forms. Marx's dialectic – a transposition of Hegel's into material life – is a process in which one of the terms – capitalism – is finally destroyed, to be replaced by its opposite: socialism in various forms, all of which still imply that capitalism will vanish to make way for a *non-capitalist society*, an economic and social system free of oppression, exploitation and alienation.

It is thus useful to distinguish between a *dialectic of evolution*, which admittedly accepts the existence of relationships based on force but rules out the destruction of the system, and a *dialectic of breakage* culminating in catastrophe, in the annihilation of the system itself. Much of the obscurity of the interpretations of Marxism stems from the fact that many of Marx's writings, from his early works to the *Capital* that he left incomplete and that Engels and the very disciples continued, may be adduced in support of both kinds of dialectic, the latter being very clearly the key to Marx's originality as a thinker and the basis of part of his influence.

Capitalism, as it develops, destroys itself. Economically, because of the relationship between surplus value, fixed capital and variable capital and because of the resulting fall in the rate of profit, it lurches from crisis to crisis, each worse than the last, until the final catastrophe. Political action can help on this progress, which remains an immanent necessity of the system, based of course on the relationship between the infrastructure and the superstructure, the dichotomous struggle between two classes and the material relationships of production.

So far, we have set out the essentially economic content of the dialectic characteristics of Marx's thought. It is based upon an economic mechanism that correlates the growth rates of surplus value, fixed capital and circulating capital and through them, under the impetus of competition among entrepreneurs, relates the rate of profit to the foregoing variables. Capital, accumulation of capital or extended reproduction, the relationship between surplus value, fixed capital and circulating capital – the mechanism wrecks itself. It may be distorted by 'exogenous' factors, but the model is *economic* in the variables it contains and the supposed interactions among them.

With Vladimir Ilyich Lenin, the First World War and the Russian Revolution, the picture changes. The expression 'Marxism–Leninism' may well mislead: Lenin's dialectic seeks vainly to reconcile the *economically* inevitable disappearance of capitalism with its disappearance through *political* action that destroys it at a blow rather than merely helping to hasten its decay. This radical change, which the Marxist–Leninists – as might be expected – deny to a man, marks a *decisive* turning-point in the history of the interpretations inspired by *various brands* of

Marxism. For purposes of agitation and political action, it is extremely convenient to maintain, as appropriate, either that capitalism is dying out of itself or that it must be vigorously helped to give up the ghost.

Great wars rend the fabric of history, they rock societies and bring to the top new teams that throw in their lot with previously oppressed or excluded sections of the population, promising them a higher position in society. But economic structures are slow to change: the French Revolution of 1789, for instance, left untouched for a very long time an economy struggling to emerge from feudal forms; and the Russian Revolution of 1917 was followed only in 1928 by the first Five-Year Plan that enshrined, after much procrastination, the option of industrialization. The assumption of power by Lenin and the Bolsheviks was no part of the requirements for economic progress, and it has been repeated *ad nauseam* but rightly that it occurred in one of the last developed and least mature of capitalist societies.

The Second World War, its progress and its outcome led finally to Yalta, where Europe and the world were divided and a political context and political constraints were imposed on the capitalist development of production and exchanges that still endure today. Two armed camps are operating as though conflict between them were inevitable. Armed insurrection, the seizure of power and the Party machinery have reshaped the new Russia, which is in no way the product of the dialectic of self-destruction of capitalism. What is more, the collapse of the Second International in 1919 attested the vitality of the nations and their ability to withstand dissolution through class struggle.

With his *Imperialism, the Highest Stage of Capitalism*, written in 1916, Lenin continued the work of Hilferding, Rosa Luxembourg and Bukharin on financial capitalism. But he carried over to the international political order and the realm of political intentions, decisions and methods, the dialectic of the destruction of capitalism through its own development by virtue of a *mechanism* of the accumulation of capital, transformation of its composition, formation of surplus value and the downward tendency of the rate of profit.

Marxism and Leninism as conceived in the original thinking of Karl Marx and V.I. Lenin are submerged beneath a mass of subsequent pronouncements by these two authors, and beneath an even greater but qualitatively inferior mass of interpretations by their disciples or their adversaries. It is, however, both possible and necessary to distinguish the Marxists' economic dialectics from their political dialectics in order to dispel deliberately maintained confusions. Obviously, that distinction is seen as nothing more than an analytical device.

For our purpose, which is to explore the relationship between Marxism and development, present reality will be better understood if care is taken not to confuse the economic message, which is Marx's specific contribution, with the political message contributed by Lenin. The import of both is that the world must be understood if it is to be transformed and even, in one sense, transformed if it is to be understood, since men admittedly understand what they themselves have made better than they do what the outside world has to offer them. One concentrates essentially on the material structures of production and exchange and the slow and laborious changing of them, while the other focuses on violent methods of seizing control of the political and administrative machinery of state, changing the teams in government, and banking on the interests and ambitions of long-frustrated social categories.

The policy of subversion wherever it is pursued, in the industrialized or the developing countries, uses both idioms with an ingenuity which does not withstand analysis. The fact is that Marx's concepts have been overtaken by history: their enduring attraction is due only to a vagueness that makes them indeterminate but politically effective. Marx's concept of 'class' might perhaps have been defined had not the manuscript of *Capital* been interrupted at the very point where such a definition was expected. 'Here the manuscript breaks off' (*Hier bricht das Manuscript ab*).

Is then the choice open between class in the sense of a group of economic interests (the Eighteenth Brumaire of Louis Bonaparte), or of an 'historic bloc' around the industrial workers (Antonio Gramsci) or even of the participatory group composed of all who have a 'class consciousness' (Georg Lukacs)?

Perhaps, but only if the economic dialectic contained in *Capital* is abandoned. That dialectic rests wholly on antagonism between two classes: one which controls the means of production, and one which is deprived of them. It is between these two that the antagonism – and not only the conflict – becomes apparent and is aggravated, being closely linked to an economic mechanism and a supposedly growing process of proletarization.

Contrary, however, to this latter view of things, the working class in the industrialized countries has become noticeably diversified; it is 'tempted' and in part absorbed by capitalism, and it does not tend to increase numerically or to undergo a reduction of its real earnings in the long term, nor a deterioration in its living standard. Apart from transitional difficulties, industrialization tends to improve the position of the wage-earners taking part in it in terms of real rewards – wages and social transfers. It is only in the areas and economic sectors, particularly agriculture, which remain closed, or partially closed, to modern technologies and financial capital, that people drop behind.

As for the developing countries, the classes and class struggle of the original Marxism are unknown in *non-industrial environments*; they occur in areas where industry has been established, in areas of foreign-based investment, in areas of indigenous industrialization and in urban areas. Elsewhere, in indigenous agricultural systems or in those which depend on traditional systems of land tenure, endemic or recurrent *group* conflicts, irrespective of the social rank of wage-labourer or small-holder or of peasants grouped in collective units, reflect a revolt against oppression and exploitation. These peasant revolts are not the result of industrialization which, if intelligently managed, could even help the rural world to improve the conditions in which its poverty is rooted. The propulsion effect that industry exerts on agriculture seems clearly to be a process making for 'deproletarization' of the peasant masses.

Cases of conflict–co-operation or struggle–synergy among social groups recur throughout the history of mankind. History cannot be reduced to a struggle between two antagonistic classes, one of them controlling the means of production and the other deprived of them. That criterion alone is not sufficient even when present: its importance depends on the organization of the social body as a whole and on the networks of information and authority that distinguish and define a given society.

The interminable discussions about infrastructure and superstructure were inevitable since Marx's thought was somewhat imprecise and gave rise to multiple interpretations. The question whether the infrastructure consists in the productive forces (*Produktivkräfte*) – roughly speaking, energy, technics and technology – or in social relations for the material production of commodities (*Produktionsverhältnisse*) in itself gives rise to difficulties, since different kinds of social relations are compatible with the use of similar techniques.

Take the example of social production relations, meaning essentially those between the heads of productive units and the dependent labour-force. Such relations cannot be apprehended apart from an organization which makes them specific and places a particular stamp on them: the very term *social* relations makes this clear. To state that such social relations – the infrastructure – *shape* the superstructure – law, beliefs, customs and ethics – is to suggest a *way of interpreting* a correspondence and to assume that one of its terms is absolute.

The confusion grows when we try to clarify the term 'shape', which we have used deliberately to point to an area of doubt which, so far as we know, has never been cleared up either by Marx or by his successors. In other words, does the infrastructure determine or merely affect the superstructure? The first alternative is the only one compatible with a rigorous interpretation in the spirit of the economic mechanism postulated in *Capital*, which is in turn the only ground for asserting that economic relations engender attitudes, the converse being considered either impossible or negligible.

In the history of societies at different levels of development, there are constant instances of attitudes being affected by economic relations and modifying those relations themselves. Marx and his first followers, more scrupulous than some of their successors, admitted the creativity of people wrestling with constraints imposed by nature or society. That creativity excludes all possibility of a mechanical, unquestionable influence of the infrastructure on the superstructure. The contemporary history of the developing countries and the diversity of options and decisions that it clearly reveals provide yet another proof of this.

Leninism, being one of many policies, makes a point of referring to its Marxist sources and stressing its fidelity to Karl Marx: in point of fact, it took over from Marx and Marxism at a time when history was refuting their tenets on an enormous scale. It holds an unquestionable attraction for countries whose economies are still to a large extent precapitalist and which neither can nor wish to wait until capitalism has developed within their territory to free their economies and societies from the grip of foreign powers: sometimes, too, it tempts countries to copy the Soviet experiment as seen from a distance and through the distorting prism of propaganda.

In these circumstances, and in view of the prestige of a Soviet state which, far from 'withering away', has rapidly become one of the foremost military and political powers, it will be realized that it is entirely unjustified to substantialize Capitalism, Anti-capitalism, Capital and Labour as major Actors in history, and to depict the world in terms of a fight to the death among these supposed protagonists. What the world showed us in the fifties, and has shown in various styles throughout its history, has been people, agents, groups in evolving structures and organizations – in fact, *unevenly active sub-sets.*

This brings us to a crucial point, the conception of capital and its nature. Capital is a collection of physically structured objects – fixed assets, raw materials and machinery – subordinated to a production plan; it is also a set of financial assets, currency and stocks and bonds subordinated to a similar authority. That is an approximate definition of economic capital and financial capital, except that, in their obsession with goods, objects and the market, some economists emphasize either financial assets or goods in isolation rather than their organization by decision-makers.

The definition that Marx made fashionable, that capital is a 'social relation' between the person controlling it (*not* those owning it) and those who serve him by their intellectual or manual labour, is due to his focusing attention on the *agents*, on people.

Subordination is a universal phenomenon, regardless of the level of development or the social system, in both East and West. It will rightly be said that neither the use to which capital is put nor power *over* or *by* capital are the hallmarks of a system. In a capitalist system, capital is applied for the purpose of securing a net profit, which never emerges from an abstract market but from markets that are regulated by their societies. The Soviet system operates to obtain a net gain, and there is no evidence that the net gain or net socialist profit deducts less from the worker's output than does the capitalist system.

Ways of extorting surplus value – to use this crude vocabulary – that is to say, of paying the worker less than the value of 'his' output (which remains to be defined), have always stimulated the ingenuity of employers everywhere. There is no reason to regard surplus value as a capitalist speciality or to suppose it greater under that system than in a pre-capitalist economy of tribe and village or in the publicly-owned units of a Soviet plan. We have no way of stating anything definite in this area. We can, however, put forward strong assumptions.

Once the individual no longer controls his own productive capital (a system approximating to a republic of small peasant farmers and craftsmen, which cannot possibly be achieved once industrialization has set in), the authority exerted over the worker is an irksome constraint from which he seeks to escape as far as possible. In the metropolis of advanced industrialization, the worker, wherever he may be, is obliged to work to earn his living: should he rebel in circumstances deemed to flout law and order, the police or army will intervene. This compound and complex relationship of dependence is not an invention of Marx and the Marxists, it is a fact of everyday observation, and the regimes that officially profess allegiance to Marxism have never eliminated that dependence nor lightened its burden. The dogmatism of totalitarian regimes, the empiricism of the highly industrialized countries and that of the countries that have no industry are all alike powerless.

The only possible way of rendering some liberation of the workers feasible lies in a very different direction. That liberation is not a direct and immediate consequence of productive forces or material production relations, nor is it directly and unequivocally subordinated to them. It is not *mechanically* obtained or impeded by the control or non-control of the means of production. The advance of liberation is also related to institutions and the rules of the social game to the extent that their impact is brought to bear. These institutions and rules are the historical products of a combination of variables, which may indeed be described as technical, political, social and moral, but which cannot be isolated or said to combine according to particular laws. This *historical* combination is the consequence of human *interpretations* of the conflicts and instances of co-operation which persist in all cases.

Conflicts and co-operation combine in variable proportions, but never eliminate inequality and the hierarchy of functions. No way has yet been found of combining the productive use of capital with freely and fully voluntary labour. Destructive violence has changed nothing. What has proved effective is regulation carried out by free trade unions in more or less democratic circumstances, and also the intellectual capacity and maturity of the parties concerned. In such circumstances, wage labour has to some extent found it possible to escape from its dependence on the factory through free time and, in terms of everyday life, by paid holidays. Not that no *quid pro quo* is exacted in return, since a fall in productivity below a certain threshold is taken as a reason or a pretext for reducing real wages. None of this is in any way automatic or mechanical, but is governed at every level by the decisions and operations of human actors or agents.

One of the weakest points in Marxist thinking is the theory and analysis of the nation. If antagonism between the masters of capital and the dependent workers is the only or decisive explanation of the movement of societies, then the nation becomes a screen, an optical illusion beyond which we come back to the class struggle. Were that so, the Marxist-inspired unitary explanation would follow logically: surplus value, the theorems of the organic composition of capital and the accumulation of capital or extended reproduction would explain all.

We shall return later to the *reality* of nationhood, which is among the developing countries' most firmly motivated hopes and the strengthening of which is among the most important objectives of the new development programme. Let us for the present confine our attention to a few observations that draw on the foregoing analyses and prefigure those that follow.

The world scale is one thing, the extent and forms of world organization are another. The difference between international capitalism in the nineteenth and twentieth centuries, apart from the disappearance of colonialism proper and the emergence of new nations, lies in the establishment of oligopolies at two levels: the organization of a few major political powers and the development of monopolies and groups connected with them. The United States of America, Japan and Europe and the associated economic and financial groups rightly come to mind. These latter co-operate and compete with one another to varying degrees, depending on the operations to be performed, and engage in oligopolistic competition, largely sustained by innovation and dealings conducted outside the market. As for the political powers, two are firmly established and the third, Europe, exists in embryonic form.

Confronted with these shifting complexities and evolving patterns, we are reminded of the dictum of that penetrating philosopher, Merleau-Ponty: 'Capitalism is confused'. It is made up of unequal sectors that engage in non-traditional but extremely effective forms of competition: and in their relations with the public authorities these sectors are in unequal and variable positions of strength. If this situation were to be succinctly depicted, we should have to speak of accumulations and markets at world level, emphasizing the plural. No one has yet dared to do so, since it would call into question the net accumulation that the major countries, clubbing together, have obtained by expropriating values from the developing countries *as a whole*.

The Marxist approach would, on the other hand, be welcome if a detailed comparison were made of state monopoly capitalism in the West and in the East. In the latter zone, the formations involved are just as 'capitalistic', even more 'monopolistic' and certainly more 'state controlled'. The transfer of all the resources of the Soviet-zone countries to the USSR is institutionalized. Analysis thereof, which has already been begun, would undeniably be useful for the scientific comparison of the two systems.

Lastly, to transpose the *class* struggle to the world scale, to claim that it 'does not take place in national contexts' but in the context of the world system, is to assume a solidarity that cannot possibly be proved among the components of the 'World Worker' in *antagonistic* relationship with the components of the 'World Bourgeois'. Karl Marx, for the purposes of argument, spoke of a collective Worker locked in struggle with a collective Capitalist within one and the same nation. But to reduce the various conflicts and instances of co-operation on the world scale to the clash between substantialized Capital and Labour, both in the singular, is to go incomparably further and to run flagrantly counter to history.

The only conclusion to be drawn, then, is that, apart from the excellent and stimulating thrust of a social philosophy that cares for deprived groups and individuals, the ideas of Marx and his successors contribute very little to the theory and analysis of development.

Motive Forces and Dynamics of Development

None of the contributions reviewed above contains a reformulation of general economic theory in both static and dynamic terms, though this is absolutely necessary for coherence when considering development phenomena. Because it postulates conditions in which the agent is a nonentity and because it is static, the traditional equilibrium based on the theories of L. Walras and V. Pareto cannot be linked analytically with decision-making, risk, information, conflict, learning and planning – or in other words with the phenomena that have to be considered in advanced research today. The traditional equilibrium theory uses a formalistic, mechanistic approach to represent the way in which objects move in a homogeneous space; since the system is at the point of equilibrium, only change originating from outside can shift it from that equilibrium.

Equilibration by the agents and their active units is not by any means a mere correction of the traditional equilibrium or a series of adjustments to it, but differs radically in its whole approach to economic activity and in its representation of it, which involves the interaction of different, unequal 'actors'; the halting of the changes they bring about is due to the exhaustion – always temporary – of their energy productive of change. So far as the system as a whole is concerned, it ceases to change whenever the continuous equilibrating mechanisms contained in it reach the point where the net overall energy productive of change is temporarily exhausted. These new sequences can be observed and constructed analytically in irreversible time.

Decision-making, risk, information, conflict, learning and planning are accordingly inherent in the new representation. Instead of a model based on a single period, since the equilibrium of the endogenous variables can be broken at the end of a period only by exogenous factors, we have a representation of successive periods, linked together because the agents carry out their activities over the irreversible course of time without their being finally stopped in any given position. It is the agent himself who changes and modifies his environment through his own activity.

Human *motive forces* and *dynamics* are quite naturally a feature of the new theory of general interdependence, whereas there was no place for them in the traditional equilibrium theory.[7]

Some economists have thought it possible to define dynamics by the fact that events can be dated. We believe – which is not at all the same thing– that it can be defined as the representation in which the agent's time is not *neutralized*. And neutralized it certainly is if it is assumed that any disequilibrium will be inevitably and mechanically corrected by a system of perfect compensation. Indeed, the agent's time is not merely neutralized but wholly voided when the agent himself and his activity are both ruled out by the hypothesis of perfect competition, in which price is the regulating factor producing an order of things that is imposed upon entities, wrongly termed 'agents', since they have no memory and no plan for the future.

Rejecting from the outset, then, the unwarranted and intolerable constraints of perfect competition, a dynamic theory can be formulated under three heads.

The first relates to the *contextual motive forces*, through which correlations are established between the great profusion of historical factors and the economic analysis of those factors.

Three groups of factors may be distinguished, concerning (1) population; (2) technology, including invention, innovation and the sum of knowledge needed to apply technology; and (3) the 'rules of the game' in society relating to the constitution of corporate economic bodies (e.g. enterprises) and the norms governing their relationships (e.g. what is termed 'private' property, contracts). There is interaction between these institutional bodies and institutional norms.

The approach adopted is to consider these sets of factors, *initially*, as moving on their own within a given complex; quantitative and qualitative changes in population, changes in science and technology and changes in the rules of the social game are considered separately. This approach has been adopted for the purpose of distinguishing manageable sub-sets in extremely complex systems.

This does not imply failure to recognize or fully to appreciate current endeavours to find out gradually how contextual motive forces *work inwardly*, in other words to apprehend and analyse the effect of the variables contained in a model on population, technology and the rules of the game.

The realities observable through such inward working, such as *Product* reaction on each of the motive forces and on all those forces combined, seem to depend on the degree of development. For example, independent research and development – as regards both structure and effects – is inadequate or virtually non-existent in the developing countries because of the scantiness of the resources they can put into it and the basic shortage of research workers and qualified personnel. Similarly, a brief analysis has already been made of the effects of the growth of global and average output and improved living standards on population growth rates. Hypotheses have also been formulated on the growing complexity of structures as a factor modifying the rules of the game. Such piecemeal studies and reflections are useful, but they do not yet form a logically organized and statistically tested set of propositions.

The table of contextual motive forces related to the other factors

Table 2.3

	Population	Technology	Institutions	Direction of actions and reactions
Context C Historical motive forces	C_1	C_2	C_3	$\leftarrow \uparrow \downarrow \rightarrow$
Structures S Structuring – Destructuring	S_A	S_B	S_C	$\leftarrow \uparrow \downarrow \rightarrow$
Functioning M Market dynamics	Product – $S.D._A$ Supply-Demand	Product – $S.D._B$ Supply-Demand	Product – $S.D._C$ Supply-Demand	$\leftarrow \uparrow \downarrow \rightarrow$

in economic dynamics (Table 2.3) classifies the relationships conceptually and shows how complex they are.

Among the sets of factors shown, which are divided significantly into sub-sets, the quantitative aspect of this complexity is brought out by such familiar procedures as combinatorial analysis and, in certain specified conditions, by the composition of applications.

Economists or sociologists will be able to give examples – though regrettably somewhat unsystematically – of linkages such as the following:

(1) Actions and reactions between macro-groups of variables: Technology–Population, Institutions–Technology, etc.
(2) Actions and reactions between macro-sets of variables and Product or significant compositions of Product.
(3) Actions and reactions between a significant combination of macro-sets of variables and Product, or significant breakdowns of Product.

If the inevitably simplified models obtained by this method set out to provide explanations, they presuppose causal relationships. But little headway has been made towards ascertaining for operational purposes the forms and degrees of development over a specified short, medium or long period.

The dynamics of structures calls in question the *structuring* structures which change an environment made up of elementary units (individuals, forms) or change other structures (industrial structures affecting agricultural structures, foreign investment structures in a developed or less developed environment, and so on).

At all events, any scientifically-minded economic theory must, if it is to become operational, take into account the very great number and virtually inextricable web of variables involved in the 'all other things being equal' from which there is no escaping but which must be subjected to preliminary investigation if we wish to know approximately *what* a scheme or model is supposed to tell us and what are the limitations of the information it provides.

Depending on the problem posed, a distinction must always be made between *structural variables*, varying less often and to a lesser extent, and *operating variables* (price, supply and demand). Any illusions about the quality and quantity of information to be derived from models of markets that are assumed to be isolated from their structural environment fall away as soon as attention is directed, following the method adopted in contemporary science, to sets of factors and the systems entering into them.

No single example can be found in history even approaching the case of a homogeneous economic context or of homothetic growth evenly distributed over an economic or geographical area, or of dialectics of development that can be evenly superimposed in different parts of an economic or geographical space. National 'wholes', and sub-sets within a national whole, combine, hold together and evolve in asymmetrical relationship.

The *basic model* is therefore the asymmetrical relationship combining a sub-set A (propelling sub-set) with a sub-set B (propelled sub-set).

The relationship may refer to a beneficial effect such as an increase in output, which may be either positive (propulsion) or negative (blocking or reduction of a previous propulsion). We have chosen the effect of the growth of a sub-set on the growth of another sub-set in order to simplify the demonstration, and for the same purpose we have taken the example of positive propulsion. Between a propelling structured sub-set – an industry for example – and another industry, the propulsion effect may be due to:

1.   the effect on prices and flows,
2.   a transfer of productivity,
3.   a transfer of information.

Expressed in the simplest terms, the effect can be seen as the dependence between the growth rate of a propelled industry (group of activities) ($g_c B$) and the growth rate of a propelling industry ($g_E A$).

This is written as:

$$g_c B = f(g_E A)$$

over a given period of time.

Determination of propulsion effect when transposing algebraic into statistical representations calls for ampler elucidation, which I have given elsewhere; so incontrovertibly important is it that it is frequently to be found in explicit terms in national accounting and official statistical documents.

As the basic model becomes more specific, it can be seen to concern a wide variety of economic sub-sets.

(a) In the *non-structured space* of elementary analysis, the basic model implicitly comes into play in static comparative analyses of elementary supply and demand curves whenever there is any adjustment (or shift in the curve) of supply to demand or vice versa.

The internal and implicitly normative logic of neo-classical economic theory places emphasis on demand as inducing adjustment of supposedly elastic supply. The system operates to satisfy the tastes of the consumer able to pay. At all levels, micro-, meso- and macroeconomic, the assumption that demand determines supply is essential in constructing the 'theorems' of the sovereignty or freedom of the consumer, who is supposed to regulate the whole system.

But even elementary theory cannot deny the effect of supply on demand in connection with the analysis of selling costs, which may be broadly equated with the costs of transforming the environment. By agreeing to assume costs in order to secure a rightward shift of the demand curve representing the initial demand directed at his firm, the head of a firm is creating certain conditions for his own success. The activity of suppliers and supply interfere with the operation of the conventional logic of neo-classical theory; where such activity is observed, the only thing to do is to find out whether it occurs in response to consumer tastes or whether it alters those tastes without any advantage for the consumer, for the purpose of securing extra monopoly profits. This distinction must be made in any context, and more particularly in a less developed

environment, since it depends on the consumer's information and conditioning.

To say that, because he has bought something, a consumer shows that his tastes have been catered for would be to refuse any analysis of objectively beneficial effects and of social utility going deeper than straightforward factual observation. Such a refusal is indeed self-evident if it has been decided once and for all to apply a set pattern of perfect competition to situations characterized by inequality in every sphere, in resources, power and information.

(b) In terms of development, the most useful applications of the basic model are to be found in *structured spaces*. These are:

> *motive investment* which – and this can never be sufficiently emphasized if we are to avoid a frequent misconception – is not Keynes's monetary investment with its multiplier effect, but a real investment which stimulates others by evoking complementarity;
> the *motive firm* in a region in which it is the leader in terms of flows of goods, investment and information;
> the *motive region* which, by the same means and through the influence of urban centres, triggers or stimulates development in a 'region of nations'.

These individual models lead us to the concept of a focal *point, centre* or *pole* of growth or development.

What this means is the *concentration* of productive agents, organized resources and technological and economic capacity within a non-geographical matrix, or a structured group of individuals in a geographical entity.

Concentration is the precondition for the subsequent propagation of effects. It would be impossible to find a single example of development since the beginning of industrialism in which there has not been this phenomenon of concentration or, as it may be termed, provided that its meaning is properly specified, *polarization*.[8]

This concept has spread throughout the world but has given rise in some cases to gross misunderstandings and in others to misconceptions.

To point out that polarization or concentration (whether geographical or otherwise) takes place at the expense of other economic or geographical areas or spheres is to state the obvious and takes us little further. The point is not to discover whether resources are initially taken from somewhere and concentrated in one sector or area, but rather whether, at the end of a particular period of observation selected according to the nature and structure of the pole of concentration, the whole set of areas or spheres over which it exerts its influence does not derive more benefit from that polarization than it would have done from more decentralized development. The historical evidence appears to be quite conclusive on this point.

The best chances of success will, of course, be obtained not by establishing any pole of concentration in any environment, but by choosing the type of focal point appropriate to the set of economic factors or geographical areas considered, and by preparing the immediate environment for outward expansion from that focal point.

We shall come back to these points in discussing development policy.

We have, I hope, demonstrated the unity of the revised general theory of economic activity.

Global equilibrating action by the agents and their active units fills the gap left by the universal, and very legitimate criticism of traditional equilibrium theory, constructed on the premiss of timelessness and without regard for the actual agents themselves.

The new theory proposes the coherent construction of a new form of static analysis or, more exactly, of metastatic analysis, and the dynamic analysis closely associated with it.

It can be applied to all countries, since not one can claim to be fully developed; it is of prime concern to the developing countries which have yet to form, at one and the same time, both their agents and their structures.

Moreover, it has its place – as I shall show – in the current trend of scientific and philosophical thought.

Having considered these questions, I shall then be able to go on to consider development policy as an extension of the revised general theory.

Development and Trends in Science. Some Guide-marks

Our precise purpose is to highlight some undeniable correlations in the second half of the twentieth century between scientific trends and this revised economic theory of global equilibration by active units. The agent and his activity are basic to the revised economic theory and are likewise central to the worldwide demand for a new approach to development.

Some convergences are consequently to be observed between changing trends in three areas, namely:

science
economics
the aspirations of the deprived peoples.

Some guide-marks will elucidate the concept of the new approach to development.

The works of those who founded the economic theory of general equilibrium – Léon Walrus, Vilfredo Pareto, Augustin Cournot and F.Y. Edgeworth – were published between 1850 and 1914. Each in his own way imposed a reduction on the broad, open descriptions of the early English classical economists and constructed a pure economic theory, sufficiently simplified to lend itself to treatment by the mathematics of the time.

The then economic situation was not too manifestly at variance with these reductionist theories. The markets in goods, shares and capital were expanding rapidly. Small-scale and medium-sized enterprises were in the majority. Wage-earning workers were docile by force of circumstance and social education; private property and commercial exchanges were challenged only by insignificant groups of agitators. The advances of science and technology aroused enthusiasm and nurtured the illusion of emancipation of the working classes in an overall climate of prosperity. Social attitudes and conventional responses to price fluctuations lent credibility to the idea that the workings of the economy were to some extent automatic. Cycles were seen as physiological phenomena in the economic organism, with the result that crises tended to be disregarded; contraction seemed to be the 'price to pay' for expansion, containing the promise of expansion which would be generated by the elimination of misplaced investment through the initiative of individuals anticipating price movements and through the reconstitution of profit margins. The gold standard was thought to be capable of correcting imbalances in international trade. The public at large grew accustomed to thinking in terms of price mechanisms and the automatic redressing of imbalances.

Academic theorists for their part – a rare species, powerless among the multitude of practical experts – tried to dismiss the layman's approximations and the reassuring commentaries of those who to a greater or lesser extent had class interests in mind; these with a scientific background were naturally inclined to draw on the mathematical theories prevalent at the time.

In a brief and striking parallel, Jean Starobinski sums up the rise and fall of classical mechanics with two quotations.[9]

In the foreword to his work *Mécanique Analytique* (1788), Lagrange described his purpose thus: 'To reduce the theory of mechanics and the art of solving the problems relating to it to general formulae which need only be developed to provide all the equations required to solve each problem . . .'.

At the end of the nineteenth century, the physicist Ernst Mach drew a parallel between the ideas of the Encyclopaedists and those of Lagrange and Laplace, concludng: 'This conception . . . seems to us to be a *mechanical mythology*, in contrast to the animistic mythology of the ancient religions. Both contain excessive and imaginary amplifications of unilateral knowledge.'

Surely no passages could have been more aptly chosen to sum up the *mechanistic phase* of Western science.

Writers acquainted with mathematics and interested in economics were to reconstruct the latter as a set of mechanisms coming under the head of a sort of 'social physics'. This appealed strongly to engineers; there was a measure of esoterism in the movement which held popular opinion at bay and on occasion facilitated the work of governments and those who controlled production and money, providing them with 'economic laws' supposed to be consistent with scientific determinism.

After the Second World War, changes which had begun long before made rapid strides. Enterprises grew bigger, more complex and financially more powerful. Economic and financial groups took on the hierarchical form of complex units, with a decision-making centre wielding a direct or indirect influence on the prices and quantities of subordinate units. With the concentration of enterprises the whole economy took on a new shape. Wage-earners at all levels, for their part, formed trade unions and also used the political parties to obtain higher wages, a share in output and productivity, and a modification of the rules of the social game.

In external relations, the inequality among nations in regard
to resources, power and scientific and technological capacity
encouraged
the formation of alliances and coalitions. Institutionalized satellites
and a train of unofficial dependents gravitated around the major
powers.

The networks of a *bargaining economy* came into being among
structured sub-sets within a nation and among nations, with the
public authorities either participating directly or having some say in
them. To argue that prices alone are enough to reconcile interests
fairly and to bring about the optimum allocation of present and
potential resources meant turning a blind eye to the facts.

As these changes were occurring in the political and economic
order, the scientific community, too, was changing its approach and
methods.

While it continued to draw on mechanics in the sophisticated
representation of quantum theory, it developed a great interest in
molecular biology, with which non-linear thermodynamics patently
had links. Following their distinctive paths, these sciences attain the
inescapable, the unavoidable, in Martin Heidegger's acceptation,
'the objectivity of the corporal, psychic and spiritual unity of man in
his entirety'. Not, of course, that they set out to penetrate his
innermost secret depths but, breaking away from the mechanistic
theories of the preceding period, they proceed, in the name of
rational coherence and experimentation aware of its limitations, to
grapple with realities that are incompatible with the conception of
the human being as a robot, with a little physical mechanism at the
mercy of relentless external forces.

The new biology and the new physics built up their theories in
irreversible time, discerning therein lines of evolution punctuated
by bifurcations or broken by interruptions and 'catastrophes', and
seeking therein constructive–dissipative structures calling for a
revision of the second principle of Clausius–Carnot; they furnish a
new concept of entropy; and lastly, without succumbing to the
temptation of predicting an auspicious or inauspicious destiny, they
hold out hopes for Man in a Nature of which he has learnt a little
more and in which he knows that he takes an active part.[10]

The social sciences and, in particular, economics, made little
effort to keep abreast of the times through a methodical study of
these changing trends. Economists read surprisingly little, said J.
Schumpeter, who read a great deal. Some, the experts, are hastily

seeking to produce practical solutions to problems taken as they stand. Others, the conformists, deliberately or involuntarily develop theories which legitimate the existing system. The very few not falling into these two groups pursue a scientific approach to economics as an organized body of knowledge which they seek to purify, master and control through science. But the way in which research is organized and economics taught does little to encourage their praiseworthy efforts.

It was practical experience in modern societies that helped to get rid of social inertia.

So-called human variables, relating to hygiene and health, education, demography and the environment, made their way irresistibly into economic theory, a domain from which they had long been banished. The traditional economic variables – price and quantity – were submerged and remodelled by variables with a revolutionary effect concerning information and communication.

Meanwhile the style of relationship between phenomena and the mathematics expressing them have changed, as attested by stochastic models, probabilistic spaces, and soft models capable of accommodating latent variables. Systems theory, games theory, combinatorial analysis and the use of pre-topology have superseded the narrowly limited, somewhat discredited mathematics of classical mechanics.

Observation of the facts has pointed to the need for something more than the traditional, mechanical equilibrium theory and this has received fresh impetus and new tools from the development of modern science.

The agent or 'actor' lives and works in irreversible time. He remembers the past and plans for the future. He represents 'negative entropy' on his own account and for his society. He fights against old age, sickness and accident. He and his group proceed from equilibration to equilibration, from one set of balances to another, from bearable existential disequilibrium to bearable existential disequilibrium, seeking always to delay as far as possible the ultimate 'equilibrium'.

His progress and that of his society do not follow a regular, linear path; that path is subject to fluctuations, accelerations, decelerations, breaking or obstruction. Actions and feedback are subject to collective regulation of a hierarchical type, however liberal the system in question may be. Such regulation is in no way mechanical. Its effectiveness and stability depend on communication and the processing of information upwards or downwards within the body social.

The new economic theory involving the actor and the extensible, compressible, flexible spaces in which he operates – purchases and sales, investment and information – can be fitted without difficulty into the context of the new scientific approach. The agent's energy for expansion is temporarily checked on achieving the prescribed aim, encountering an obstacle or meeting with opposition from another party. Temporary equilibrium between two agents is the result of a temporary cancelling out of their two opposing energies for expansion. Equilibrium – always temporary – of the whole will be established at the point at which the *net* energy for expansion is around zero.

This new approach, the transition from mechanical explanation to thermodynamics, is beginning to modify all aspects of economic thinking: the theory of motivation, optimum, so-called economic rationality, and the relationships between static (metastatic) and dynamic analysis. It is bound to be criticized, since it shakes inertia, disrupts routine thinking and shows up the implicitly normative character of traditional economics.

The new theory elaborated by reference to science and by following its example leads on directly to the demand for a new approach to development. It is clearly due to the work of active elites in nations which are becoming active and quite rightly believe that markets are made for men and not the reverse, that industry belongs to the world and not the world to industry, and finally that the sharing of resources and the product of labour depends on strategies centred on man if it is to have any legitimate basis, *even in economic terms*.

It has not, therefore, been irrelevant to make it clear that traditional economic theory remained *outside* the movement of science, whereas the new economic theory is part of that movement.

It now remains to explore trends in philosophy, simply to seek out some correlations with the most recent developments in advanced economic research.

Development and Trends in Ideas. Some Guide-marks

We have just drawn attention to some correlations between the present trend of scientific thought and the attempt to renovate economic theory. It may be noted that, to all appearances, there are only two general theories of economics.

In the one, the market is taken in isolation and considered to be an intelligible entity having no connection with its environment; its paradigm is a mechanical model.

In the other, emphasis is placed on the agents, their activites and the equilibrations resulting from the exercise of their energy productive of changes when applied to modifying their material environment or resisting the effects fo their co-actors' energy; its paradigm is a thermodynamic model.

The first of these theories places emphasis on the market, the second on organization; the first is expressed in instantaneous, static and timeless form, while the second is constructed dynamically, in irreversible, directed time which is not regarded as neutralized from the outset. While this notion of time is not to be confused with historical time, it affords room for novelty and invention but also for duration: the agent lasts, he has a life cycle; fixed capital lasts; and so do institutions.

The opposition between the two general theories points up the fact that they have a philosophical foundation which they do not as a rule formulate clearly.

At first sight, the new approach to development and the new international economic order are akin to the second of the two theories, as shown throughout this study. Development is activity, dialectic and deliberate organization; the forms of self-organization of individual systems, fraught with conflict, call for some higher organization to render them mutually compatible.

Apart from the early classical authors, and with a few honourable exceptions, economists have not been trained as philosophers, or if they have, they prudently conceal the fact, since it is frowned upon by their fellows. This makes the task before us even more difficult.

It is out of the question to associate *any one* economic system with *any one* philosophical system in Europe since the Second World War, but it may still be useful, for our purpose, to single out a few *guide-marks* for the reader interested in the links between economics and philosophy. They may be regarded as marking out the path of a research process which, as in the case of the investigation of scientific trends, is more than any one researcher or even one team can undertake single-handed.

It is a fact that today even British or American economists seem to be influenced by Utilitarianism; the work of John Stuart Mill is not an inappropriate starting-point for any study of the kind on which we are now embarking.

The Utilitarianism of the founding fathers came, for diverse though concurrent reasons, to be schematized, adulterated and degraded, to such a point as to become, in extreme cases, that caricature of thought ironically termed '*economism*'.

The reactions to these extremes can be discerned at several levels. No philosophy of any consequence today falls into the trap of plain deterministic materialism. It might be said that all are philosophies of action, some of them by considered choice. It is in their thinking that the most striking correlations are to be found with equilibration by the actors and with those deliberate, complex, often contradictory *activities* which yet combine in a movement supported by the upsurge of Third World forces, directed against the present economic and political 'order' and towards the reconstruction of a more intelligible and more avowable order.

John Stuart Mill's Utilitarianism[11]

To my mind, a careful reading of Chapter VI of Book IV of the *Principles of Political Economy* (1848), entitled 'Of the Stationary State', and comparison with Mill's essay on *Utilitarianism* (1861), are all that is needed for an understanding of the creative concern and the underlying coherence and perseverance inherent in Mill's well-known line of thinking as it developed and gradually matured. It may be added that this will also help to avoid confusng respectable Utilitarianism with the spurious versions of it produced subsequently.

In the chapter referred to above, John Stuart Mill launches into an ambitious anticipation of the future of capitalism. He sees it as heading of its own accord towards a stationary state through the lowering of profit rates in conjunction with capital accumulation. But this is not the main point that concerns us here.

Mill does not see this slowing down of economic activity as being an evil for which there is no compensation. On the contrary, he welcomes it as providing an opportunity to escape from the hubris of gain and from a mismanaged effort to 'get on' which jeopardizes higher values. The fact that capital and population may cease to grow, at a pace intolerable for a human life, may have good effects. A stationary condition of capital and population 'implies no stationary state of human improvement'. There would always be scope for 'all kinds of mental culture', for 'moral and social progress', for improving the 'Art of Living', and much more likelihood of its being improved when minds ceased to be 'engrossed by the art of getting on'. Even the industrial arts could be used to abridge labour. Mill the liberal Utilitarian leaves no doubt about his innermost thoughts when he writes that he hopes 'for the sake of posterity' that human beings will 'be content to be stationary long before necessity compels them to it'.

Could one imagine a clearer and more strongly asserted profession of faith in a human destiny which is in no way confined simply to enjoyment of material things?

After composing a long treatise on political economy, John Stuart Mill set forth his doctrine in a short, methodical and closely argued essay, *Utilitarianism*.

A distinction is usually drawn between Mill's Utilitarianism and that of Jeremy Bentham, who held that all human activity could be reduced to a calculation of pleasure and pain, which is either a tautology or the reflection of the sketchiest of philosophies. It is not redeemed by extending *this* sort of 'happiness' to the greatest possible number of individuals. This latter restriction makes the theory disturbingly vague. Some commentators have pointed out the 'radical' aspect of Benthamite thinking in contrast to the prevailing ideas of the time; however, especially in a period of *industrial* capitalism still fairly close to its origins, to ask the ruling classes or the state to do all they can does not seem to be asking too much of them, particularly when one considers that Bentham was not concerned with moral issues, or, if he was, only very covertly or too discreetly.

With Mill we are in an altogether different climate of thought; the change is in what traditional philosophy calls the right direction, that which leads to the intellectual and moral values held to be the constituent properties of the human being.

From the very first pages it is made clear that the purpose of the book is to establish the criterion of good and evil which can be grasped by our 'rational faculty' – neither pleasure by itself, nor utility as opposed to pleasure, as some moralists of the time feared. Man's only end in life is happiness as perceived by his intelligence, sensibility and moral feelings. Some kinds of pleasure are 'more valuable' than others; it is for able men to judge and to say which pleasures are associated with the exercise of our highest faculties.

Hence the celebrated passage: 'It is better to be a human being dissatisfied, than a pig satisfied; better to be Socrates dissatisfied, than a fool satisfied. And if the fool or the pig are of a different opinion, it is because they only know their own side of the question.'

The utilitarian ideal is happiness for all. Sacrifice has no moral value unless its object is to secure happiness of others. Moreover, in the imperfect state of our social arrangements, sacrificing oneself for others is the supreme virtue.

Have economists, who have made considerable use of personal interest in evolving their doctrines, reread John Stuart Mill? Immediate interest, what is '*expedient*', far from merging with the useful, has a detrimental effect; the moral person will not agree: to shape his behaviour in accordance with what is expedient once there is a 'superior' interest for himself or for society. Falsehood and the love of money for money's sake are judged by this standard. The love of virtue is a sentiment which contributes most to happiness for all. All the applications of utilitarian doctrine derive from the same basic approach.

The rereading of John Stuart Mill gives us some insight into his underlying intention but may suggest some misgivings about the vocabulary he uses.

The intention is a moral one, the pursuit of an exacting, and undoubtedly lofty, morality.

The vocabulary is that of an Englishman who has no intention of breaking with a certain tradition of his country. Utility designates the pursuit of a practical form of happiness which can and must be made appealing but can in no way be suspected of base materialism; it must spread through life as it is; its strictest requirements must not be enlarged upon, so as not to discourage good intentions; that happiness is nonetheless rooted in elevation of mind and draws sustenance from justice and solidarity. It precludes the perpetual 'demand for more' and is concerned not with the quantity of wealth enjoyed by an individual but with the intellectual and moral quality of the choices he makes.

Schumpeter is probably right when he says that Mill's doctrine is merely a new way of expressing natural laws, a statement of the natural laws of man in society, where the society is considered to be extremely stable and the nature of man greatly simplified.

These reservations in no way detract from the certainty that Mill's Utilitarianism is founded on a scale of values.

Degradation of the Original Utilitarianism

This high-minded, but not austere doctrine, which relies on moderation rather than on asceticism, has suffered a *diminution of truth*. Even the most deeply pondered thinking cannot be entirely isolated from the society that the thinker has around him. It is not arbitrary to take the view that Mill expressed in philosophic terms the ideal of life held by the worthiest representatives of the contemporary English aristocracy and their emulators, and that he desired to see it spreading among the people at large. If so, the implied examples or explicit references running through Mill's writing have gradually lost their relevance and force. The relative importance of the aristocracies of birth has declined; their prestige and their power to call forth a pale imitation among the people kept at a distance have certainly waned. Social circumstances have changed radically and the pursuit of plain happiness has, on the whole, acquired a growing appeal without being associated with the high values which are the hall-mark of happiness as conceived by the elite of 'competent' judges, as our author would put it.

The evolution of the industrial and mercantile economy did not temper the desires of capitalists, nor of workers, nor of the middle classes. Education spread but was not accompanied by ethical training. There was more but certainly not better information and, as the gaps between social classes narrowed, Mill's moral doctrine *lost its meaning*, its practical significance. There was a time when happiness of a high standard and the scale of values that went with it were accepted as a matter of course. That time has gone. Getting richer has become, as it were, an end in itself, contrary to what Mill was seeking in his optimistic attempt to make virtue 'attractive' without slackening its moral force.

The mathematically-minded economists of the following century, with their theories of 'neutral' utility and 'ophelimity' (for economic satisfaction), were in no position to check or slow down the movement. The very few people who actually read them were tempted by a mechanistic interpretation of economics which was all the easier to regard as 'neutral' in that it was dissociated from man by being depersonalized. At the end of this train of 'scientific' thought, we find the autonomy of the market and the interaction of its allegedly automatic mechanisms.

Meanwhile, basic needs, real needs were less directly perceived by broad sectors of the population. The production offensive backed up by advertising stimulated the desire to buy, or 'consumeritis' as it has ironically been called, showing it up as a fashionable disease. The novelty of a product became a value in itself, and the exploitation of artificial needs created for the purpose of selling more took precedence over the real consumption of the more privileged strata, the middle classes and the better off sectors of the wage-earning class. History said 'no' to Mill's excellent intentions and cast doubts on his utilitarian ethic as a substitute for that of effort and duty.

The spread of the *American way of life* after the Second World War and its infiltration into European lifestyles was to add to the general confusion. The obsession with consumer goods and with financial profit as the means of acquiring them, the quickening pace of society's life and the growing laxity of morals led to the emergence of that profoundly debased form of Utilitarianism which helped to give rise to, and spread the use of, the term 'economism', now employed quite casually and carelessly to describe what is, in fact, an inversion of values in which *chrematistic* or money-making values take precedence over the *economic values* of traditional practices bound up with a system founded on the family and society. We need to appreciate the tragic ambiguity of such terms as the 'consumer society', the 'welfare and leisure society' and the 'permissive society' which, whether we will or no, reflect the devaluation of social ties. A society in which consumption can be regarded as 'legitimized by' or 'closely dependent on' the level of consumption – even if this is merely a clumsy way of putting things – will, if that level declines, lose its cohesion and soundness. When prosperity wanes, demands are exacerbated in an environment that had become accustomed to thinking of growth as self-sustaining and of rising wages without extra work or invention as being one of society's dues.

In a Ferment of Research, Two Philosophies of Action

The degeneration of the original Utilitarianism into commonplace hedonism, accelerated by the moral confusion resulting from the Second World War, is the scourge of European societies today. They are readier to indulge in drug-taking or facile pleasure-seeking than they are to heed philosophies of any kind, set about as they are by those *brands* of ideology that are crystallized into formulae sufficiently elementary and approximate to become effective weapons in social conflicts.

What people in general extract from J.P. Sartre's atheistic existentialism, assuming they know of it, is the appeal to absolute freedom, but in so doing they reduce it to the lowest levels.

Althusser's Marxism, the complicated and indeed debatable interpretation of Karl Marx that he puts forward, transforming the reasoned interpretation of an historical evolution into a 'scientific' theory, is seen as yet another justification of Marx, without anyone's taking the trouble to analyse it in greater depth.

The greatest bodies of thought are always liable to fall prey to a reductionism which betrays them enough to make them superficially accessible to lazy readers and to professional agitators.

Nonetheless, the extreme seriousness of the present crisis makes it absolutely essential for any thinking person to reflect on the *action* that might go with and support the major purposes of a revised economic theory based on the agent, i.e. on the individual acting individually and as part of a group to modify his environment and weaken his adversaries. Such a philosophy would run counter to those which once decreed that 'God is dead' and now decree that 'man is dead'.

Some of these philosophies put forward a structuralism which, if it amounts to a doctrine advocating fixity, renders human activity meaningless and, if it is understood as a means of disrupting the intellectual and moral patterns, is no more than a method from which reflection can fan out in all directions.

Others tend to reduce consciousness and intentional activity to the subconscious and its drives. Taken to the extreme, they destroy the active subject and the agent; if they do no more than qualify consciousness and activity, bringing to light the turbid, threatening admixtures that they see in the obscure movements of the infra-human, they call for increased vigilance on the part of the intellect and greater discipline of the will.

These philosophies, which we need not examine as such, tend to run counter to the concept of the agent and the interpretation of action which we so urgently require in order to interpret the historical movements which hold out for the most active individuals the promise of the great and glorious schemes of a new society and a new approach to development.

However difficult and subjective a choice may be in this area, we suggest that, in the research prompted by the sight of the upheavals in the world, invaluable lessons can and should be learnt from Karl Marx's philosophy of *praxis* and from the Christian personalists' philosophy of *action*, derived directly or indirectly from Maurice Blondel.

Action, conditioned by its technological, economic and social environment, is not determined by that environment but derives from it the specific characteristics which indicate where it can be applied and clarify the ways in which it may be effective. The constraints of this kind which affect our framing of our schemes for life and our choice of means are undeniable. Theory and doctrine in the human sciences do in fact seem always to be to some extent axiological: the human phenomena observed cannot be reduced to the status of objects except by destroying their essential characteristics, and when the theorist applies his own interpretative matrices to them, he does so with the avowed or secret intention of influencing action in the societies in which he lives, and of affecting one aspect or the course of such action. He can only choose between conceptualizations that are more or less implicitly normative and those that are explicitly so. In economics, for instance, pure subjectivism is not tenable; there is no perfectly isolable and rational economic man any more than there is a perfect market. Nor is the notion of an agent entirely conditioned by external factors any more acceptable. This is attested by a massive body of evidence difficult to refute; since the beginning of the industrial era, capitalism has been modified by the deliberate action of the workers, their groups and their leaders. It has been modified not by the workings of an inexorable, blind mechanism derived from the proportions between profit, surplus value, fixed capital and circulating capital, but by planned action on the part of organized trade unions and parties.

Colonialism did not disappear as a result of economic contradictions, but in consequence of organized political pressures and the militant conquest of power.

What remains of Marx's original theories is the exaltation of the desire for freedom on the part of the deprived and the oppressed when, at favourable times in history, they succeed in combining political action with a widespread, latent refusal to accept institutional abuses.[12] It is a lasting lesson, even when one considers that Marx's thinking is much more than 'the spontaneous philosophy of the proletariat'; but it is clearly not a complete philosophy of action.

A clearly designed and remarkably well-structured philosophy of action is, however, to be found in the work of Maurice

Blondel[13]. Even those who do not accept it, forming as it does a coherent whole, may find in it an example for the construction of their own doctrines.

In Blondel's view, action cannot be reduced to a sort of activism or operation external to the person; it is, taken as a whole, the activity which constitutes thinking, willing and doing. It is both living freedom and intellectual lucidity. It is the very basis of the individual human being and deserves to be considered as an existential *cogito*. It is that synthesis of willing, knowing and being without which the personal individual would cease to exist. It is impossible, Blondel tells us, to 'abstain, to stand aloof'; I am incapable of 'self-satisfaction, self-sufficiency and *self-liberation*'. The individual is not a natural product of the Universe, nor a successful achievement of life, but an *act* whose consciousness comes 'as it were from above'; it emerges from the Universe which 'calls it into existence with all its constituent effort'.

This doctrine, which implies faith in God, discovers in nature the source of free, spiritual order; it sees a religious dimension in all thought and the elements of thought in action.

This philosophy – to which one cannot do justice in one page – is one which can guide and regulate the action of every human being and human group aspiring after and striving towards 'reciprocity of consciousness'.

Even those who do not subscribe to it are bound to concede that it offers us the most coherent and noble interpretation of the living synthesis of intellect and action in every human being.

Notes

1. For a criticism of the tradition equilibrium theories as stated by Walras and Pareto, see: Perroux, François. 'Sur le degré de généralité de la théorie de l'équilibre général', *CISMEA*, No. 9, 1967, p. 227. 'La mathématique walraso-parétienne et l'unité "active"', *Mélanges en l'honneur du doyen Teixera Ribeiro*, Portugal, Coimbra, 1978. 'Notion d'équilibre et mathématisations actuelles. Une interprétation', *MED*, No. 8, 1974. Bernis (Destanne de), Gérard. 'Les limites de l'analyse en termes d'équilibre économique général', *Revue économique*, November 1975.

2. Perroux, François. 'La généralisation de la *general theory*', *Revue de la faculté des sciences économiques*, University of Istanbul, 1949 (booklet). 'La généralisation de la théorie de l'intérêt chez J.M. Keynes', *Banque*, March 1950. 'J.M. Keynes, l'homme et les problèmes de son époque', *Economie contemporaine*, January 1951. Barrere, Alain. *Théorie économique et impulsion keynésienne*, Paris, Dalloz, 1952. *Déséquilibres économiques et contre-révolution keynésienne*, Paris, Economica, 1979. Leijonhufund, Axel. *On keynesian*

116   *Theoretical Formulation*

economics and the economics of Keynes, Oxford, Oxford University Press, 1968.
    3. Lesourne, Jacques. *A theory of the individual for economic analysis*, Amsterdam, North Holland Publishing Co., 1977. Perroux, François. *Unités actives et mathématiques nouvelles. Révision de la théorie de l'équilibre économique général*, Paris, Dunod, 1975. 'L'équilibre des unités passives et l'équilibration générale des unités actives', *EA*, No. 3–4, 1978.
    4. Lewis, Arthur W. *The theory of economic growth*, 1st ed., London, Allen & Unwin, 1955. *Economic development with unlimited supplies of labour*, Manchester School of Economic and Social Studies, 1954.
    5. Rostow, W.W. *The stages of economic growth. A non communist manifesto*, Cambridge, Cambridge University Press, 1960.
    6. Perroux, François. *Karl Marx* (Introduction de l'oeuvre de), Paris, Gallimard, Pléiade, Vol. I. With a critique by Maximilien Rubel. Amin, Samir. 'L'accumulation à l'échelle mondiale, critique de la théorie de sous-développement', *Anthropos*, 2nd ed., Paris, IFAN, Dakar, 1977.
    7. Perroux, François. 'Résumé des cours donnés au Collège de France', *Annuaire du Collège de France* (1955–75), Paris.
    8. Perroux, François. 'L'effet d'entraînement. De l'analyse au repérage statistique', *EA*, Nos. 2, 3 and 4, 1973. 'La firme motrice dans une région et la région motrice', *CISMEA*, A.D. series, March 1961. 'Les industries motrices et la croissance d'une économie nationale', *EA*, No. 2, 1963. 'Note sur la notion de pôle de croissance', *EA*, Nos. 1 and 2, 1955. 'Les pôles de développement et l'économie internationale', *The challenge of development*, Symposium, 1957–8. 'Une distinction utile à la politique des pays en développement: points de développement et foyers du progrès', *CISMEA*, F Series, No. 12, November 1959. 'L'idée de pôle de développement et les ensembles industriels en Afrique', *Sentier d'Europe*, No. 1, 1957. 'Les pôles de développement et la politique de l'Est', *Politique étrangère*, No. 3, 1957. Lajugie, Joseph, Delfaud, Pierre, Lacour, Claude. *Espace régional et aménagement du territoire*, Paris, Dalloz, 1979 (an excellent treatise – scientific, rigorous and operational).
    9. Starobinski, Jean. *Les emblèmes de la raison*, Paris, Gallimard, 1978.
    10. Jacob, François. *La logique du vivant*, Paris, Gallimard, 1971. Monod, Jacques. *Le hasard et la nécessité. Essai sur la philosophie naturelle de la biologie moderne*, Paris, Seuil, 1971. Prigogine, Ilya. *La nouvelle alliance*, Paris, Gallimard, 1979. Nicolis, G. and Prigogine, I. *Self organization in non equilibrium systems*, London, John Wiley & Sons, 1977. Caillois, Roger. *La dissymétrie*, Paris, Gallimard, 1973.
    11. Mill, John Stuart. *Principles of Political Economy with some of their Applications to Social Philosophy*, Vols. 1 and 2, University of Toronto Press, Routledge and Kegan Paul, 1965. *Utilitarianism* (French version translated, with chronology, preface and notes by Georges Tanesse), Paris, Garnier Flammarion, 1968.
    12. For a study of the movement of Marxism towards 'utopia', see the very interesting collection: *Utopia et Marxisme selon Ernst Bloch*, Hommages published by Gérard Raulet, Paris, Payot, 1976.
    13. Blondel, Maurice. *L'Action. Essai d'une critique de la vie et d'une science de la pratique*, Paris, Alcan, 1893. Dumery, Henry. *La philosophie de l'action. Essai sur l'intellectualisme blondélien* (with a preface by Maurice Blondel), Paris, Aubier, 1948. Lacroix, Jean. *Maurice Blondel, sa vie, son oeuvre* (with a summary of his philosophy and a short bibliography), Paris, Presses Universitaries de France, 1963.

    To make the points mentioned in the text a little clearer, the following are a few preliminary ideas on (a) human Activity, and (b) the concepts of *Praxis* in the writings of Karl Marx and Action in those of Maurice Blondel.
(a) Activity is inherent in the human being. It may be defined in terms of *creating*

(*poiein*), *doing* (*prattein*) and *struggling*.

The individual creates a distinctive image of himself that is a compound of what he desires and a projection of himself, of others and of the world. That image precedes its verbal formulation and conceptualization – in other terms, it has a precognitive content.

By working on himself and his environment, the individual comes to construct a dynamic and evolutive world; his successive actions are, to an extent that varies greatly according to persons and circumstances, governed by a purpose whose thrust or outlines may change as he acquires experience and learning.

In his activity the individual struggles *against* nature and time; he generally functions by negentropy. He also struggles against his adversaries and enemies, who are always to some degree his partners (according to the Littré dictionary, a partner is 'an associate with whom one plays'). Human relationships are ambivalent, combining conflict and co-operation, struggle and synergy. The co-operation component may or may not be conscious, perceived and intentional: if it is so, the changes wrought by time will generally amend the original intent.

Activity thus advances from the creative image to *doing* (work and struggle). This rudimentary interpretation is borne out by countless observations: to extrapolate, it might be said to run throughout world history. It helps in making groups of active individuals easier to understand, but only if strict specifications are imposed.

For the group, *creating* stems from that compound image of which we spoke above, and which in turn arises from the life of the group itself. That image is incorporated – and distorted – in the mentality of individuals; it exists prior to its spoken formulation and to cognitive procedures, arising from daily contacts and the influences exerted by the gestures, behaviour-patterns and collective life-style of the group.

Each individual may interpret and formulate the image. As a rule, however, it is put into words by a handful of active interpreters and by *leaders*. Modern communication techniques confer great powers on the few who control them.

The group's *doing* is its work, organized synergically for purposes of adapting to or changing the environment. It also results in the formation or deformation of active individuals through the conditions and content of the organized work.

Struggling is the instrument of group formation and identity, which result from the situations of conflict–co-operation within the group or between it and others.

These features are to be found in local, coactive and kinship groups. In no case can these groups be reduced to things or abstract structures.

There are countless junctions and intersections in individual and group life spaces. What is important, in a large group such as a nation–state, is the *whole*. This defies our formal instruments of analysis or description; whenever they are applied, the choices that underly them must be *defined explicitly* (see the Appendix: Models, their Limitations and their Proper Use).

(b) *Praxis*, as conceived by Karl Marx, is the result of labour, defined in relation to society by institutions that reflect a power relationship and allocate *social roles*. It applies above all to dependent wage-labour; when the capitalist stage is reached, it transforms nature and the human habitat. The labourer, although not directly and spontaneously conscious of the fact, is the Worker who reconstructs the world and humanity; he is associated with a historical process whose outcome is *preordained*.

To this background Marx applies an emotive picture of redemption through suffering, and another of conscious struggle that is assured of victory through its collusion with an economic mechanism: that of the declining trend of profit rates. The combat must be carried on, but in the conviction that it will hasten the collapse of a system that is irrevocably doomed by its internal contradictions.

Through action the individual creates himself and, in the course of history, the group of workers recreates itself through *auto-praxis* (Maximilien Rubel, 'L'auto-praxis historique du prolétariat', *Economies et Sociétés, Cahiers de l'ISMEA*,

1975). In its origins and development, this process is quite unrelated to strictly deterministic materialism, and is specifically contrary to political dictatorship: it is touched off and kept alive by a cumulative realization of its legitimacy and effectiveness, in which rational analysis plays a great part. What is the origin of this chain reaction? It stems from a fundamental fact of life over which the actors have no control: man's intrinsic nature. Human beings are *creators, workers* and *strugglers*: they find satisfaction and fulfilment in and through the exercise of these innate capacities.

Now let us turn to the philosophy of Maurice Blondel as expounded, since his thesis of 1893, in *La Pensée* (Alcan, Presses Universitaires de France, 1934), *L'Etre et les êtres* (Alcan, 1935) and *L'Action* (Alcan, 1893, Presses Universitaires de France, 1936-7).

To understand the individual in action, Blondel goes back to the 'common source' of intelligence and will, to that '*dynamism* of the spiritual being from which they draw *their force of action*' (Lacroix, Jean: *Maurice Blondel*, Presses Universitaires de France, 1963, p. 60). The entire work is a study of 'the relationship between *thinking* and *being* as revealed in *action*' (*op. cit.*, p. 63).

Blondel's philosophy of action is the end-result of a rational inquiry and the product of an intellectual effort. That effort is *not sufficient* to overcome a dilemma that cannot be dealt with by rational investigation, requiring the attestation of faith. Active individuals and groups thereof are *by their nature* capable of reason and of rational investigation of their actions. In the long run, that reason brings to light the question that was from the outset lurking in their subconscious: action for what?

Is man 'flung down here for no purpose' or 'destined for and capable of satisfaction and fulfilment'? The reply is an act of faith that transcends all logic.

Let us agree for a time, and for purely heuristic purposes, to leave aside Blondel's distinctive, personal and coherent views, and to accept his system without reference to what the unbeliever sees as the mere hypothesis of God. *On the other side* of reason and rational argument there is a dynamic of the active individual; *beyond* them, faced with the inscrutable choices to which the boldest and most rigorous rational inquiry leads, there is something – a belief, a faith in a future, in ultimate values and a purpose. A fundamental example, albeit one of many, is this: 'Man *is* freedom; each man *is* freedom' – an assertion that transcends all the certainties of rational knowledge, its abstract constructs and its experiences. Seen in this light, action is in some way a pledge of faith in freedom and its deployment; it testifies to freedom in its observable forms, which are those of *liberation*.

Praxis as Marx saw it before his thought was betrayed, Blondel's Action interpreted without reference to God (*only* to explain it *better* to those who reject the hypothesis of God), suggest aspirations and intellectual movements in the two systems which are not mutually incompatible. This intellectual dynamism flows from a source that precedes rational inquiry, and stems from man's original being. Both lead to a place where belief and choice attribute values but which reason alone can neither elect nor foster.

It will remain for the active individual to propose, through rational inquiry, paths that are considered possible for mankind's adventure in the context of place, time and circumstances. But regardless of the content of the strategy and tactics, Action would betray its essence and its dignity *were it to invoke* 'so-called historical requirements' in order to evade or flout the values by which history is judged.

Hence there can be no multidimensional human development without the irrepressible dynamisms of the development of the individual himself.

As the only irrefutable earnest of values, action endorses the multidimensional investigations of the *mind that both knows and wills* and, through the inexhaustible strength of a belief, is capable of obtaining through experience the proof of its objective sincerity and historical effectiveness.

3 POLICY AND STRATEGIES

Power, Powers and Human Societies

The relations between people are ambiguous and ambivalent; conflict and co-operation are so intimately interwoven that the term 'conflict co-operation' may be used to bring out their joint presence in a 'Janus bond'.[1]

Once this is grasped, it will be seen that in the course of irreversible time the two are not exactly co-extensive: their frontiers vary in response to different operations and to changes in the size and structure of two contiguous societies and in the information available to them and, equally, to the development of the so-called 'global' society of which they form part.

Analytically, everything may be explained in terms of asymmetries between physical entities, agents and groups of agents – whose economic importance we have discussed elsewhere in some detail – the asymmetrical impact of one unit on another calling forth a matching, excessive or inadequate compensatory reaction. This last gives rise to (a) influence, or (b) dominance (coercion), or (c) subordination, whether institutionalized or not. For simplicity's sake, (b) and (c) may be viewed as the chief forms of power.

Intentionality is introduced when power is defined, in Jeanne Hersch's words, as 'the ability to impose one's own will on things or human beings'.[2]

Power is involved in every human activity, and the proponents of the traditional equilibrium theory or neo-classicism needed all their ingenuity to exclude it from the market, which they made simply the place where objects moved. That ingenuity was wasted: history and analysis have restored power to its rightful place in any realistic, operational form of economic thinking.[3]

The forms of power are multidimensional, technical, political and social. Since individuals belong to several groups, and in consequence of the division of labour and social stratification, there are countless intersections between different areas of power. Because agents or actors are different and unequal, conflicts of interest, and clashes between aspirations or values sought, are the rule. Political Power, written for convenience with a capital 'P' (or

119

Government with a capital 'G') plays a part in every observable society. The functions traditionally ascribed to it are to protect the group's physical and cultural heritage, to act as an arbiter of conflicts that might jeopardize the group's existence, and to promote its purposes.

In order to exercise these functions, Government must seek the consent or acquiescence of the individual within what is now somewhat obscurely called the 'collective consciousness'. Constantly assailed, called into question and precarious, it is obliged over and over again to plead its own cause and justify its action. This political power is engaged in a constant search for legitimacy, which alone makes it a political authority. The essence of the new approach to development with which we are concerned is a worldwide challenge to Power and a demand for a form of legitimation untainted by what J.-P. Sartre called 'bad faith' within and among nations. From this it derives a virtue that transcends conflicts of interest, the ethical significance of which accounts for the depth and gravity of the crisis through which we are passing.

Since an exhaustive survey of the encounters between the traditional powers in the West and in the developing countries is completely out of the question, two general models may be put forward as a basis for a systematic classification and investigation of the conflicts of legitimacy between the West and cultures to which it must now give serious thought after long ignoring or neglecting them.

Neither model completely matches any observable situation, and they are no more than guides for the study of specific cases.

One is the *Max Weber model* and the other the *anti-Weber model*. The first is widely known, having been much mooted since the publication of the study on the types of Power (*Typen der Herrschaft*). Force becomes Power by the acquisition of legitimacy, which it draws from tradition, from utility or from charisma – three ideal forms (*Idealtypen*) which in practice are intermingled with one another. We would point out that this legitimacy remains philosophically very dubious. Its salient point is the transformation of violence into strength through a process of social legitimation. The extreme case of violence is the putting to death of individuals by other individuals by due process of law – meaning by virtue of the purposes or values enshrined in the law, which is itself legitimized by one of the sources of legitimation mentioned above.

Whatever the source may be, it is incommensurable with a

human life in the view alike of many world religions and of any philosophy that recognizes the uniqueness, irreplaceability and unpredictability of every human being. The society that takes the life of but one of its members literally does *not* know what it is doing, since it thereby proves its contempt for life, whereas the commonly observed respect for life is one of the keys to its own proper functioning and stability. This is not, however, the point to which we wish to draw attention here. Our question is whether there is any consultative procedure at all whereby the members of a society may properly be asked to give their views on the legitimacy of taking life by order of a government acting through administrative machinery. Let us say that there are at least very strong reasons to say that there is none.

Whether we assent to another's death or refuse it is a moral issue: no institutional procedure organized at a given point in time by institutions – that is to say, under given *constraints* – is sensitive enough to reflect faithfully the moral decisions which, if they are to have any ethical force, must be considered in the light of essentially personal knowledge, for which each is answerable only to his conscience, and in circumstances that are as free as possible from all constraint.

This thesis points up but does not justify the grave inadequacies of the ballot-box and the law courts. The electoral system rests on parties whose motives are always mixed, their moral stances being tempered by their ambitions. The law courts base their rulings on police inquiries not wholly immune from bias deriving from the reconstruction of the offence – yet the *entire truth* can never be fully reconstructed, just as the judicial decisions of the bench or jury cannot but be influenced both by personal cnsiderations and by society's *unacknowledged but very real* caste hierarchies.

At most and at best, Weber's model is a sociological construct of little real benefit even in the investigation of cultures that differ from our own. What do we gain by labelling an Oriental or African culture as 'charismatic' or 'traditional' when it stems from a living faith? In what intellectual or moral debate could the West's pragmatic atheists engage it from the standpoint of their utilitarian legitimation, based as it is on social benefit measured by the yardstick of Western rationality?

Even in the West, Weber's model probably has less explanatory force, less 'realism', than is commonly credited to it. It fails to account for and transcend the deep-rooted oppositions to which the aspirations of those who advocate a new form of development for all bear witness.

The *anti-Weber model* cannot therefore be rejected out of hand, and it is worth while to give some thought to the questions it sets Western cultures and those of other continents. These other cultures are exploring their own identity and attempting to redefine it without detracting from, betraying or destroying it. All the evidence suggests that they are neglecting none of the assets this gives them in their contracts with Westerners, but are nonetheless seeking within themselves a recipe for autonomy and identity in the circumstances that the modern world imposes and that are essential to the quest for modern efficiency.

The anti-Weber model is summed up in a single formula: politics begins where violence ends. This calls for some comments.

Acts of violence – crime, murder, armed robbery, the burning down of crops or forests, kidnapping for ransom, the destruction of inhabited houses and so on – are, regrettably, the work of individuals and of groups that reject law and order or claim that their action is prompted by such rejection. The authority invoked for the suppression of crime, apart from a quasi-instinctive, reflex-like reaction, is – consciously or unconsciously – the *reaffirmation of that law and order*. And there can be no affirmation without proofs either drawn from reasoning which furnishes something tantamount to clear moral right or justifies a lesser evil, or deduced from practical experience of the attitudes that have brought about lasting peace in a community. Suppression therefore posits an evaluation, a judgement of violence felt to be such by certain members of the body social and enshrined in the society's institutions.

In the penetrating view of Maurice Hauriou, institutions represent 'social armistices'. They establish a sort of formal record of a situation that has become stale thanks to the temporary exhaustion of the energy productive of change vested in adversaries who, after confronting each other, have at least temporarily agreed on a basis for co-operation. When circumstances change, struggles are resumed.

What Western societies now see as their most valuable political and social achievements have no other historical origin. They are considered legitimate largely because they have made violence less frequent and less deadly by substituting trials of *strength* for the exchange of blows. The circumstances in which that strength is distinguished from violence consist in protracted struggles; they cannot be reduced to the action of the governments considered legitimate at a given time, nor to the rulings of their judicial bodies.

These struggles were not and are not silent exchanges: they were and are vocal, using speech to put forward, if only in embryonic form, communicable statements. The verbal exchanges in the struggle are not dialogues, but describe human combats in terms of values that are upheld, consciously or otherwise, by intellects. Attempts are made to justify the trial of strength by a rudimentary statement of the values involved, justice or freedom. These values are deliberately couched in opaque and nebulous terms, interwoven with arguments that the adversaries know to be dishonest, but which they press the more unscrupulously in that they feel, or are convinced, that they are fighting against social dishonesty.

Hence both *hypothetically* and *legally*, the motives for violence can be abolished or reduced only by a critical study of the violence that forms part of institutions. It has been pointed out very rightly that in every institution there is the spoken and the unspoken, the things proclaimed and the things left unsaid. Societies being hierarchical, the 'spoken' is generally favourable to the higher strata, while the 'unspoken' reflects the subordination of the lower strata. Institutions can become more widely understood only through discussion of them: their acceptance can be measured in terms of the numbers of informed and aware supporters they attract, as opposed to those who acquiesce out of ignorance or apathy.

The analysis thus takes us to the verge of dialogue,[4] or in other terms, of a free exchange through which such values as freedom and justice may provisionally be agreed upon.

Each party to a dialogue risks his all: his first position and the statement he has made of it may well be totally destroyed. Dialogue is nothing if not *active*, being a sublimated form of conflict-co-operation governed by the age-old rules that the West has inherited from the Greeks and from the Judaeo-Christian tradition, but also to be found in other, non-European, traditions.

These rules automatically exclude violence and even force, other than that of compelling or persuasive argument. The proponents of dialogue open, pursue and conclude it in a human space that is devoid of violence.

This is an exacting requirement, but it points to the intellectual attitude and social framework without which dialogue can only be false or, at worst, a verbal exchange as destructive, albeit by other means, as a violent exchange.

We have so far considered dialogues between hypothetical persons acting quite separately from the social groups to which they belong – which already verges on the impossible. Political dialogue is obviously another matter altogether, being essentially a dialogue between organized social or national groups. Even the choice of a spokesman for each group compromises the rules of dialogue: being made up not of philosophers but rather of individuals collectively aware of special interests, the group is inclined to prefer a spokesman who is effective in the particular circumstances of place and time rather than one obedient to the dictates of truth and justice. Generally speaking, it is not his job to place even his *own* truth at risk in an exacting dialogue, and still less to jeopardize the truth of the group that has placed its truth in him.

Such is the painful situation of 'dialogues' between trade unions or between nations.

Political 'dialogues' are relativized, just as politics itself is inherently relative. The political motor of human progress lies in the fact that the individual conscience cannot be reduced to a social standard or an array of institutions. The way ahead lies not in the forcible suppression of conflicts, but in the creation of conditions conducive to *helping* all parties to appreciate that conflicts may *bear fruit*, quite distinct from the decrees of the government in power or the constructs of an intellectual elite.

The new development movement, if it is not to lead to the world's going up in flames, must at the least adopt a line of research, a guiding principle and, basing itself on the anti-Weber model, a course of slow, patient and cumulative advance.

That model leaves room for the cultural exchanges which go far beyond economic exchange. It underpins the demand for a regeneration of the spirit of development policy before its content is decided. It is to this that we now turn.

The Economic and Social Dialectics of Development

'More and more, development is thought of as *an awakening of the very soul of society*' (Unesco, Medium-Term Plan for 1977–82, p. 64, paragraph 3106)

Fewer and fewer competent economists or observers now maintain that uncontrolled market forces can of themselves produce a soundly-functioning economy.

Throughout the West, the logic of market economics is corrected by that of the economics of solidarity. Mercantile exchange must therefore, following the example of the American economist, K. Boulding, and my own example 10 years earlier, be restored to the context of enforced transfers – taxes, public levies, etc. – and social transfers such as gifts, grants and social policy.[5]

The logic of solidarity is couched in terms acceptable to every modern mind in Article 3 of the Universal Declaration of Human Rights, which proclaims that 'Everyone has the *right* to life . . .', thereby outlawing all acts of destruction or violence against another living being, and directing attention to the harm done to the integrity of the human being by social organization, regardless of whereabouts. If the right, thus formulated, is to be effective, something more is needed than to record the commercial equality of debit and credit, of benefit and contribution, seemingly so obvious: their direct and indirect effects on the integrity of the human being must be investigated. A remarkable sequel to Article 3 may be found in Unesco's recent work on the universal right to complete development of the personality.

Both at national and world level, these principles are still considered to be revolutionary by the open or covert advocates of the status quo, since they run counter to and conflict with national and class egoism.

In the twentieth century, however, they are supported by extremely powerful social forces – those of the deprived nations which have, in one sense, taken up the demands of the deprived classes of the previous century. Decolonization, the political rise of the developing countries, and the dissemination of information are all contributing to the challenging of the mercantile economy throughout the world. Absolute and relative poverty have been 'discovered'. Terms such as 'justice', 'equity' and human 'solidarity' are creeping into the economic reports of the most highly qualified experts. The supposed impartiality of economics, the alleged separation of means from ends, and the so-called absolute divisions between economics, politics and social matters are now seen for what they always were: ideologies designed to serve vested interests.

Scientifically verifiable and economically operational laws may be identified and applied without necessarily reducing man to the robot status that he has in the market mechanism.

The conflict between the doctrine of the 'pure' market and that of the market 'corrected' by the principle of solidarity has been a constant feature of Western economic history since industrialization. It has since the Second World War spread throughout the globe, with a frightening intensity exacerbated by the crisis. During the period of exceptionally high growth rates, the costs of solidarity were borne without difficulty: since the crisis, they have given rise to great acrimony between both classes and nations.

Above all, the very foundations of economic oganization in the West – private ownership of the means of production and national sovereignty – are now being questioned. Can the decentralized capitalist economy escape all criticism when, while dominated by its monopolies and its financial groups, it cannot rid the world of hunger and poverty? And what is the meaning of national sovereignty in the light of the flagrant inequalities between *nation-empires* and lesser nations which are, in plain fact, *quasi-nations* lacking both real internal cohesion and effective power against the outside world?

The demand for a new approach to development thus arises in an historic climate compounded of doubts about the ability of liberal economics to cope with tasks and difficulties for which it was not designed, and doubts as to the sincerity of the principle of national sovereignty.

Development policy is here at one with the policy of the *building up of new nations*: they combine to challenge political and economic orthodoxy. The former aims to structure badly developed economies and to rectify their poorly co-ordinated flows, foreign dominance and wastage of human resources, while the latter seeks to reshape every aspect of a young nation's relations with the world around it, easing the grip of the dominances to which it is subjected, strengthening its cohesion and increasing its negotiating power.

Hence all aspects of the new approach to development are closely interdependent.

1. It seeks the degree of freedom from the limiting conditions of the domestic and foreign markets that is essential to human dignity: this is the dialectic of fundamental needs and purchasing power.

2. It likewise seeks to reduce the structural ascendancy imposed by the powers and to find points of entry into world economic networks: this is the dialectic of independence and co-operation.
3. It seeks to strike an optimum balance between industry and agriculture: this is the dialectic of domestic and external economic structures.

The Dialectic of Fundamental Needs and Purchasing Power[6]

This dialectic, which assumes tragic dimensions in the poorest of the developing countries, is also at work in the developed countries, since they have proved unable to do away with poverty altogether. Furthermore, despite the great progress made, the private and social accounting in which they engage may be misleading in regard to the respect accorded to the integrity of the human being at work and in life.

National accounting systems are derived from private book-keeping, which is basically individualistic and narrowly economic. They therefore make no allowance for the amortization of man, as Simon Kuznets long since pointed out.

The amount and structure of social costs should be subjected to a long-term investigation of their effects as regards 'manpower amortization'. The amortization of fixed capital and the means of production is calculated as a matter of course, but this is not yet properly done in respect of the human agent, despite the progress made in ergonomics and the study of worker fatigue.

What is more, even in the most developed countries, some of the population do not enjoy a minimum living wage, or the minimum income needed for a decent life in the society to which they belong.

As far back as 1952, French schools felt it necessary to calculate the *coûts de l'homme*, meaning the costs of a truly human life for all. These costs are broken down into three groups: those which safeguard the individual's physical and mental equilibrium, those that enable each person to have an intellectual and moral life (education), and those that provide everyone with the minimum leisure without which self-awareness is impossible.

The introduction of these costs into private and social systems of accounting in itself runs counter to the logic of ability to pay, since it acknowledges that the living individual takes priority in the distribution of product and income. Human life has precedence *in law* over an increment of enrichment, although this imperative, like any other, is conditioned by time, place and cultural environment. Clearly, too, it may come up against absolute impossibilities. In any case, it calls for a rigorous inquiry into what is possible, and acknowledges a *hierarchy* of satisfactions and uses that is radically different from that dictated by ability to pay.

The imperative and calculation of the *coûts de l'homme* involve consideration of:

objectively 'useful' effects;
the potentialities of the human being;
multidimensional maximizations.

Even this bald statement brings us back to some of the demands inherent in the new approach to development. They come hesitantly from institutions and give rise to emotive reactions, but do at least point to striking convergences between scientifically-minded economics and the general trend of science.

Objectively 'Useful' Effects. Current economic theory has been built up on the basis of subjective value and neutral utility (ophelimity or economic satisfaction). Its strength lies in its claim to respect the freedom of individual choice, in contrast with authoritarian rationing by a Planning Centre under party control. Its weakness is that, before one can choose, one must *be* and survive, and that the freedom of subjective choice can be complete only when the subject is informed and capable of rational judgement. Markets, however, are only partially explained by scientific reasoning, whether they be viewed with production or with consumption in mind, and the solvency of those who have access to the market is bound up with historic circumstances that have nothing to do with even the least exacting economic reasoning. The result is that the appetite for luxury and semi-luxury products is satisfied *before* everyone's vital (or biological) needs and existential needs, meaning those which relate to a human living standard, are met.

The objective is not in the least to force people willy-nilly to be fed like cattle or to bring them up as perpetual children; nor is it to seek the ultimate liberation of future generations by crushing today's people in the machinery of planning enforced by a state policy. It is to *enable* people, through a collective effort, to feed themselves, to educate themselves consciously and to achieve their own liberation without violence.

Polemics and counter-polemics have created more and more confusion and cast discredit upon observations which albeit summary and crude, are nonetheless incontrovertible, and cannot be gainsaid by irony or a conspirarcy of silence. While today's wealthy talk of slimming diets, what sun-tan preparations are safest, or the comparative merits of cocktails and whisky, it is hard to agree that a thorough knowledge of the objective requirements for human health has no part to play in remedying certain destructive consequences of solvency-based economics or in informing the customers' choices. André Mayer's work on the composition of normal diets in terms of calories, ingredients and trace-elements is an incontrovertible guide for self-criticism by individuals and governments, helping those concerned to judge attitudes and behaviour patterns that are irrational *in every way*, without forcing them to adopt the rationality of the laboratory.

The World Health Organization has already, for the benefit of peoples and political leaders, identified and classified objectives based on the soundest medical knowledge, which are pursued primarily through market control: to prevent illnesses, to cure curable diseases and reduce the sufferings caused by incurable diseases, to help those who suffer lasting effects to win back their place in society and a job, and to provide for the needs of the patient and his family. Which of us would reject such a programme on his own behalf? Nor can what science teaches us about the quantity of air and light and the hygiene required in homes be overtly neglected by those in charge of municipal or national policies . . .

Objectively, 'useful', beneficial or detrimental effects have gained acceptance in scientifically-minded economics: despite fierce resistance, that discipline is turning its attention to the lessons to be learnt from them. It is moving away from the subjective utility of the Vienna and neo-classical schools, and moving beyond the neutral ecnomic satisfaction of the disciples of Pareto, who bracket together all desires to use or purchase goods.

The Potentialities of the Human Being. The economic development of a developing country starts off with a purpose in mind: the future prospect of what it *may become* precedes projects and plans. Mineral or energy prospecting is carried out to identify subsoil resources, and the physical and chemical nature of the sea-bed is investigated. Investment for prospecting purposes comes before investment in capital construction, infrastructures, buildings and machinery for the production and distribution of the product.

Prospecting goes on over periods of several decades, calling into play the vast resources controlled by financial groups, with or without the help of the authorities. Where the developing countries are concerned, the economics of private profit therefore stakes everything on the potential so-called natural resources, with the object of using them to make products intended for customers who can pay: it remains true to its own commercial economic logic, undervaluing or neglecting the identification of the potential resources that people themselves represent. Those resources are not seen as such and for their own sake, but are considered only insofar as they provide a workforce for the private firm. The state in the developing countries being poor, human potentialities are neither detected nor tapped by an effective strategy for nutrition, hygiene, health and basic education. This paradox, of which the public and the extremist parties are fully conscious, is at the root of the violent reactions which regimes not subject to democratic control attempt for a time to repress.

The true remedies lie in a profound change in the very conception and practice of economics. The first signs of this can now be seen, but the movement is thwarted by a misconception attributable to the mentality propagated by mercantile economics.

A good example of this in 'academic' economics is the attempt to calculate the worth of a man,[7] for which several methods are used. An individual's contribution to the gross national product may be calculated in constant terms for the probable duration of his life. Leaving aside the technical difficulties of this calculation, this worth of 'value' is clearly not the same to society as it is to the individual concerned. Equally, reference to the gross national product fails to measure properly the individual's multidimensional contributions to the society in which he lives. An alternative is to calculate the loss at any given time that the disappearance of an individual would cause society by reducing consumer spending. If the individual was unproductive, his death reduces the society's net costs: the possible implications of this method are obvious. Lastly, there is the insurance premium that an individual pays to cover himself against the risk of a fatal accident. But this relates to the financial compensation that he wishes to obtain for his family, and is in no way an indication of the value of his life.

These defective techniques suggest that society has no scientific way of calculating, in the strict sense of the term, the consequences of the loss of the multidimensional contributions of one of its members.

This clearly does not mean that it cannot, in the case of statistically homogeneous social groups, evaluate very approximately the cost of training an adult for work and his anticipated social product. For the group selected, one would take, in the first place, the executed product over 40 years of working life (board and lodging, the product of an effective working career, taxes and social charges) and, in the second place, the cost of 20 years of training (subsistence, education and vocational training). What price references should be chosen for the two periods? What allowance should be made for new commodities and techniques? The difficulties of current statistics are further complicated here by the inability to take account of *qualitative* differences among the individuals living in society, which were not reflected in the product or the cost that the market is supposed to set on them.

In the developed countries that pay most attention to people's fate as such, social policy anticipates the calculation, and while this may give rise to difficulties over a long period, it must be said that, in the final analysis, despite hitches and crises, the lot of the workers and the 'rejects' is probably improved thereby.

There are still unexplored reserves of human energy in the developed countries: what could be said of the developing countries?

Multidimensional Maximizations. Clearly, the human being has energies other than those that he exercises as a buyer or seller in a market, or as the producer and consumer of commodities. The findings of biology, ergonomics, occupational medicine and psychosociology are fertile in countering the narrow so-called calculations of market economics: they open up new prospects for the economist, obliging him to pay heed to facts that he used to overlook.

By way of example, the consumption of perishable goods is not the end of a line; scientifically-minded economics cannot allow itself to ignore the consequences which consumption, by its volume and structure, has on the agent's psychosomatic equilibrium and his ability to make intellectual, social and economic contributions. No one denies that it has specific implications, but neither is it recognized that those consequences condemn *pure* market economics and prompt what are known as 'enlarged consumption' policies entailing public assistance, social control over consumer spending and the education of the purchaser.

Production does not merely transform the structure of inanimate objects but also affects the worker, shaping him for better or worse, enhancing or detracting from his overall worth.

In general terms, life in society represents a combination of activities and the bringing together of agents who furnish one another with an evolving array of external social economies. These are ignored in the study of markets, but must be 'discovered' if we are to build up a body of knowledge which is less incomplete and more efficient in economic and human terms.

'An economy which takes account of the whole man and of all people' is not a mere moralistic recommendation, a comment derived from the Christian ethic and directed against what are claimed to be economic mechanisms. On the contrary, it is an objective coming under the head of scientifically verified economic knowledge; it helps us to understand that we cannot know whether we are rich or poor until we have accepted the task of exploring, using and developing the potential of our human resources. This is true for the older countries which are concerned with the accumulation of capital and the manufacturing of products for customers able to pay for them; and even truer for the developing countries which are seeking to take their place in the modern economic networks.

This needed to be pointed out so that the discussions on fundamental needs can be seen in their proper context.

Aid policy and advantageous conditions in the area of foreign trade (such as across-the-board preferential terms) have yielded only very inadequate results. Now, at the end of the second Development Decade, policy-makers and people in general are entertaining doubts about the validity of the strategies so far applied.

In the case of the poorest countries, no one questions the need for further aid. In the case of intermediate countries, the question raised is whether the strategy of industrialization should not be reviewed with respect to its content, orientation and rate of progress.

This strategy, initiated by the developed countries for their own advantage, results in the formation of small islands or enclaves of industry in economies with rural populations engaged in agricultural production. It encourages the production of crops for export at the expense of crops for local consumption, and this maintains or aggravates the deficit in the balance of trade of the country concerned, because the export crops necessitate the import of fertilizers and machinery.

Advanced technology is never introduced in isolation, but is invariably accompanied by local changes in lifestyle and by uncritical mimetic behaviour, a virtually reflex imitation of the wealthy countries by producers and consumers in the developing countries. Such imitation, which has frequently been criticized, breaks down the traditional forms of solidarity and causes the needs and aspirations of the population in general to be overlooked. In order to do as well as the foreigner, in order to make up the technological lag, people are sacrificed and their dependence is perpetuated.

As a reaction against this error, the doctrine of *fundamental needs* and *self-reliance* is beginning to take shape. Fundamental needs are never reducible to normal subsistence rations; the availability of these is merely a necessary condition, a first step.

Everywhere, regardless of the cultural environment, man, who is a 'sympolizing animal' (Ruyer), attaches symbolic values to his food, shelter and work; it is dangerous, even for the mere maintenance of a minimum of law and order, to seek to deprive him of them. If he evolves through education he will replace his inherited symbols with other symbols, but he will never abandon them altogether. The working or living environment, workshop or village, transmits messages. The economy of signs is not restricted to physical structures, but imbues whole societies; it has an efficiency of its own which is not reducible to physical productivity or profitability in market terms.

The developing countries help us to understand the *real-real* economy, which is not expressed by market values subject to deflation by means of a price index; it concerns physical goods and their symbolic significance, before and after market operations. Development, which is always both *cultural* and material, is more than a matter of buying and selling; the preferences that it reveals are only a part, and probably the least decisive part, of the preferences revealed by the environment. The instruments, the means of production constructed by men, have significances which are accepted or rejected; they stimulate or discourage effort, for a given level of remuneration.

When the population of a developing country awakens to freedom, its political leaders are inclined to take up the weapon used by the former colonial power to maintain its domination, i.e. nationalism, and turn it against that power.

On the other hand, the example set by the industries which have been introduced exerts a fascination of its own.

Lastly, it is clear that, subject to many conditions, the industrialization of developing countries tends, over time, to bring their balance of payments into equilibrium.

As a result, we find a variety of factors working together to promote hasty and unco-ordinated industrialization, before the ground has been properly prepared.

As a reaction against this state of affairs, *self-reliance* is now quite rightly being advocated. Self-reliance means a form of development in which full advantage is taken, and full use made, of the people themselves, who are taught to use appropriate technology to produce locally what they require for their subsistence, with no disruption of their customary ways and traditions. This is perfectly compatible both with the judicious step-by-step transfer of up-to-date technology and with endogenous industrialization financed from local savings.

During the transition phase, at all events, self-reliance inevitably has to count upon two genuine, basic propensities: the propensity to work and the propensity to change (innovate).

The former is defined by the *additional* quantity and quality of effort which a group, above some specified standard of living, will be willing to make in respect to a particular stimulus.

The latter means the actual change in the organization of product-manufacturing units which those in charge are capable of effecting in the hope of achieving some additional result other than profit exclusively, starting from some specified level.

The formulation encompasses all types of motivation (wealth, power, prestige) and is applicable to all units (private, public or mixed). It remains open to what Adolf Berle has termed the *transcendental margin*, i.e. the margin of results, over and above private interests, that a society can achieve if it succeeds in arousing enthusiastic, lasting support for some great common undertaking. It is true that there are two methods by which fundamental needs may be met, the aid method and the income method: people may be given things, or work may be found for them to do.

It is perhaps not entirely opposite, however, to treat the second of these methods as parallel to the first, as Paul Streeten does in an interesting essay.

Let us assume that the means of production have ben set up. The question then is whether the people whose fundamental needs have still not been met possess the energy and training they require in order to be employed. If not, an advance will be required in order to enable them to find employment. Once they are employed, we must ask whether the pay received will be adequate to enable them to go on working without physical detriment; the prevalent devotion of the principle of productivity, as calculated by the employer, wore out many a man in colonial and post-colonial history.

Furthermore, quite apart from employment for wages, self-reliance may involve improved forms of craft activity, co-operative associations of small units, or production groups, depending on local customs. Instructors, recruited in the country itself and suitably trained, can help to improve techniques, increase production and free the inhabitants of rural areas from one of the worst forms of subjection, namely dependence with regard to food.

No one denies that the satisfaction of fundamental needs on a worldwide scale is contingent on changes in the consumption structures of both developed and developing countries; the evidence of independent experts and detailed studies alike point to precisely that conclusion. Nor are there any insurmountable obstacles as regards technique or organization. Until such time as *something* at any rate is done along these lines, we must agree with Julien Benda's view, as expressed at the end of one of his books: 'All in all . . . a rather nasty species!'

The Dialectic of Independence and Co-operation[8]

To varying degrees, all developing countries are heavily dependent in terms of their foreign trade. In that field they are subject to asymmetrical effects of influence, dominance and partial domination:

influence in that the better-off classes follow the ways of the wealthy people with whom they deal, aping their lifestyles and patterns of consumption (Duesenberry); they in turn are imitated by the new middle classes and envied by the people at large;

dominance in that the threat of the interruption of trade (A. Marshall) and the overwhelming inequality as regards technological knowledge and financial resources exert constant pressure, to their disadvantage, in the preparation of private or public agreements and in the drafting of specifications;

partial domination in that, in particular sectors, the quantities sold and the prices paid are virtually determined by oligopolistic middlemen supported by their respective states.

These unquestionable facts cannot be fitted into the conventional models of foreign trade, whether of the Ricardo-Hume type or of the Heckscher-Ohlin type. These models share the feature of being constructed in static terms: on the hypothesis of full competition, the factors of production being homogeneous, technology given and constant, and product substitution being assumed to be perfect.

These models have been successively amplified and rendered more complex with great ingenuity, but they remain basically unchanged. They are constructions which destroy the phenomenon of international trade, rather than simplifying it in the interest of intelligibility; they seek to apply the pure market theory to organizations – but that theory, by construction, excludes any form of organization.

In connexion with the developing countries, the following question must be asked: is the trade in question trade between large firms, or is it trade between small units and individuals within a network of foreign trade activities which afford them an opportunity to express their tastes and preferences?

The interposition of monopoly barriers between producer and consumer, between the producer in a wealthy and powerful country and the purchaser in a poor, weak country may well empty current theorems about terms of trade and gain from trade of much of their substance.

Recent theses such as the technological-gap theory (M.V. Posner) and the product-cycle theory (R. Vernon) quite rightly treat nations as structures different from one another; these theories consequently represent a break with the classical models.

The structure of the developing countries forces them, in the context of foreign trade, into the position of serving their foreign partners.

Their development is turned outward by the direct investment which they receive; this leads to distortions in the trading pattern and places certain lines of trade at an advantage.

In many instances, developing countries are exposed to a process of *decapitalization*: the flow of capital exported by foreign firms exceeds the inflow of new capital.

In addition, the flow of commodities is established in such conditions that the terms of trade suffer lasting detriment in certain cases.

Yet another factor is the *brain drain*: the best engineers, scientists and technicians are enticed into leaving their native lands by the salaries and facilities available in the wealthy countries.

In short, the developing countries are suffering from a loss of substance, with their economies slipping into the control of foreign decision-makers, both private and public. These are the conditions in which what is probably the decisive foreign policy problem in the new approach to development can be defined: methodical, persevering efforts to achieve compatibility between the necessity of co-operating with outsiders and the need for autonomous development.

The Content of the New Development Policy. We may begin by considering the purpose and objectives of this policy as a whole, before going on to analyze the conditions and resources for carrying it out.

The purpose is quite simply the liberation of a people from foreign control, concurrently with the material and intellectual development of its members. A nation is a people ascendant, the culmination of a process of instilling vitality into the very being of society.

These two objectives are not necessarily compatible in themselves.

History offers many instances of peoples who have acquired material wellbeing and prosperity by accepting servitude or subordination.

Furthermore, material development as assessed by others, as for example by a vendor in search of customers, is altogether diffferent from material development as assessed by a people concerned to preserve its cultural identity (a possession which is fruitful in every sense, even in terms of the production and exchange of goods). We are confronted at the very outset with *multicriteria* decisions, and these are always difficult and virtually impossible to represent in model form when they involve psychological and cultural values.

However, to omit the concept of national interest and national good would be to overlook the concrete, positive and immediate problem; that concept is very much alive among the intellectual and spiritual elites and among both the ruling classes and the people they govern in the emergent nations, so that this discussion cannot be restricted to the area of *pure* market economics, especially as the present state of the world constitutes an invitation to open our eyes to the 'impurities' of market economics and indeed of 'pure' economics. These are circumstantial reasons, but there are plenty of analytical reasons as well.[9]

A nation and a national economy are *organizations*. Organization comes into the field of abstract, formal economics; it presupposes the establishment of a hierarchical order of entities which are regarded as components of a larger entity regarded as a whole. This is true of single firms and groups of firms; industries and regions, they include an element of organization, and so do nations and groups of nations.

Closely related to organization is another fundamental characteristic which marks out a nation: a nation is a *structure*, a set of proportions and relationships which cannot be altered without time, effort and expense. A nation may be described as 'industrialized' or 'agricultural', as an 'exporter' of industrial products or raw materials; it may have a full industrial set-up with the whole range of light and heavy industries or it may have a processing industry unrelated to centres of heavy industry . . . and so on. Nor must it be overlooked that a nation or 'national' economy is made up of economic spaces that are dependent on decisions made by nationals and of other economic spaces that are dependent on decisions made by foreigners. Evolution, clearly, consists in structural changes. The malleability of a unit or a whole, the change impressed upon its volume and composition, is neither nil nor infinite: it is contingent on prices and many other parameters. The extensive use of localized fixed capital and the inertia of organization serve to restrict it. On the other hand, the spread of general technological information and multi-dimensional training for skilled workers and managers tend to augment it. All in all, insufficient malleability, and indivisibility phenomena, as opposed to the fluidity and divisibility assumed in conditions of perfect competition, precipitate structural crises with catastrophic consequences in the developing countries.

To sum up, the 'nation', as an *organization* and as a *structure*, cannot be left out of the theory of inter*national* trade. The nation is a structured set, made up of structured sub-sets (whether localized or not). The mere presence of a government and a state administration alters the functions of production as these are described by the adherents of the pure market theory.

The consequences of all this are manifold, and all of them unfavourable to the developing countries:

(1)   The structures of the 'national' sets are unequal in relation to one another. Those which have reserves and credit at their disposal can absorb shocks from outside, at any rate under normal conditions, whereas the others are extremely vulnerable owing to the concentration of their foreign trade.

(2)   Strong structures are capable of 'pushing' exports with the help of subsidies and market organization, in contrast to the exports 'pulled' by pre-existing outside demand, which are the only variety recognized by the conventional models.

(3)   Strong structures permit not only non-price competition (through diversification and selling costs) but also *mixed competition* by major firms operating symbiotically with a great power and selecting relatively weak economies and states as the area for their expansion.

(4)   The cumulative effect of all this is to give the former a lasting *structural ascendancy* over the latter.

Inequality and asymmetries are thus the rule. The facts of the present help us, as we look back, to understand the expansion of world trade in the nineteenth century, which was characterized by British hegemony, the generation of markets through investment abroad, and close links between trade relations and monopolies in the areas of production and finance.

The new development policy, the great liberation game, thus assumes a specific, clearly determined content:

A – The developing countries have been subjected to a *structuring process* determined by and for outside interests.

B – Those countries are engaged in an economic and political struggle to achieve *restructuring* along lines desired by their governments and designed in the interests of their own people.

A. Structuring imposed from without finally results simply and solely in 'imported' inequalities in development and the outward direction of trade and production; it also involves the configuration of investment for infrastructure and means of production. It affects life-styles, the training of entrepreneurs and managerial personnel, and customers' tastes; there is a general distortion, with the weight of the richer and more powerful economy acting consistently against the fundamental needs of the masses.

B. When the government of the developing country resists, there is no need for it to search for new arguments, since it can find them ready-made among those put forward in some very old theories.

The protection of nascent industries was an argument advanced and developed by the United States in its early days, and one which has been repeatedly called in, and brought up to date since. One serious implication of this argument, however, has not been appreciated: the element of truth which it contains ultimately compels recognition of the inevitable conclusion that competition ceases to exist if the parties are too unequal.

Competition is a spot with its own rules and yields none of its advantages when the outcome is decided in advance. Economic competition is supposed to result in the triumph of the 'best' producer, the one who produces at the lowest cost and can thus sell at the lowest price. It becomes a mere sham if one of the parties is strong enough, in practical terms, to produce whatever it decides to produce and *compel* acceptance of its output at a cost and selling price set by itself, whether temporarily or over a long period of time. I am fully aware that this is an exaggeration; what I wish to do is to direct attention to positions of dominance which are ignored in the current theory of monopoly or oligopoly, based as it is on two parameters only: prices and quantities.

Developing countries wishing to break free from this structural ascendancy might also have recourse to the concept of anticipated comparative costs. The countries with the most powerful economies argue for the reduction of tariff barriers on the basis of actual contemporary comparative costs. The liberalism they recommend, regardless of the initial position, is a doctrine which may be neutral in appearance but is actually unilateral.

Let us consider, for example, a long-established and flourishing industry in the United States of America, operating in a high-technology sector. Its costs (the example is not an imaginary one) will be from one-fifth to one-sixth of the costs of similar industries in a European country. A 'purely economic' case for absorption can be made out. To avoid that outcome, and to give the industry which is at present less competitive the time it needs to adapt and to achieve efficient production and marketing capability, a *strategy* is called for. Such a strategy will depend on variables which a study of current costs and quantities is, in itself, unable to integrate. What then of a trial of strength between an economic and financial group in the United States and an industry in a developing country?

Strategies designed to counter structural ascendancies are well known: they consist of import substitution, diversification of exports, and the careful and persistent search for specialized points of entry into world trade. What the developing countries lack is the dimension represented by financial resources and bargaining power. At all events, they cannot solve their problems by means of isolated actions concerning particular products, costs or prices; what is required is a global, endogenous, integrated strategy of resistance, until such time as it is possible to move over to the offensive.

The strategy for the offensive is quite simply the structuring of the economy of the developing country concerned through measures which give the local population a larger share in the management of local resources and in the distribution of the profits generated thereby. We do not speak of the exclusive benefit of the local population, because, assuming that all desired corrective measures have been applied, the question of the international division of labour would still remain.

Of the many interrelated aspects of this structuring policy, we shall select those which are emerging in regard to polarization.

Throughout economic history, there is not a single example of different populations or territories having experienced similar, balanced and evenly distributed growth; nor is there a single example of different populations or territories having experienced unbroken growth, evenly distributed between them.

It is a fact that growth and development are associated with territorial grouping and with the concentration of investment, population, trade and information at specific points. This is true of very large firms, combinations of firms, nations with regions of uneven economic density, and the world as a whole.

We may focus our attention on a *single* one of these forms of polarization, namely *industry*, which is exceptionally significant for any country in the modern age.

A group of industrial firms is located within an *economic* space not referred to as a territory (a matrix without any specified location), or within a *territorial* space (a matrix with a location reference).

Such a group will be termed a pole of growth or pole of development when it generates growth and/or development phenomena asymmetrically in its environment, the converse not holding good, at any rate for a period.

Let us consider only territorial space. Experience has shown that an industrial grouping, or, as we may term it for the sake of convenience, a Large Unit (LU), acts as a magnet for a cluster of additional establishments and firms (in retail trade, transport, communication services and the like), if at the outset the space in question was, in economic terms, 'empty'. The additional means required for this process of concentration are either borrowed from other points within the same region or nation, or imported from outside. Where they are borrowed from other points, the integration in question is accompanied by instances of disintegration, which have given rise to the misunderstandings indicated above, as well as to a good deal of irrelevant polemic.

These dynamic complementarity phenomena are the result of the forces of attraction exerted by the Large Unit, which becomes to some extent a propellant. Once formed, it acts to further expansion, either through demand for raw materials and labour or through supplies of products. Regardless of whether pre-existing lines of transport and communication are available or whether the Large Unit is instrumental in getting them built by the authorities, linkages between different places result. At the ends of the axis so created, the horizons of economic agents expand as new opportunities for investment open up before them, while information and consumer demand are stimulated.

These linkage effects are reinforced by interface effects between different areas of technology (including manufacturing, organization, transport, and human resource training).

In contrast to the mobilization of idle resources over a short period, it is the combined action of complementary factors which produces the 'propulsion effect' over a long term. This can be clearly seen if we examine two groups of sequences: *investment sequences* and *distribution sequences*.

(a) A typical investment sequence describes the relationship between one act of investment and subsequent acts of investment induced by the first.

Total investment (I_T) is, in any growth process, the sum of an initial growth-inducing investment (I_E) and an induced investment (I_c), the latter being itself the sum of the induced investments, over the itineraries of induction (induced investment lines $(1, 2 \ldots n)$).

$$\Delta I_T = \Delta I_E + \sum_1^n \Delta I_c \tag{1}$$

As a result, of course, the transition from additional investment to additional product (P) is ordinarily expressed by applying to the investment the reciprocal of the capital-output ratio (1/K). This is a distinctly unsatisfactory method which could be improved by applying a product formation factor (S), inasmuch as product formation does not depend solely upon the quantity of capital.

We can thus write the usual formula:

$$\Delta I_T \frac{1}{K_T} = \Delta I_E \frac{1}{K_E} + \sum_1^n \Delta I_c \frac{1}{K_c} \tag{2}$$

or the following:

$$\Delta I_T s_T = \Delta I_E s_E + \sum_1^n \Delta I_c s_c \tag{3}$$

If we add terms representing the products (P) and the respective periods within which the effects are observable $(T, t, t + \theta)$, we arrive at the following:

$$\Delta P_{T_E} = \Delta P_{E_t} + \sum_1^n \Delta P_{e_{t+\theta}} \tag{4}$$

These equations dispel the obscurity surrounding the transition from capital expenditure to product over any period, particularly a medium or long period.

They also emphasize the radical difference between Keynesian effects in the true sense of the term (mobilization) of unused resources by an injection of money into a stable structure) and complementarity effects resulting from changes in structure (new industries, interface effects between technologies, and linkage effects between localities).

(b) Typical distribution sequences relate investment to earnings from work.

These *distribution sequences* have been, implicitly or explicitly, accepted in the case of the industrialized countries.

They can be used directly for industrialized areas in developing countries, and, with some appropriate adjustments, they can also be used to describe relationships between investment and earnings from work in countries in which industrialized areas are incompletely integrated into an agricultural environment.

In developing countries, even favourable and optimistic scenarios applied to industrial areas result in an array of reasons why the beneficial effects of investment and accumulation in such areas are not propagated, or are only partially propagated, outward toward agricultural areas.

In the industrialized countries and so far as industrial areas are concerned, the effects ascribed to investment (I), the source of which may be the supranormal profits of the private sector or, subject to certain conditions, intervention by the public sector, produce an increase in the supply of capital (K) available to the workers (W). Hence an increase in the product (P) obtained by the workers (W), and hence in turn, subject to certain conditions, an increase in the real earnings (S/P) of the workers.

In other words:

$$I \rightarrow \frac{K}{W} \rightarrow \frac{P}{W} \rightarrow \frac{S/P}{W} \tag{1}$$

or, in terms of increases referred to periods,

$$d\,I_{t0} \rightarrow d\frac{K}{W}\,{t1} \rightarrow \frac{dP}{W}\,t2 \rightarrow d\frac{S/P}{W}\,t3 \tag{2}$$

There is nothing automatic or inevitable about the transition from one of the terms in this sequence to another, despite certain sketchy presentations which may give a different impression. At every such transition, observation and experience have shown that the process of propagation is interrupted; given imperfections in the market, such interruptions are analytically inevitable.

Discussion in the developing countries should focus not on wages, with the usual connotations of that term in the industrialized countries, but on earnings from work, in the broadest sense of the remuneration of small farmers and *peons*. It is easy to understand why the transition from one term to the next, in the sequence given above, has every reason not to take place. Capital (assuming that it does not leave the country) tends to flow toward or be reinvested in the sectors with the highest rates of profitability; an increase in capital per worker affects only workers who are already trained to some extent; given a situation of high and lasting inflation, increases in figures do not mean increases in purchasing power.

The analysis outlined here can readily be carried out in greater depth, made more specialized, and applied to the relations between agriculture and industry.[10]

The result is that the motive industry and/or motive region exert an overall propulsion effect on the rest of the economy. Major poles generate secondary poles. A new structuring of the economy takes shape as these poles are linked with their environment.

In the simplest possible terms, this analysis shows how a large firm which moves into a developing country destabilizes the original environment and directs it outward; it also suggests the content of a policy specifically designed to turn that environment inward again. Such a policy must consist in laying down conditions for the establishment of large firms such that it becomes advantageous for such firms to direct some of their activities toward the domestic economy, or to use appropriate investments to link local activities with their own. The organizational action stimulates or controls the propagation of effects and the emergence of new markets.

The Industry–Agriculture Dialectic

Throughout the world, industry and agriculture are unsatisfactorily associated. This is true of the advanced capitalist systems, headed by the United States of America, which have recourse to extensive intervention to maintain the prices paid to farmers and to absorb surpluses; of the USSR where agricultural yields are inadequate; of continental Europe where the importance of agriculture rules out the possibility of sacrificing large sections of the population on the altar of the 'world price'; and of the developing countries with their highly concentrated agricultural (and mineral) exports, which are seriously exposed to the fluctuations of foreign markets. More generally, the problem of world hunger has not been overcome and food dependency among the developing countries remains an unsolved issue.

A number of obvious confusions obscure the scale and urgency of the present-day problem of the relationship between agriculture and industry. One springs from a false historical analogy and the other from the unjustified application of a conventional theory.

In English-speaking countries, there is sometimes a tendency to confuse the situation in England in the early stages of industrialization with certain situations observable today. The view that the earlier advances in agriculture in England were one of the things paving the way for the development of industry there – which is highly debatable in itself – should not be put forward in assessing the current situation in developing regions or countries. The reason for this is simple: a well-established industrial sector is today operative throughout the world and has long since set up bases in the less developed countries. The initial situation in these countries is in no way comparable with that of England at the end of the eighteeenth century; the suggestion that industrialization must await the constitution of a local market and the growth of a body of customers for firms among the rural population is therefore based on a false analogy and a questionable transposition. Even in the nineteenth century, the opening up of markets owed much to domestic and foreign investment.

Furthermore, the conventional theory of foreign trade throws little light on our problem. It assumes a homogeneous world of perfect competition, as well as homogeneous factors, and it is formulated in purely static terms. The factor endowment rule derived from this theory (the relative scarcity of capital or labour) is similarly flawed and disregards structural phenomena. Fortunately, it has not prevented the developing countries from asserting their right to industrialization, which is today officially conceded to them by the international authorities.

To varying degrees, the developing countries all have economies marked by the preponderance of agricultural production and the rural population, despite some progress towards industrialization and the rapid advances of urbanization. For this and many other reasons, these countries are in a position of dependency in relation to the outside world. Their weak internal co-ordination, which impedes the quick and proper propagation of economic effects, is often aggravated by climatic conditions and almost always by the inadequate educational level of the population. The underdevelopment of human energies is constantly depressing the level of production and productivity, leading to a cumulative deterioration of human potential. The new approach to development demands the *total restructuring* of the less developed nations and of the world. This restructuring relates basically to the association between industry and agriculture or, more precisely, between the various forms of industry and agriculture.

If this association is to be improved, two types of contradictions will have to be overcome.

(1) For structural reasons, industry stands in an asymmetric relationship to agriculture. Industry is therefore generally found to exercise a structural ascendancy over agriculture. The operation of the market by itself does nothing to alter this inequality. It can only be overcome by appropriate organization. This raises the question whether it is possible to make industry *serve* the needs of agriculture instead of allowing agriculture to be, in many respects, dominated by industry, and, if so, how it should be done. Although the question is relevant to many countries, developed or otherwise, it will be examined here only in relation to developing countries.

(2) Such restructuring is conceived very differently by less developed countries and by developed countries when they embark on trade relations. Similarly, the 'world' viewpoint, the evaluation of advantages from the world standpoint, coincides neither with the developed country's assessment nor with that of the less developed country. It is not enough, then, to say that the international division of labour is not very marked in the field of agriculture: this judgement applies to the current functioning of the market, whereas the problem to be solved is a long-term *structural* one. Structural change calls for sustained efforts over a long period and involves great expense. Unless the populations at risk are to be abandoned to their fate, the present circumstances of international competition stand in great need of correction; and this is all the more justified – to underline the point once more – since no developed country can really pride itself on the relationship it has established between its agriculture and its industry.

That, then, is the problem to which we have to address ourselves.

Before specicfying its terms in detail and considering possible solutions, let us dispose of one possible confusion.

Our chief concern is not with industrial products and agricultural products. Agricultural products are in any case obtained with the help of industrial products, even if this involves, as in the case of the least advanced forms of agriculture, no more than working implements and rudimentary means of transport. Once modern industry has penetrated a given region by means of trade, its products are used there without its having to establish its own production apparatus in the region. The sale of imported industrial products is one thing; the establishment of industrial units in an agricultural zone is another. And it is with the latter case that we shall be primarily concerned. Our attention will be focused on the relationship between organized industrial production elements and organized agricultural production elements within a given economic space.

In this context, we shall analyze:

(a) asymmetries and their intersections;[11]
(b) the role of the political Power (Government);
(c) the control exercised by the latter over production bodies and the organization of the environment in which they work;
(d) the new financing essential to the new development;
(e) the specific factors involved in the operation of multinationals.

(a) Industry generally enjoys relatively higher rates of production and productivity growth than agriculture. Cumulative effects are accordingly commonly observed. To the extent that earnings are linked to productivity, therefore, they tend to be higher within the industrial zone.

Industry and agriculture are also in an unequal position with regard to innovation. Once a broad and progressive industrial sector has been established, the transfer of technical and economic innovation proceeds in a clearly discernible direction. Innovation passes *from* the industrial sector *to* the agricultural sector. Tractors, bulldozers, electrical apparatus, self-propelled and mechanical equipment, antibiotics, defoliants, insecticides – such artefacts all stem from the efforts of industry, which develops them and often plays a part in their spread to country regions by financing their initial launching. The history of the established industrialized countries leaves no doubt as to the main direction in which innovation is transmitted and spread. It is the industrial centres in the older developed countries which are today supplying the less developed countries, and within a given country the less developed regions, with innovations. At those points where innovation makes its impact, the growth of output and the increase in productivity accelerate, the structures generating novelty and the *structures accommodating* it always having to be considered together. In the case of the major innovations of our time (the peaceful use of nuclear energy and data-processing), the source of innovation and the direction in which it flows are obvious and the 'revolutionary' consequences stemming from them are already clearly perceived.

When we come to look at the life-styles, the social attitudes and the patterns of durable-good consumption and use, the asymmetry under consideration is undeniable. In the industrialized countries, changes in the most of everyday living stem from imitation of urban centres and use of the apparatus produced by industry. Expanding possibilities with regard to the transport of people and things and the circulation of information through the press and the mass media, the growing taste for novelty, and the trend towards more or less slavish imitation, are at the root of the far-reaching changes that have been observed throughout the country districts of Europe. The cinema, television and the butane gas container have had a destabilizing effect on the habits of rural producers and consumers.

Comparatively speaking and having due regard to the great disparities involved, similar processes are clearly evident in the developing countries. These have been studied in sociological monographs: it is well known that the motor car or the tractor transforms the face of a village or region, and that the good or bad effects of such change cannot be assessed in terms of market prices, profit levels or local wage-increase rates. The developing countries' propensity to imitate goes beyond the *demonstration effect* described by Duesenberry, which relates mainly to consumption; it also influences the conduct of producers, those in authority and all economic agents in their everyday life.

Asymmetries of a quite different kind from those described above call for separate comment. Semi-feudal landholding systems, such as are found in Latin America for example, show a great capacity for resisting land reform. In such cases, industry is not directly involved; we are dealing here with an historical survival, the persistence of 'social armistices', of *institutions* which perpetuate the ignorance and subordination of the rural masses. The dominant classes in this instance merit the reproach of *not* using foreign or domestic industrialization to help in liberating their *peons*. It is only very *indirectly*, to the extent that the dominant classes are in league with foreign enterprise and 'export' their profits and their capital, that industry contributes to maintaining the formidable social gap between powerful landowners and dependent workers.

The situations described are well known; on the other hand, the asymmetries with regard to financing – which represent a crucial factor in the relations between developed and developing countries and have not gone unnoticed : are very far from having been methodically and exhaustively analyzed. Any major industrial or commercial venture requires pre-financing as a prelude to financing proper. Long and costly preliminary studies have to be undertaken to identify mineral and energy deposits, suitable sites for the establishment of production units and possible backers and periodic cash suppliers for the project. This pre-financing comes before the purchase of equipment and the hiring of services for the carrying out of the venture; when risks are foreseen, provision also needs to be made to guard against them. Foremost among such risks are those connected with technical changes involving *obsolescence* which may jeopardize the execution of the most carefully devised plans and programmes.

Such are the main aspects of that *financial power* which assumes greater importance than either organizational capacity or technical competence.

All this raises the serious question, which is broadly summed up in a slogan reflecting the experience of those directly involved and an intuitive insight on the part of that section of the general public that concerns itself with such matters: 'Finance creates industry; industry creates the economy'. The formula highlights, in succinct and exaggerated terms, a supposed and frequently confirmed relationship between different branches of economic activity, namely a power relationship between structured sub-sets. This relationship eludes both microeconomics and macroeconomics since, in their present state, neither can take account of structures and their interconnections or of evolving asymmetries in irreversible time. Development and the new approach to development depend precisely on these factors which cannot be fitted into the current models – and are therefore disregarded or neglected.

Taking up again the formula: 'Finance creates industry; industry creates the economy', we may ask whether industry 'creates' agriculture? Or does finance, directly or through the agency of industry, 'create' agriculture?

The reply will obviously depend on the particular cases and circumstances considered: it will relate to special models *when* it is *possible* to construct them. The issue, however, goes beyond relative statements of this kind, useful as they may be: what we have to discover is whether the logic of the market-based capitalist economy allows of a general hypothesis which can serve as a basis for specific enquiries.

The logic to be considered here is that of financial solvency or, which comes to more or less the same thing, anticipated profit. When over a long period, for structural reasons, a sector experiences relatively higher growth rates than another for its production, its productivity and the earnings of those engaged in it, it becomes an object of preferential interest to finance.

In the developed countries, finance has close links with industry; it tends, save in exceptional cases or as a result of government intervention, to neglect agriculture and, more particularly, the backward parts of this sector.

In the developing countries, finance is interested in those activities which serve industry, and, unless corrective measures are taken by government, is much less concerned with agriculture and still less with farmers.

Asymmetries in financing are of crucial importance for an understanding of non-harmonious development and mal-adjustments between branches.

We have just reviewed the asymmetries observable in developing countries. Technical and economic asymmetries, asymmetries in the spread of innovation, asymmetries in the systems of landholding, and asymmetries with regard to financing – these are all aspects which elude current theory.

These asymmetries are not found juxtaposed but rather interwoven with one another in networks of extreme complexity. Development centred on people cannot disregard them since they affect the population concerned. The propulsion effects defined and analyzed in spearhead economic research are at once distinguishable from one another and compounded with one another. The propulsion effects exerted by the various branches and the overall propulsion effects on the product of one of their combinations need to be defined and described in relation to the population as a whole. Ensuring that they serve human needs is not only a matter of seeing that they help to raise material living standards; it involves employing them as tools to raise the cultural level of society and its members. The market and capital cannot fulfil this function. A great *Actor*, belittled by the liberalism and individualism of the neo-classical schools, needs to define his purposes and prove his efficacy.

Recognition of the Actor's importance brings us up against yet another asymmetry, one which governs a great many others: it involves the relationship between governments and their administrative apparatus, on the one hand, and the whole body of agents governed and administered, on the other; it produces favourable results in the long term, provided that it does not stifle the sources of creativity that well up or spring forth in every human being.

(b) It is a striking fact that current theory, instead of considering the decisions and actions of those who govern, is focusing attention on things and objects, discoursing with analytic subtlety on *public goods collective goods*, and *meritorious goods*. The inconsistencies of terminology reflect the uncertainty of the thought process; at all events, the reference to goods opens the way to their incorporation in the conceptualizations and formalizations of the market – a market characterized by perfect competition, naturally.

Instead of identifying the distinctive features of the public sector and defining its specific activities, writers tend to reduce it, whether explicitly or not, to the laws of the market as operative between private units and to the price system formed by those units at their point of meeting. This in fact means applying to the public sector the yardstick used to measure the functioning and performance of the private economy – a paradox which tends to be overlooked in the everyday business of economics education.

Government is not the 'void' to which an old French liberal, Julia, chose to liken it ('The State, that void'). It is a decision-maker, an active participant, and not an inert apparatus; it emanates from the nation and permeates the entire nation in all its aspects; it is Government, in 'complicity' with the nation, in conflict-co-operation with its constituent parts and its individuals, which brings out the force of the dictum: 'The *nation* is an Actor, it is not an Object'. The nation becomes a decision-maker and an actor through Government.

For the developing countries, even more obviously than in the case of the developed countries, the defence of their specific interests and the protection of the personal dignity of their citizens *involves the existence* of the nation, while not being its unique responsibility or dependent solely on the choice of its rulers.

Personal development is the responsibility of individuals themselves; no one may shrug off on to someone else the responsibility for his own human development and self-fulfilment.

This requirement is recognized in many cultures and reinforced by a great many religious doctrines. Viewed from the quite different standpoint of empirical observation and history, however, it is likewise clear that personal activity represents the mainspring and the ultimate test of any form of development. Traditional peasant communities and populations retaining close links with their soil are endowed with energies stemming from the inmost depths of their ancestral past, which cannot be completely destroyed by any external action.

To say this does not in any way mean subscribing to the myth of the 'noble peasant', but simply draws attention to the durability of cultural and traditional values among populations which are directly in touch with nature and engaged in a daily effort to transform it in accordance with human needs and aspirations. When accepting, in the case of developing countries, the idea that the peasant creates the nation, one must be careful not to transpose a European experience. It is, however, a largely attested and irrefutable fact that the emergent nations, given their present situation, will not be able to consolidate their status unless they renovate their economies and policies in such a way as to make their agricultural producers and rural societies an integral part of the nation. This is an essential social and psycho-sociological component of development policy as applied to the industry-agriculture dialectic.

In the developing countries, Government faces the task of:

1. stimulating and strengthening organizational structures so as to provide the population with institutions conducive to the multidimensional creativity of informed and responsible elites, drawing support from the population as a whole, rendered capable of consciously living out the values implicit in its own distinctive culture;
2. linking the structures it supports so as to generate a preferred overall structure, chosen after due consideration;
3. operating an enlightened market system, based on the education of producers and consumers.

This three-fold approach to the organization of a mainly rural population limits the danger of recourse to a coercive and virtually 'forced' labour system. It represents the closest approximation to a system that makes the fullest use of the human resource while respecting its multidimensional potentialities; it is contrasted with a policy of modernization for its own sake and with the training of a section of the population on the basis of imported models, thereby in fact putting it at the service of foreigners and cutting it off from the mass of the people.

The most recently emergent nations, which are seeking their way or coming in to their own at the present time, would obviously be well advised to reject *economism*, which is destructive of that human substance that is the surest guarantee of their freedom.

Is the state – whose role it is to inspire and guide this transformation – powerless in the face of foreign states having greater military might, financial capital and technical capacity?

On the evidence of post-war trends and in the light of various unexpected developments, it is clear on the contrary that the government of a new nation, even a relatively weak one, retains a considerable margin of effective action *vis-à-vis* capitalist or totalitarian aspirations, provided it is well-informed and resolute. It can take advantage of its strategic value on the political chessboard. It can make use of alliances and coalitions. It has access to international organizations. It possesses an independent negotiating capacity in a world characterized by the increased circulation of information. In short, the state is far from being powerless to assert a degree of national autonomy, which represents both the strong mode of interdependence and the expression of its cultural identity.

(c) Against this background, the *economic* side of development policy concerned with the co-ordination of industry and agriculture involves two closely related tasks: (1) the choice and regulation of activities, and (2) environmental planning in the area where development takes place.

1. The new nation does not start from scratch. It will already possess industrial centres whose effects need to be *introverted*; new industrial centres will need to be created, a matter which should be largely in the decision of the government. The restructuring of the whole system will depend on the links established between the new centres and the old. From the outset, this approach distinguishes between the various *sorts* of industry *and* of agriculture and aims at the stimulation of the latter by the former.

To consider the question in terms of 'agriculture first' or 'industry first' is to pose a false dilemma. It does not help us to understand the real situation or suggest an operational strategy. The real issue is: which industries, linked to which forms of agriculture?

There is usually much to be done in the way of helping domestic *food* production to regain the ground lost to agriculture for export, proposed or imposed by foreign interests and giving rise to increasing imports of fertilizers and machines. The development of domestic food crops can be promoted by local capital, by the use of technologies appropriate to local needs, and by the training of native farmers. Food 'scarcity' is a striking example of a scarcity resulting from erroneous practices and from imported rules of the game. There can be no doubt that the scale and structure of domestic foodcrop production are not sufficient to meet the basic needs of the populations: this is not a fact of nature but a result of the strategies imposed by large firms and economic and financial groups. What seems to be a growing reaction against this inequality of powers is currently taking shape.

The 'agriculture first' strategy is based on the maintenance of the established patterns of trade and the gradual building up of domestic saving. History has shown that 'wise' counsels of this kind have more than once been given by industrialized countries with the object of slowing down the industrialization of their clients. The latter have come to see that such advice is far from ingenuous.

The 'industry first' strategy places the emphasis on capital accumulation, gains in productivity and increase in the value added per unit of output. Advocates of this strategy gloss over the price to be paid in terms of cumulative debt and foreign structural ascendancy. When the new industrial countries are quoted as an example in this respect, nothing is said of these long-term disadvantages, just as it is common to disregard the very different aspect of technological and social damage.

Starting from a given situation, the best results are generally achieved by combining industrial sub-groups and agricultural sub-groups so as to achieve the desired overall structure. The aim is to take advantage of the propulsion effects of industrial investments within the industrial sector itself and of the propulsion effects of different forms of industry on forms of agriculture.

A few examples will clearly have to suffice in this connection. For instance, mining for export can provide the basis for primary processing industries. Single-crop exports can provide the basis for processing industries that will diversify the product. Heavy industry introduced from abroad can provide the basis for the co-ordinated creation of light industries. Food-crop production can provide the basis for the establishment of small industries financed by local savings and employing appropriate technologies. Consideration also needs to be given to the possibilities of co-production or, more simply, sub-contracting by arrangement with large foreign enterprises.

The important thing is to get away from the abstract idea of agriculture's being led by industry and to think in terms of specific forms of agriculture being led by specific forms of industry within a general environment characterized by propulsion effects.

Organized sub-groups likewise often call for the regulation of prices and flows; systems theory provides a reasonably accurate idea of such regulation. Some form of agriculture, for example, may be associated at the input stage with a machine industry and a fertilizer industry and, at the output stage, with a primary processing industry and a canning industry. At both the input and the output stages, regulators can be introduced to control prices and flows over a given period.

2. Such a combination of activities yields results only when accompanied by environmental planning. In the case of developing countries, this involves forging links between industry and agriculture at both the *physical* and the *social levels*.

The transport network may reflect one of two possible approaches.

On the one hand, the main consideration may be the principal products – generally agricultural if they originate in the country itself, or introduced by foreign interests for their own benefit when they are industrial. In this case, the development of the transport network, aimed at improving communications with the interior or facilitating the shipment of goods to the ports, will be carried out with the chief products in mind. This was the approach until lately adopted by the colonizers; it continues to be so under *de facto* neo-colonialism. The calculations needed for such an approach are relatively easy; but the result is that the whole hinterland or large parts of the interior are not 'irrigated' and have only a small and very indirect share in the development activity of the chosen zones or sites.

On the other hand, the object sought may be to give the whole population a fair chance, making the best use possible of present and potential human resources. The procedure in this case is to 'irrigate' the territory at suitable points with the aim of promoting *external economies* for the benefit of largely agricultural, underprivileged and long-neglected populations by means of new communications. In such cases, precise calculations give way to global evaluations based on the somewhat imprecise but inevitable scenario approach. The choices involved in this case are, however, less difficult. It is frequently a case of linking up main production centres with secondary production centres; all the known cases show that considerable advantages flow from the linkages thus established between places and the interface effects between technologies.

Environmental planning aimed at ensuring a proper linkage between industries and forms of agriculture also has a social aspect. The establishment of networks for the communication of information to the rural population goes hand in hand with the setting up of schools and vocational training centres. Overall education policy is the means whereby a nation in the process of self-creation, a quasi-nation, progressively acquires the crucially important characteristic of being 'a distinctive locus for the circulation of information' (R. Caves). This is essential for the proper cohesion of the agricultural and industrial sub-groups. National unity and its economic consequences are equally dependent on the success of a multidimensional communication policy.

(d) The relatively unfavourable position of agriculture in respect of immediate profitability and the subjection of some types of agriculture to foreign structural ascendancy are factors crucial to a proper analysis of underdevelopment; the availability of finance is the necessary (but not sufficient) condition for overcoming these major difficulties.

What has been said regarding combined strategies for the purpose of arriving at a chosen structure for the 'national' whole presupposes the availability of finance.

Any hope that national savings may be sufficient for the purpose or that financial capitalism may be converted to an approach which is at variance with its logic can be dismissed. Fields must therefore be intensified in which capitalist interests are both served and unwittingly and indirectly serve the long-term interests of countries whose development is dependent on the reform of their agricultural systems.

In one field at least, historical experience is conclusive: capitalism has never declined to shift the financial responsibility for infrastructures on to Government or to divide it among its own financial groups. Those responsible for the new form of development should take very careful note of this fact and should collaborate, within the limits of their resources and those of their allies, with the bodies concerned with the new financing and participate in their operations.

The new financing is *mixed* (private and public); *multinational* (bringing together several developing and several industrialized countries among both the lenders and the borrowers); and *collective* (i.e. designed to promote the long-term interests of populations, via the realignment of world forces and the vigilance of Government).

A style of financing that breaks with the doctrines of traditional finance has already started in the advanced capitalist countries, but it has yet to be accompanied by the change of mentality and outlook necessary if it is to have a decisive impact on developing countries.

It is through political pressure on the part of the new nations and in the course of better informed negotiations among the major powers that objectives less narrowly defined in terms of the profitability of *specific projects* stand the best chance of being accepted.

Dependent as it is on political decision and backing, the new financing vital to the new development can become, and is indeed becoming, a reality:

- through appropriate *institutions* (semi-public companies, holding companies with state participation, multinational consortia, companies involved in the transfer of techniques and technologies, undertakings co-operating with the World Bank in the joint financing of common lists of goods and services or in schemes whereby certain goods are financed by the Bank and others by private capital);
- through appropriate *operations* (interest subsidies, state guarantees, exchanges of techniques and technicians in association with loans, exchanges of information, joint training of staff, joint ventures, market sharing, production sharing, etc.).

These financial techniques, provided they are conceived with the new approach to development in mind, open up very flexible regional and multinational economic and financial spaces which may be extended and modified according to needs and circumstances. Just as monetary regionalism is not incompatible with a worldwide currency system, so economic and financial regonalisms have a co-operative role to play in the development of the world economy.

To achieve the combined objectives of a policy aimed at optimum co-ordination between industries and forms of agriculture, national planning would seem to be essential. The plan remains an obscure concept until such time as its content is defined.

Some kinds of propaganda attempt to persuade us that the mass mobilization of the population's labour is the most effective and rapid way of increasing the national product. Development centred on people is incompatible with this approach, to the extent that it is destructive of human lives and energies. The criterion to follow in considering planning must be the full development of human resources.

In the USSR today, attempts are being made to improve planning processes.

The friends and allies of the USSR among the countries of the Danube region have continually come out in favour of decentralization, either with the aim of reforming their price system (Hungary), or as a way of maintaining their autonomy (Yugoslavia, Romania). None seems wholly prepared to accept the subordination of its agriculture to foreign interests.

When the situation of developing countries allows it, the 'indicative' plan – more appropriately called an 'active' plan (Pierre Massé) – is an effective method for attempting to achieve the co-ordination of industry and agriculture for the benefit of the population as a whole. The prerequisite for such an approach is the ability to recruit political leaders and technicians within the country itself, to have statistics available in usable form, and to persuade the population to accept the overall discipline involved.

Planning without planners provides a negatively formulated indication of the conditions for the success of a plan, which are *political* and *technical*. Given both, planning is a most suitable means of reducing external ascendancy, offsetting price and income fluctuations, and correcting inequalities in bargaining power in relation to foreign countries by means of additional information.

Within the nation, planning can provide guidance for choices and can identify the priorities on which the choice of the sub-groupings to be established and the planning and adjustment of the environment in which their effects will be propagated has to be based. At quite another level, and indeed, we believe, particularly in political emergencies, it may well make the exploitation of what Adolf Berle calls the *transcendental margin* of motivations, taken to signify the additional effort and sacrifice accepted beyond immediate personal interest, which may be obtained from a people passionately intent on a common purpose. Some young nations engaged in struggles for liberation are quite well aware of this possibility.

The important thing seems to be to grasp the fact that, in more or less peaceful times, active planning is a means of gathering together information that has been sorted and is consequently more readily assimilable, even *before* serving the purpose of adapting means variables to objectives variables. The decision-makers and agents in the various branches thus understand their respective places in the whole and the probable limits set to their activities. The rulers, senior administrative staff and executive personnel are better able to appreciate how their co-operation interconnects and to initiate more enlightened collaboration with the populations concerned.

Developing countries that set out to combine their industries and forms of agriculture by reference to considered criteria, come up against conflicts of interest between the parties concerned, aggravated by differences in rural and urban life-styles and in some cases exacerbated by ethnic and religious animosity. When confronted with such potential or overt strife, in which passions and emotions play a greater part than reason, it is preferable not to expect too much of the virtues of columns of figures, even when accompanied by ingenious commentaries. Competent and skilled interpreters may nevertheless, at intermediate levels, put forward arguments based on some particular aspects of a plan or the plan as a whole.

For the same reasons, the services that a plan can render for the purposes of arbitration in a developing country should not be overrated. The experience of countries that have long been industrialized and have an extensive agricultural sector shows that industrial producers and agricultural producers are not readily reconciled by arguments derived from a plan.

A further complication is due to the fact that planners have usually been trained in a foreign country, which inculcates in them its own methods based on its own experience. The regular training of technicians who will be able to adapt the methods taught to them by Westerners to the distinctive structures of their young countries, and in those countries' interests, is a long and difficult process. In view of the diversity of types of agriculture and the fact of their being relatively scattered and remote from urban centres, *multilevel planning* would be advisable; but where are the necessary skills and capacities to be found?

To relate the foregoing observations more closely to practical life, we may consider, in simplified terms, two methods of interconnecting industry and agriculture.

One approach works to the advantage of big farms, which tend to come into being, sometimes with direct encouragement from Government, as soon as the market is in operation. They provide the best structure for the reception of *packaged technology*, which was one of the hopes of the 'Green Revolution'. Grouped components designed to raise yields are offered to farmers as a *package*. The farmers will need to use inputs, tools and methods which will be made available to them but which depend for effectiveness on judiciously studied and tested complementary adjuncts.

On reflection and in the light of initial experience, however, this method, impeccable on paper – maybe the actual paper of a plan – seems likely to prove disappointing if the geophysical conditions have not been properly studied, market conditions anticipated and the motivations of farmers correctly foreseen. When the incentive to which they respond is profit, the aggregate profits to be expected by them must exceed the total associated costs.

Detailed studies have shown that, in many developing countries, the peasant farmer seeks a result in which we call *real-real* terms, as opposed to a real result obtained by deflation applied to market prices. The person concerned wants goods, in kind and in tangible quantities, to be available to him and his family. He may be said to have a subsistence motivation; the levels hoped for change, but in sequences different from those linking monetary profits and monetary costs. Forecasts concerning monetary variables may therefore lead to error.

The second approach covers the *peasant base strategies* which seek to ally the peasants with a government. Peasant families are given access to the land on terms substantially similar for all; efforts are made to avoid monopolistic capital accumulation; and emphasis is placed on small or medium-sized industries, the guiding factor being technical skills and methods suited to their needs.

This sketch brings out not only the variety of objectives that may be served by planning but also the limitations of the extent to which it can actually bring about social and economic change. In a plan, just as in an imperfect market, the various authorities come up against one another and also, taken as a whole but in shifting clusters, against the political power, Government.

(e) Application of the active-units theory gives us the necessary basis for an understanding of the specific significance of transnational corporations (TNCs),[12] or multinationals, in regard to the association of industry and agriculture.

The TNCs, those 'major Actors' as Pierre Massé calls them, generate *their* own economic spaces for the exchange of goods, investment and information. They apply them to the economic spaces lying within the territorial space of a nation. If we had all the necessary statistics, we might regard each nation as being made up of two kinds of spaces: one subject to the decisions of the national authorities and the other to those of non-national authorities. This distinction would lead us to look more closely into what the nation really is and would provide us with a number of quantitative coefficients that would help us in attempting to appraise specific aspects of national sovereignty. Investigation of the effect of TNCs on the agriculture of predominantly agricultural countries would be particularly interesting.

TNCs, whether they be highly or less highly centralized, are *private organizations* both in status and in their objective, which is to maximize the private profit generated by all the units they control (subsidiaries or associated firms) in all the countries in which they have established themselves. This is the general objective; its achievement may involve a great many profit strategies, according to period and place.

As private bodies, TNCs inevitably come into contact with organizations – the political authority (Government), the civil service and the authorities of the intermediate communities – in the host country. Government and the public authorities are responsible for ensuring the general good of the whole population in regard to which they discharge their specific function. The result is expressed in abstract terms of social utility, social product and social cost. Failing such references, it takes on practical shape in the needs and aspirations of the population.

The encounter of major private and major public units, both endowed with energy productive of change and expansion, results in intersections or conflicts over the course of time. Such conflicts cannot be exhaustively anticipated and settled in articles of agreement or any document of that sort. Time, which constantly brings with it something new, alters the scope of the various exchanges, transfers of utility and power relations initially agreed upon at a given point in time.

The TNC maintains close contacts with its country of origin, from which it derives capital, R & D, general and professional information, and its relations with the public authorities. When it moves into a developing country, it discusses the conditions of its operations with the public authorities there and with the private-sector enterprises. The inequality in these operations stems from the economic structures of the corporations concerned and from the respective externalities procured for them by their nations and their political powers.

A 'major Actor', such as a manufacturing TNC, has a place in a *network* of other TNCs involved in transport, trade and banking and of information centres. Comparison of networks of this kind for United States TNCs and for units in a developing country is significant in that it reflects a complex inequality prior to any explicit collusion or legally established coalition.

These factors make it easier to understand the distinctive forms of competition practised by TNCs originating in the most powerful economies, such as those of the United States and Japan.

The oligopolistic competition between TNCs is closely bound up with all the means of action of their respective countries. They are associated with the rival endeavours to the nations themselves to conquer foreign markets. These nations stand out in obvious contrast to the 'nations' of the neo-classical models, constituted by small units obedient to prices, or even reduced to factors and products considered in isolation and moved by price differences.

TNCs are powerful private organizations existing in symbiosis with powerful public organizations. It may truly be said that they tend to detach themselves from their respective countries, but this altogether relative 'autonomy' never involves a radical break with the structure, principles and prestige of the original environment or with the zones of influence available to its public authorities.

Furthermore, the TNC, as compared with a major company of similar size and structure, carried out its activities in quite different conditions which give it a special advantage in cumulatively increasing its power: it can transfer its procurement or marketing operations from one nation to another; it can attract a proportion of local savings in the host environment to itself; and it operates its own networks for the circulation of commodities, capital and information.

Taking the example of a country as powerful as Canada, an

economy made up of business markets, with over 80 per cent of its total investment accounted for by direct investment from abroad, it may be stated in very moderate terms, that the neo-classical interpretation has long since entered on a phase of 'diminishing intellectual returns'.

The implications of the entire foregoing analysis as regards the association of industry and agriculture that a developing country would wish to bring about for the benefit of its people seem fairly clear.

Notes

1. Perroux, François. *Pouvoir et économie*, 2nd ed, Paris, Dunod, pp. 43 *et seq*.

2. *Le Pouvoir*. Rencontres internationales de Genève, Neuchâtel, La Baconnière, 1978. Hersch, Jeanne. 'La nature du pouvoir', p. 75 *et seq*.

3. Arndt, Helmut. *Markt und Macht*, Tübingen, J.C.B. Mohr, 1973. Lhomme, Jean. *Pouvoir et société économique*, Paris, Cujas, 1965. *La grande bourgeoisie au pouvoir*, Paris, Presses Universitaires de France, 1960. Myrdal, Gunnar. *The political element in the development of economic theory*, London, Routledge and Kegan Paul, 1953. Hirschman, Albert O., *National power and the structure of foreign trade*, Berkeley and Los Angeles, University of California Press, 1945. Russell, Bertrand, *Power: A new social analysis*, 6th ed., London, George Allen, 1948. Morgenstern, Oskar. *The limits of economics*, Edinburgh, Hodge & Co., 1937 (English translation by Vera Smith: German edition published in 1934). Wieser, Friedrich von. *Social Economics*, New York, Adelphi Company, 1927 (English translation by A. Ford Hinrichs).

4. Bernis (Destanne de), Gérard; Tiano. 'Conflits et dialogue social', *Encyclopédie française*, Vol. IX, Larousse, 1960.

5. Perroux, François. *Economie et société*, Paris, Presses Universitaires de France. *Economie et société. Contrainte, échange et don*, 2nd ed., Paris, Presses Universitaires de France, 1963. Boulding, Kenneth. *Beyond economics. Essays on society, religion and ethics*, Ann Arbor, Mich., University of Michigan Press, 1968. Perroux, François. *L'économie des Jeunes Nations*, Paris, Presses Universitaires de France, 1962.

6. Green, Reginald Herbold. *Basic human needs, concept or slogan, strategy or programme, mobilisation or mystification?* Institute of Development Studies, University of Sussex, 1977 (roneotyped). See the important article by Paul Streeten, 'Basic Needs, Premises and Promises', *Journal of Policy Modelling*, 1979. ILO. *Employment, Growth and Basic Needs: A One-World Problem*, Geneva, 1976. Perroux, François. 'Les coûts de l'homme', *EA*, No. 1, 1952.

7. Mishan, E.J. 'Evaluation of life and limits', *JPE*, July-August 1971.

8. Perroux, François. 'Le théorème Heckscher–Ohlin–Samuelson, la théorie du commerce international et le développement inégal', *MED*, No. 1, 1971. 'Pour rénover la théorie de l'équilibre économique intérieur et extérieur', *MED*, No. 16, 1976.

9. Perroux, François. *Indépendance de la Nation et interdépendance des nations*, 1st ed., Paris, Aubier Montaigne, 1969; 2nd ed., Collection 10–18, 1971. Levitt, Kari. *La capitulation tranquille*, foreword by Jacques Parizeau, Diffusion Québec, Ottawa, La Maison réédition Québec, 1972. 'Conflits de classes et conflits

de nations', *MED*, Vols. 1 and 2, Paris, Economica, 1979. Perroux, F. *Dialogue des Monopoles et des Nations*, P.U.G., 1982.

10. Systems analysis may usefully be applied to the classification of the ways in which the propulsion effect may be used to promote agriculture and counteract the structural ascendancy of industry over agriculture in the developing countries. Cf. 'Equilibre et Régulation', *EA*, Nos. 3–4, 1978; and 'Théories des systèmes et théorie de jeux', *CISMEA*, E.M. Series, No. 6, 1980.

11. There is a whole series of the *Cahiers de l'ISMEA, Economies et Sociétés* (A.G. Series) devoted to a new analysis of the dynamic relations between industry and agriculture (editors: Michel Cépède, Louis Malassis and Joseph Klatzmann). Of particular interest are the following issues: No. 13 (1976), Groupes complexes et combinats agro-industriels; No. 10 (1972), Le développement agricole intégré (especially Bernard Rosier's article entitled 'Notes sur l'analyse des structures économiques et de leur dynamique', pp. 1163–83); and No. 11 (1974), Agro-industrie. Attention is drawn to the fundamental articles by Louis Mallassis.

Emphasis must be placed once more on the fact that it is misguided to apply models based on the pre-industrial 'agricultural revolution' in England to contemporary situations. In this area not enough is known about the relations between earlier advances in agriculture – brought about by land reform and improved farming practices far more than by mechanization – and the astonishing progress of industry. The historians W.W. Flinn and H.J. Habakkuk consider that agricultural improvements played only a minor role in *triggering off* industry.

There can be no breakthrough in this area until *historians* ask these questions basing their interpretations on models that allow for *propulsion effects* and giving forecasts of the duration and succession of the *periods* involved. Maurice Niveau has done just that in a concise treatise entitled *Histoire des faits économiques contemporains* (Paris, Presses Universitaires de France, 1970, pp. 14–17, Collection Themis).

12. Perroux, François. *Les entreprises transnationales et le nouvel ordre économiques du monde*, Introduction by Gilbert Blardone and Daniel Dufourt, Lyons, Institut des Sciences sociales appliqées, 1980. Modelski, George (ed.). *Transnational corporations and world order. Readings in international political economy*, San Francisco, N.H. Freeman, 1979. OECD, *Transfer of technology by multinational corporations*, Vols. I and II, Paris, OECD Development Centre, 1977.

Decisions on transfers of techniques and technologies are, unless a political agreement has been reached, taken by the TNCs with an eye to the benefit of their own strategy. Within the same limits, the same decision-makers – the TNCs – may contribute to attenuating particular food shortages, thereby acquiring a formidable *food power*. Lastly, without taking a direct interest in the agriculture of the developing countries, they may subject it to the effects of input (fertilizers and machinery) and output (processing and marketing).

In the special area we are considering, the bilateral counter-forces have only a limited impact, for international trade unionism has little muscle-power and codes of conduct do practically nothing to alter bargaining strength.

Worldwide political action, backed by the gradually increased influence of the developing countries in international organizations and by a firm stand on the part of local national governments, seems so far to be the only recourse against a *transnational power system* whose logic cannot, without self-destruction, satisfy populations otherwise than in proportion to their purchasing power.

4 PURPOSE AND VALUES

The new approach to development and the new international economic order are evidence of much more far-reaching changes than the demand for a redistribution of resources and for radical changes in the rules of the game among nations. Feelings of resentment that have long been building up in the Third World are rising to the surface and showing themselves in hard bargaining, threats and outbursts of violence.

The West was, on the whole, a not particularly scrupulous colonizer. It did not use its military and economic superiority to impart its science and technology to the colonized peoples and to give elites selected *by them* the means of gradually bringing about the form of modernization of *their choosing*.

Qualifications are, admittedly, called for in this assessment but it does describe, in rather extreme terms, an uneasy phase in European expansion. It will be conceded that colonization led to a degree of training of local elites and initiated economic activities, which were, however, dominated by the parent states. Viewed in the light of developments since the Second World War, and with some substantial reservations, colonization can nevertheless scarcely claim to have been fully warranted by the benefits it bestowed.

The colonial system consisted in a specific political and legal status backed by overwhelming scientific, technological and economic superiority. That status has changed nominally with accessions to independence, which, whatever may have been said about them, have profoundly altered the relative situations. Since real economic changes are always slow and gradual, however, the inequality of resources remains, so that the term 'neo-colonialism', contentious though it may be, does contain a large measure of truth.

The emergent nations may be regarded as *quasi-nations*, since they have as partners nations which, owing to their size, the nature of their activities and their bargaining power, exert *de facto* influences and ascendancies which, even if the will were there, could not be eliminated in a short time.

These after-effects of inequalities of strength are active, and the popular memory of them gives the nations every reason to try to struggle free of them.

This is borne out by the severe judgement passed on the behaviour of Europeans, and more broadly of Westerners. From the standpoint of Asia or Africa, they seem to be exhausting themselves in self-interested quarrels after slaughtering one another in deadly wars. They have enriched themselves by any means, regardless of the rules of conduct prescribed by their religions or philosophies. They act indeed like atheists and their mores are evidence of the crudeness and triviality involved in the unbridled pursuit of gain. The pattern they follow seems to be that of the man concerned with earthly accomplishment, constantly haunted by the idea of getting the most out of things, who can not refrain from exerting his will to power whenever a material interest is at stake.

Faced with the hunger and poverty of the world, they have not succeeded in putting into practical effect the development policy that they proclaimed aloud. When the general crisis came, they were able, not altogether unjustifiably, to invoke it as a reason for further restricting the aid they were providing with such seeming reluctance. Weakened as it now is, the West cannot make good a claim to continuing respect on the score of past benefits at a time when its relative strength is declining.

Until recently, the West maintained that it bore a message of civilization, a sort of culture of universal value from the point of view of its substance, combined with political and legal ways of doing things that were worth copying. The substance is now suspect and the ways of doing things challenged.

This crisis of civilization goes deeper than failures in the economic system: it lies in the minds and hearts of men.

The developing countries are becoming aware of their own cultural values and finding in them comfort and reasons for maintaining their dignity and identity. It is possibly easier to reconcile opposing material interests than to find comprehensive values and to transcend historical cultural conflicts sustained by barely compatible images of man.

At the same time as they are accepting the other party's ways of doing things and turning them against him, the so-called underdeveloped countries, which have known substantial intellectual and moral developments in their centuries-old past, are looking to that past for new ways of expressing their own culture – without betraying it.

A new *frontier* is thus emerging, in the Anglo-American sense of the term, an area of mental-energy resources as yet very imperfectly identified and exploited. It lies in the qualitative realm which largely eludes the statistics of moral phenomena and the 'sociometry' or 'primitive' societies.

The best-informed Western observers recognize that we have something to learn from these revivified lands inhabited by groups of people *vis-à-vis* whom we were prone to set ourselves up as teachers ready to instruct them.

Treatment of development issues inevitably remains superficial unless we get down to the deeper intellectual and spiritual levels from which political and economic debates spring.

All nations and all peoples throughout the world are, without saying so, looking for *meaning* in human destiny and the strivings of human beings and, in the light of the world crisis, we can more readily perceive the fact that all are in the same situation, together with the tragic threat lowering over the world community.

Leaving aside the political quarrels of the divided world, could the West as a whole remain indifferent to Solzhenitsyn's moving admonition in his address at Harvard in 1978? What you are doing, he said, is not high enough, pure enough or warm enough to win universal support. Not high enough, because morality loses its virtue when it is mingled with mercantile economics. Nor pure enough, because the quest for supreme values can scarcely be combined with the use of covert violence under the guise of freedom and equality. Not warm enough, because that movement of the heart which might betoken brotherhood is not often apparent in either your private or your public life.

The good thing about philosophical reflection and the world bodies that engage in it is that it brings to the fore those questions, considered inopportune, which are implicit in development policy when the latter is taken seriously.

An intelligible and avowable meaning for economics cannot be dissociated from an intelligible and avowable meaning for human destiny. Such a meaning must at least be sought and I shall do no more than suggest, with all due modesty, some of the avenues that might be explored in seeking it.

The Possible Conflicts Between Economic Considerations and Cultural Values

The West, because economic activity there is disquietingly remote from cultural values, which are insistently proclaimed but not experienced, offers the developing countries its technology as an extension of its science and its art of economic calculation.[1]

Calculation, the preferred and too frequently used way of expressing economic considerations, consists in translating costs and outputs into algebraic quantities or numbers. By its very nature, it concentrates on things, material objects that are counted, that are supposed to be measured, and on the basis of which are largely conventional arrangement of figures permitting the statement of a net maximum. The fact that this maximum tends irresistably to be confounded with an optimum is revealing.

Nevertheless, whatever efforts may be made to introduce what are termed human variables into the calculation, it will never be possible to take *account* of the multidimensional and infinitely complex aspects which, we know, from direct experience and from analysis, distinguish each human being and each society of people.

When economic calculation boasts of being 'operational', it raises serious issues. Operational for what kind of operations? Operational in regard to whom? The operations referred to are those of the market economy, which *presupposes* the equivalence of services rendered and values. Economic agents and economic subjects never stand in a relationship of perfect reciprocity of intentions and situations. These elementary observations take philosophical reflection a very long way since the first leads on to the very concept of value and the second to the ideal of reciprocity of consciousness.

Without carrying the challenge to economic trading as far as that (though it has been fruitful whenever it has been ventured), one cannot help being struck by the narrowness of calculations based on market values. The biologist's calory and energy counts are, after all, calculations as precise and legitimate as price calculations. There can be no question of using them as a substitute, but to admit them is to introduce a judgement of market values based on objectively beneficial effects.

The quantified evaluation of normal food rations, to give just one example, has led to a timely broadening of the economist's interests, directing his attention to discovery of the deadly effects of the rule of 'ability to pay', pure and simple.

Extra-market operations, when due account has been taken in them of some of the objectively beneficial (or destructive) effects brought to light by science, have been regarded by the people directly concerned and by public opinion as more deeply worthwhile than the functioning of the market as it is everywhere except in the textbooks.

We are still a long way from cultural values, which are of quite a different order from bodily health.

In the developing countries more obviously than in the developed countries, where it seems to be blurred in the universe of artefacts and the staccato rhythms of machinery, culture is perceived as a set of standards and values pervading the outward expressions of human life and the depths of the consciousness. These standards and values may, through the reflection of those sharing in them, be translated into concepts and more or less reasoned; but they exist before conceptualization and extend beyond such more or less organized translation.

They are transmitted orally in the family and elementary communities. Culture emanates from the living environment that enshrines and transmits images. These images are formed in association with the subconscious and what might be termed the super-conscious, the evaluations and rules of life that tradition, day-to-day contacts and social learning have imprinted in the memory and in habits.

Between the culture spread in and by a living environment and the individual sharing in it, communication is direct, prior to criticism and even to spoken expression, furnishing a pre-reflexive view of man, nature and society in their interrelations. It precedes the formulation of language, though everything therein – vocabulary, syntax, sentence melody and emotional impact – conveys and attests it.

When we begin to reason, we never start from *nothing* but from a substratum, a cultural acquirement that life has given us in distinctive circumstances of place and time. This is no doubt one of the reasons why communication through language differs from cultural communication.

The latter is possible on another register. It is established by images arising from the dwelling-place, the environment and socially organized activities. Landscapes, monuments and gestures 'speak' before words come to help; they suggest an inherited life-style and prompt projects and forms of activity.

Culture is 'incorporated', 'incarnate', but it is nonetheless inward and intimate; it operates by way of ceaseless interchange between the existential environment and the consciousness.

The signs transmitting it concern the 'symbolizing animal'. They are social symbols short of being ritual symbols. Each society has its own rites, usually influenced by religious rites but remaining distinct from them.

Symbols of union go hand in hand with symbols of separation, even in societies which are beginning to open up. The social consciousness draws an invisible but real dividing line between 'us' and 'foreigners', and there are enough differences and contrasts between human groups for the distinction to harden into a division between 'friend' and 'foe' in private or public relationships.

When it is suggested that culture is a set of values lending cohesion to a group and enabling it to communicate with other groups, nothing is said about the kind of communication involved. For those who, in any case, find in human relations the dual components of struggle and co-operation, of conflict and agreement, this brings out the compound – even in the most pacific exchanges – of sympathy and hostility, of benevolence and ill-will. For this *compound* to become *harmonious union*, no common measure of self-discipline, and the acceptance of values which are in theory all-embracing, are required.

This shows clearly enough that the cultural relationship defies calculation, and more particularly economic calculation.

In the works of Western writers, two modes of apprehending the relationship between economics and culture can readily be discerned. Some engage in economic analysis of such cultural phenomena as politics or religion – an enterprise which is doomed to failure. Others consider cultures are regulating economic activities. They are on the right track but they need to give up the quantitative methods favoured in their specialist field and to recognize that the understanding of cultural phenomena requires those attempts at *qualitative* description and interpretation which are abominated by a large proportion of those who presume to practise the 'human sciences' according to the current vogue.

A significant lesson in this respect is suggested by the fact that there is no satisfactory mode of remunerating works of art, as careful thought about the facts of history seems to make quite clear.

In a variety of societies, the fixing of remuneration for a work of art by the market has proved unsatisfactory: it makes the artist dependent for a living on customers who will pay, and the fact that an art gallery may act as an intermediary does not help matters much, since the gallery will certainly expect to be paid for its services. If the state or some other public authority supports the artist, it turns him into a civil servant and subjects his creative powers to the dictates of an administrative department. In the days when a high standard of culture usually went with great wealth, patronage offered undoubted advantages both because it was exercised by intellectually and aesthetically educated elites and because it established emulation among them in regard to protecting the artist, or at least the major artist. Times have greatly changed since then!

Nowadays, in an atmosphere of cold warfare and latent political conflict, it is significant that governments should be concerned to recognize the persuasive virtue and communicative powers of the work of art. Whatever the system of government followed and the level of development, the political authority takes care to make the creative achievements of its artists and the imperishable riches of its cultural heritage known abroad. Schemes have even been mooted for appealing, by means of travelling exhibitions, to those sensitive depths of the heart at which political divisions may be forgotten in the response to beauty.

Many other instances can be cited to show the strength of cultures in resisting invasion by economics. At all events, the point is most directly demonstrated once it is grasped that:

(a) economic phenomena and institutions depend for their existence on cultural values; and
(b) the attempt to separate collective economic objectives from their cultural environment has finally ended in failure, despite the most ingenious intellectual acrobatics.

Not a single basic economic concept can be really thought through if its cultural grounding is shaken.

Competition, for instance, regarded as the 'pillar' of economics, is an activity through which the 'best' emerges, that is to say, the one that proves, by experience, to be able to satisfy the customer at the lowest cost and for the lowest price. It is a form of sport and, like any other sport, it has its rules. The rules of the competition game distinguish 'fair' competition from 'cut-throat' competition; they even go further in trying to reduce the social losses caused by the elimination of the unsuccessful competitor. However little it may be observed in practice, the law, reflecting a minimum moral standard, draws a dividing line between competition which is acceptable and that which is not, with due regard to what is considered the normal life of society as a body.

It is easy enough to demonstrate the same subordination of the economy to cultural values in connection with property ownership, contractual relations, business organization, the protection of the wage-earner, and the like.

Still more conclusive is the utter inability of generations of well-known economists to fit collective benefit into the market economy set-up and to find a way of gauging it. Welfare is a somewhat obscure notion derived from market-formed prices. Since prices are not strictly additive and subjective elements are irreducible, the *theoretical* construction of collective benefit necessitates laying down practically impossible conditions:

> superimposable indifference curves of the individuals concerned (K. Wicksell); or
> similarity of the general progress of economic welfare and social welfare (A.C. Pigou): or
> the supposition that producer and consumer surpluses are economically homogeneous quantities (Hotelling, J.R. Hicks).

The economist, abandoning these intellectual exercises, will be obliged to concede that there are as many forms of welfare as there are major political parties (Gunnar Myrdal) or organized human groups in society (G.J. Stigler). For the purposes of a descriptive study, these are devices that cannot be entirely left aside; and it has already been noted that they refer very largely to cultural values and phenomena.

It is culture[2] and the social hierarchy engendered by cultural values that determine the allocation of the *roles* preceding any economic analysis of production and distribution. These economic and social roles are not laid down once and for all; they may be challenged and may be the subject of social conflicts: over a long period the agents involved are not content to progress within the role assigned to them; the most active seek to move up through the social hierarchy and, by means of alliance and coalitions, to modify its form and signification.

Two very rough-and-ready outlines can conveniently be put together to contrast the society built on social distance and domination with the society seeking to reduce inequalities and promote participation. The first fits the structure of nineteenth-century industrial societies fairly well, while the second reflects the beginnings of a profound change in that structure, much desired by the working world and grudgingly accepted by the ruling classes under the pressure of labour's demands. On the assumption that the grading of social strata is marked by economic status, by education, and by the actual contribution to the formation of political will, a parallel may be drawn in very summary terms (see Table 4.1).

Table 4.1

A. Advancement observed in the nineteenth century	B. Advancement initiated in the second half of the twentieth century
Rise of individuals and elites who keep very much aloof from the immobile mass	Higher material and cultural level of the mass, enabling it to produce its own elites
Power of dominant groups serving a privileged class which forms a screen-structure	Power of functional and social elites serving new groupings of activities
Formation of value systems in the upper part of society, which transmits them to the mass	Formation of value systems through active interchange between the mass and the new functional and social elites

In the developing countries, where individuals working in industrial and urban areas come into contact with those living in agricultural and rural areas, it would be interesting to see whether the 'B' form of advancement does not conflict with the 'A' form associated with the persistence of feudal-type systems.

Economic and social roles are played out everywhere within an evolving environment in which cultural factors are decisive.

Cultures defy quantitative measurements and oversimplified motivations based on patterns of behaviour assumed to be reducible to hedonism in the light of the further assumption of a calculation of pleasures and pains. This is so because the arts entering into the calculation, more particularly in pre-capitalist economies and societies, are associated with and influenced by acts which, for want of a better description, may be said to be *conditioned* and *inspired*, provided that these terms themselves are defined.

The most extreme behaviourism has given up seeking for actual reflexes in social relations, but it admits the importance of socially conditioned activities which owe very little to conscious and considered intention. Such acts are to be observed in any social complex.

Inspired acts are those motivated and regulated by *purposes* set by moral and aesthetic values. These cover acts generally regarded as the highest testimonies to human dignity, such as the love of a mother for her child to which she sacrifices her life, and the love of the soldier for his country, prompting him to serve it by readiness to die for it.

In the sphere of poetry and art, it will be found profitable to reflect on Paul Valéry's saying that: 'the law of *non-poetic* but useful acts . . . is that they are effected with the greatest economy of strength and by the shortest ways'.

To round off this analysis of the possible conflicts between economic considerations and culture, emphasis needs to be placed on a point which is extremely important in all cases and especially so in that of the developing countries.

The point in question is that the market and capitalism 'consume' cultural and moral values that they *do not replace*. The processes used, in their contemporary form, do not match the available descriptions to be found in textbooks. Through the obsession with material goods, the depersonalization of human relations, omnipresent advertising, and the lure of monetary gain in all its forms – including financial speculation – the market and capitalism in fact tend to destabilize cultural standards and to 'reify' minds. Not to mention the corruption they encourage in the relations between public administrations and private interests.

Consideration of the new approach to development and of the total restructuring it postulates would be superficial and serve little purpose if it did not reach down to the innermost depths of human beings and of the ever-fragile societies they attempt to put on a durable footing.

The most devastating defeats and the most fruitful victories are the outcomes of a tragic game played out in the depths of the human mind and consciousness. The worldwide scale of this game might well create a false impression. We shall see that it in no way changes the essence of the diagnosis. Every person and people's societies are seeking *significance* for their destiny; and that is cultural.

World Values and Aspects

Sir Dennis Robertson, looking into the economic efficacy of motivations, was thinking in terms of the private economy when he distinguished the *strongest* forces and the *highest* forces, giving precedence to the former.

When the economy manifestly calls for organization, and public organization, there is every reason to doubt whether personal interest, profit-seeking or the pursuit of monetary gain can suffice to mould it into a human order. The market and capitalism – motivations and mechanisms – have not succeeded in overcoming hunger and the most abject poverty all over the world. After two development decades, the prospects are indeed still tragic and call for a radical change in the policy and strategies hitherto followed.

Three approaches or views of the world show it as a whole made up of structured sub-sets, the relations between which are highly asymmetric and the inequalities profound and universal.

The *world of nations* is that depicted – fallaciously in fact – by the flat tints of a political map of the world. The nations are unequal in population, in resources, in wealth and in level of development. What is more, their frontiers are crossed by the *orbits of influence and dominance* of the superpowers and the major nations. No territorial representation provides an accurate reflection of this state of affairs. If they overlooked it, the nations would run serious risks; it is better for them not to be obsessed with their purely legal sovereignty or their cultural zones of influence.

They can be neither self-sufficient nor fully 'open', because they have the custody of their populations, who cannot be sacrificed either to unreserved acceptance of the dictates of the 'world price' or to the protection of a foreign power. Unless it is to renounce its own identify, every nation, however poor and weak it may be, is seeking autonomy within the system of interdependences by which it is linked, unequally, to others.

The *world of development zones* comprises industrial and financial aggregates whose propulsion effects (and stoppage effects, too, in some sectors) are exerted on the rest of the world. In the

East, there is the USSR, acting on its satellites; in the West, the United States, Japan and Europe in the making constitute the three major zones of world development. In each of these zones, the policies of states and of the major economic and financial groups do not, of course, always coincide exactly. And the policy of these privileged human groups suggests the need to discover – according to the areas and circumstances involved – where the true *decision-making centres* are situated. Nor are these zones of development equal among themselves; their influence on the world varies in intensity according to the world's forms of government and their own expansion plans.

In the forms of competition or the political alliances of the political powers and the informal powers operating in each major development zone, nations of secondary importance and the nations of the developing countries cannot keep out of the game conducted by the main partners. They are never mere pawns moved around on a chess-board, because their political resolve is a factor with which the bigger parties have to reckon, not least because they too have a certain freedom of manoeuvre by means of alliances and coalitions.

Lastly there is the *world of the masses*.[3] This aspect of the world is at times somewhat eclipsed by the previous two. But in point of fact, it is the one that lends our age a dynamism unprecedented in the history of mankind.

The masses, the multitudes reduced to the elementary conditions of life and condemned to exist at subsistence level, have always been there, excluded and silent. Today's masses, however, cannot be disregarded, whether they be the thousand million people starving on the earth or the multi-class masses of the cities or of farming communities that are backward as a result of being dominated.

Class, in Karl Marx's connotation, is losing the more or less homogeneous features it had in the nineteenth century in the developed countries. It is becoming diversified and splitting. The upper strata are by no means anxious to give up the advantages bestowed on them by capitalism and stand apart from the deprived strata. Taken as a whole, the wage-earning working class in the industrialized countries can no longer be regarded as a reference and symbol of human destitution. The masses in the developing countries are the most representative victims of such destitution.

Higher incomes and increased resources concentrated in chosen territories and economic spaces have not spread; local and individual *advances* have not turned into overall *progress*; the results of the staggering developments in technology, production, transport and communication are, generally speaking, chiefly of benefit to the relatively affluent countries and classes.

As already noted, the world, considered under its three main aspects, is neither a system regulated in the light of the interests of the whole world and the aspirations of that *whole*; still less is it a human home, with all that the notion implies in the way of security, trust and regular intellectual and moral interchange.

The human home has not come into being and has no chance of doing so spontaneously; it is one of the names – and there are others, as we shall soon see – denoting the Great *Enterprise* of Humanity.

To use a form of words which requires correction before it can be made explicit, the new international economic order indicates a line of progress. There can clearly be no question of an exclusively or even mainly economic order in the usual sense of the term. It is a political order that is needed to regulate the functioning of the vast structured sub-sets linked by a basically asymmetric relationship. The notion of order nevertheless calls for thoughtful comment.

In the eyes of the 'orthodox' economist, who posits the absolute separation of economics and politics, economic order is that established by the market. It is consistently extolled in the best treatises: without it, chaos would reign; thanks to it, the tastes and preferences of the economic units finds the law of their compatibility and become mutually possible.

Transposed to the scale of nations and the relationships between them, the order of the market has been advocated since the first English classical economists right up to the present day. This is the logical course of an analysis which leaves out national reality and considers only factors and products in a homogeneous space. The fact that markets are imperfect and depend on organization is totally discounted. Power, which means in practice Government, is entrusted to the meditations of political scientists or specialists in public law and to the vigilance of rulers and diplomats. It is their responsibility to define law and order for the world, the purpose of which is to ensure the free operation of the market without any outside interference likely to disturb it.

This division of labour between the intellectual architects and builders of economics and those of politics, with the economic norm on one side and the political norm on the other, may well prove misleading. In point of fact, it brings us up against a profound contradiction.

The inalienable object of politics is the fate of people living in society; it is essentially an hierarchical organization. *Orthodox* economics deals with individual economic units linked with one another by the market alone, receiving all the information at their disposal simply from the price. The 'purity' of the economic model is due to the lack of hierarchy, *except* in the matter of purchasing power, and to the active presence of hierarchy and power in the political model.

The contradiction can be resolved only if it be assumed that *de facto* equality among all economic units rules out any power of some over others in any respect and in any field. In that case the functions of the state and the functions of the market exactly coincide. In both cases, they consist in establishing and observing the equality of all the units. The distinction between the role of the state and the role of the market fades away, leaving only economic units which can all be substituted for one another and are in perfectly symmetric relationship with one another.

Starting from *watertight compartments* separating politics and economics, we arrive at a construction in which politics and economics become *indiscernible*. The society formed by the market, the *pseudo-market society* stigmatized by J.M. Clark, and the society without Government – anarchy in the etymological sense – are two equivalent terms describing one and the same conceptual form, the spontaneously pacific and fruitful encounter of atoms driven by a law of nature external to them, or of identical units co-operating spontaneously under the binding effect of a law of *their* nature. It is a natural order in either of these acceptations which arises from simplifications and sublimations inspired by implicitly normative considerations.

Such a conception contradicts the reality observable from the earliest days and throughout human history. It is radically at variance with the hypothesis of the composite human relationship (conflict co-operation, struggle-agreement, hostility-sympathy) whose content is in keeping with the implications of science and the lessons of history.

Between agents differing from one another and unequal among

themselves, asymmetry is the rule. It calls for regulation in the name of values which have arbitral force only if they are held to be superior both to the established political order and to the established market. What is true within a nation is, *a fortiori*, true in the relations between the structured sets which go to make up the world as we see it, as we live in it and as we act in it.

The possibility of introducing a humanized order into those relations by structural dialectic systems and in inter-cultural dialogues does not depend on a beneficient law of Nature or on the 'natural' goodness of the human being.

Should the new world order, then, be deduced from political power scaled up to the world as a whole? This is the thesis accepted or implied by those who place their hopes in the formation of a World State, that is, so far as the dominant theory is concerned, of a constraint legitimized, for example, by democratic procedures as practised in the West.

In attempting to evaluate this thesis, we are not concerned with the possibility or probability of its realization in a particular form and in the short, long or very long run. The reader is simply referred to what has already been said about the morally *insuperable distinction*, in questions of life and death, between the legitimation of Government and its legitimacy in the ultimate judgement of the human conscience.

It must also be borne in mind that personal development, the freedom of persons fulfilling their potential in the context of the values to which they subscribe and which they experience in their actions, is one of the mainsprings of all forms of development.

When these *explicitly* normative presuppositions, derived from experience, are accepted, the inescapable conclusion is that the World State could be as brutal and as deadly – albeit in other ways – as the national state we know. The hypothetical operations of a world army or police force necessarily involve reference to the mentality of the rulers who would control their use and to the ideals in conformity with which they would take their decisions. The combination of intellectual and moral values is unavoidable; they are in fact the basis of approximations to legitimacy and of acquiescence in the decisions of the legitimate authority.

There can be no foreseeing the course of history, and the more or less plausible scenarios put forward are pitifully mediocre. Unblinkered analysis of the facts of world history and of the present state of the world seems at least to indicate the general line of humanly acceptable research and the *direction* of the multidimensional, overall development of each person and of mankind as such.

The order envisaged in people's minds assumes a *comprehensive purpose* and a *common plan*.

It is this endeavour, supported by immense forces all over the world that forbids us to 'dismiss' as 'Utopian' the three grand designs outlined below.

Popular Mobilization of Resolve and the Formation of Public Opinion

The countries subscribing to democracy in the West have all the necessary means of informing their citizens and inducing them to desire less of a contradiction between the values they profess and the things they actually do. The general policy and the content of education and teaching bear a large share of responsibility here and leave much room for improvement.

Structural Reforms in Consumption, Production and Distribution in the Developed Countries and the Developing Countries

We know that, if the former consumed less meat and alcohol, the latter would be better off. We know that, for any action on an effective scale, the developed countries would need to shift the emphasis in production towards essential goods. We know that the distribution of wealth and incomes is open to much criticism in both groups of countries. What is lacking is the will to carry out the necessary changes and to overcome the inertia of structures.

The Strategy of Gradual, General and Controlled Disarmament[4]

The re-allocation – in accordance with procedures already studied – of even a modest fraction of what is expended on the preparation and perpetration of collective slaughter would change the face of the world. Mankind will indeed have to choose between the propensity for 'legitimized' murder and the propensity for saving human lives, in other words, a preference for life.

Such major offensives do not remove the necessity for the patient and gradual elimination of injustice in the basic communities and in daily life. It is in the minds of a few that the greatest currents of human thought take shape, but the desire to harm or to save may spring up in the minds of all.

Having taken as my subject the new approach to development considered as inseparable from the new international economic order, I did not start out with the idea that these sets of demands represent wild fancies or monstrous deviations that can be discounted, being condemned by a proper analysis of 'normal' economics, the economics at present practised, taken to be the only possible economics and supposedly controllable by the prevailing orthodoxy.

The growing consciousness of development and of underdevelopment has helped us to understand that the dominant theory is implicitly normative; it is constructed *by* and *for* the world's most developed nations and, owing to the inadequate spreading of surpluses throughout the people of a nation or the peoples of the world, this theory works preferentially and cumulatively to the advantage of 'the upper part of society' (John Stuart Mill). It imposes the law of ability to pay and of the market on populations seeking to meet their needs and to achieve some of their aspirations.

I have not regarded the new development movement as representing a catalogue of demands drawn up, with the exaggerations usual in such cases, for the purposes of argument in negotiations. Even if some people have such an intention and it can be discerned in some overstatements, the movement, itself associated with *a period of the history of mankind*, seems to me to be consonant with a broadened spectrum of economic considerations, backed by new analytical instruments. The leading formulations and models are applicable to structures, to sequences of structures and to what are termed human variables, observable or latent. The energy productive of change inherent in the agents, the people capable of transforming their environment, is central to the regeneration of general economic theory. These are, I believe, indisputable and encouraging signs. Case studies, statistics and special, well-delimited econometric exercises are necessary but must be *placed in context* in order to nurture economic thinking. Accurate detail is one thing; rigour is another. It calls for a general interpretation, basic knowledge and the conscious and pondered acceptance of the paradigm from which the algorithms and calculations are derived.

For the rest, since I can obviously do no more than suggest guide-marks here, I have indicated a few ways in which the new economic theory ties in with developments in science and philosophical reflection.

Since the century before last, the philosophy, whether explicit or not, in the study of societies and their economic aspect has been a philosophy of Nature. This was at first interpreted in the light of theological conceptions and ideas of providence and expressed, from Newton onwards, as a kind of mechanistic social physics. The laws of nature may be discovered but their operation must be suffered without any hope of controlling them. When the philosophy of Enlightenment began discussing human nature, after abandoning the providential interpretation, it branched out along paths where it finally came up against the choice between total, incurable scepticism and the strict determinism which excludes objectives and purpose.

Some major aspects of science and philosophy in the twentieth century are profoundly changing our intellectual atmosphere and seem certain to influence that body of gradually organized and verified branches of knowledge that we over-optimistically refer to as the human *sciences*.

If man is programmed, and the programming includes the possibility of learning, we are very far removed from the deterministic materialism propagated by nineteenth-century scientism. If the most recent thermodynamics is right in its teaching about constructive-dissipative structures, the world and man are not condemned to evolve towards chaos.

As for contemporary philosophy, no one can fail to be impressed by the force with which some of its schools have extolled creative freedom and the virtues of action which brings about a practical synthesis of the intellect, the imagination and the aspiration of every human being to be of value. These statements, understood by all and spontaneously appealing to the oppressed and the unfortunate, are in line with the hopes and endeavours of the new approach to development.

These are merely partial indications – proposed staging-posts – and calls to send the mind adventuring forth.

They warrant our accepting the viaticum offered us by André Mayer[5] at the end of a very fine exposition in which, beyond the Great Work of Nature, he affirms his faith in the Great Design of Man.

Notes

1. Perroux, François. 'Critique de la raison économique et raison statistique', *Hommage à Mgr H. Van Camp*, Brussels, 1976. Chanier, Paul. *La critique de la raison économique*, doctoral thesis (typescript), Paris, 1972.

2. Saint-Sernin, Bertrand. *Le décideur*, Paris, Gallimard, 1979. Krishna, Daya. 'Culture', *International Social Science Journal* (Paris, Unesco), Vol. xxxix, No. 4, 1977. Ibrahim, Saad Eddin and Hopkins, Nicholas S. (ed.). *Arab society in transition. A reader*, American University in Cairo, 1977. Cazeneuve, Jean. *Les rites et la condition humaine*, Paris, Presses Universitaires de France, 1957. Ruyer, R. *Le monde des valeurs*, Paris, Aubier, 1948.

3. Perroux, François. *Masse et classe*, Paris, Casterman, 1972.

4. Myrdal, Alva. *The game of disarmament. How the U.S. and Russia run the arms race*, New York, Pantheon Books, 1977. Myrdal, Gunnar. 'The equality in world development', Nobel lecture, 17 March 1975, in *Swedish Journal of Economics*, Vol. 77, 1977. *Asian drama; An inquiry into the poverty of nations*, A Twentieth Century Fund Study, New York, NY, Vintage Books, 1970.

5. Mayer, André. *Nourrir les Hommes*, Brussels, 1964. UNESCO. *Birthright of Man*, a selection of texts prepared under the direction of Jeanne Hersch, Paris, Robert Laffont, 1968: French and Spanish editions available. Lacroix, Jean. *Le désir et les désirs*, Paris, Presses Universitaires de France, 1975.

APPENDIX: MODELS – THEIR LIMITATIONS AND THEIR PROPER USE

The intuitions underlying the new approach to development spring from experience of reality and prompt action. They all run counter to the static expression of growth in orthodox economics. This is amply demonstrated by the implications of the new development (see Table A.1).

Table A.1: Implications of the New Approach to Development

1 Concepts	2 Implications	3 Formalizations

DEVELOPMENT	(a) – Evolution
	 – Structures
	 – 'Activity'
		(a') – Linked growth rates
		    of sectors in
		    irreversible time
		 – Consequent structural
		    shifts

GLOBAL	(b) – The whole unit – Each of its aspects	(b') – Sets – Spaces – Partition – Topology
ENDOGENOUS	(c) – Self-reliance 'from within'	(c') – Human variables – Power

INTEGRATED	(d) – Interconnection
	    of structures
	 – Consistency of
	    structures
		(d') – Power
		 – Systems approach
		 – Cybernetics

It may be wondered, then, whether the new approach to development can ever lend itself to formalization, mathematical expression and even modest quantitative treatment of projects and plans.

Is not the new approach to development, on the other hand, quite in keeping with the changes already initiated in the types of mathematical tools used by the economist? May it not therefore throw some light on the serious difficulties encountered by economic thinkers and on the soundness of the most recent research?

Do not the developing countries rightly demand some relaxation of the restraints imposed by narrow theories and market analyses, arbitrarily disconnected from the dynamic forces of history and consequently mutilated and severed from human agency? Are not the formalizations and mathematical expressions applied to economics gradually being improved as allowance is made for long-neglected variables and relationships, some of which are in fact implicit in the new approach to development?

In preparing to provide answers to these questions, we shall consider:

The mathematics of general interpretation
The formal representation of action
The extension of cost-benefit analysis
The models 'of' the Club of Rome and reports 'to' the Club of Rome
National plans and world models.

This review will be followed by a brief assessment of the limitations and the proper use of modelling.

The Mathematics of General Interpretation

The most notable change has been the shift from the somewhat discredited mathematics taken over from Lagrange's classical mechanics to topological mathematics, following G. Debreu and K.J. Arrow.

The former describes the movement in space of indeformable *objects* and their halting (point of equilibrium when two equal and contrary forces are applied to them). The latter admits of spaces lending themselves to contraction, expansion and deformation and representing the operations of economic *agents*; it describes the successive equilibria while setting limiting conditions; it amplifies all the models of monopolistic competition, while retaining all they have to teach us.

Furthermore, in close conjunction with this change, probabilistic and stochastic models are preferred to deterministic models.

Probabilized spaces afford an opportunity for testing in the economic field the various contentions advanced in connection with subjective and objective probability (R. Radner, K.J. Arrow, P.

Massé, H. Savage, N. Georgescu-Roegen, J. Lesourne). This was bound to be so once the economist had elected to refer to irreversible time, introducing novelty, and attempted, without so far entirely succeeding, to gain control over uncertainty and risk.

The needs and aspirations of differentiated and unequal economic agents are not spontaneously inter-compatible. Operations projected and operations effected involve intersections, once allowance is made for systems of monopolistic competition. *Conflict* has been introduced into present-day theory following the work of Oskar Morgenstern and J. Von Neumann on games.[1] Marked progress has been made in formalizing it (Martin, Shubik, Schleicher) to the point of including sequential games and even (Marchi) struggles making for change in the rules of the game. Nash's model,[2] which, in cases of duopoly, makes a distinction between equilibrium under threat and equilibrium after agreement, or models of games with superadditive properties (C. Dagum) highlight the usefulness of agreement as a means of transcending struggle.

The systems approach at all levels (micro-unit, industry, economic groups) takes advantage of the representation of directed paths (graphs) (J. Lesourne, R. Vallée, F. Lemoigne, Ponsard, R. Lantner, J. Gazon, M. Mougeot); it also assists in representing the hierarchical interconnections of subsystems and their control.[3]

Cybernetics (following such classic writers as Norbert Wiener and C.E. Shannon, O. Lange, Louis Couffignal and G.T. Guilbaud) sets out to study organized systems including a target function and admitting of feedback.[4]

Information theory draws on the present forms of mathematics and is introducing new elements into all areas of economic thinking (Jacob Marschak, R. Radner, Octav Onicescu).

The thermodynamic analogy, used cautiously and in a strictly scientific way, provides the basis for models of equilibrium which allow for differences of size among units, complex units, intensive and extensive variables and the coupling of these units with a 'reservoir' of money or resources (model of A.L. Lichnerowicz).

The analogy, used under the same conditions of scientific control, suggests the desirability of drawing upon the constructive–dissipative structure models put forward by Ilya Prigogine and the Brussels school.[5]

The underlying key idea is that of an evolution which may lead to metastable states of matter and energy, far removed from the equilibrium position. Provided that purely verbal transpositions are rejected, it opens the way to research on *physical* (N. Georgescu-Roegen), *biological* (Atlan) and 'informational' (O. Onicescu) entropy-negentropy and to the study of their consequences in economic and social systems.

No informed observer can stand in doubt about the extent, direction and nature of the progress made as a result of these formalizations. They are quite distinct in nature from the mechanical equilibria of things, of inert objects; they set out to reproduce more pertinently the networks of projects and operations of the *agents*, the *active* units, and of the struggles–synergies and situation of conflict and co-operation between the units and their alliances or coalitions.[6]

They describe structures acting upon other structures; they begin to satisfy the 'demand' of the components of development for representation (see Table A.1: 2(a), 3(a′)).

Instead of applying solely to individuals, to individual units and to goods taken *ut singuli* and tied down to the rudimentary sequences of comparative static analysis, recent analyses use the necessary instruments to arrive at combinations of units and sectors (matrices) and the way they are connected (transition matrices), with the possible inclusion of asymmetries (diagonalized matrices). What is more, a bold conception – which is still, for the time being, mainly speculative – situates the matrices of successive dates in vector or tensor spaces where they are deformed (Guiseppe Palomba, Cherubino). This clearly involves integrating into an evolutive representation the parts in the whole (see Table A.1: 2(b) and 2(b′)).

The application of economic spaces, taken in their three canonical forms (space as a structure, polarized space, space as the content of a plan) and combined with the spaces relating to functions (decision-making spaces, operational spaces) makes it possible to describe the heterogeneity of a territorialized structure fairly accurately and opens the way to formalized representation of the 'nation' (see Table A.1: 2(c) and 3(c′)).

Furthermore, all the mathematized expressions of asymmetry, organization (Herbert Simon) and decision-making, mainly multiple-criteria decision-making (Bernard Roy), lead to the formalized approach to the interconnection of powers (see Table A.1: 2(d) and 3(d′)).

We thus have a whole set of references which, within the limits laid down, are sufficiently numerous, precise and systematic to warrant an overall judgement: the mechanics of general equilibrium is losing ground to more relevant, more flexible and in a sense more complex and sophisticated formalizations, covering the agent, activity and the structures of agents and activities, which are consequently suited on the face of it to those forms of global, endogenous, integrated development which are intuitively demanded by the developing countries.

This judgement is borne out by consideration of formalizations with a more specific object.

The Formal Representation of Action

Optimization, in its present forms, is connected with the work of L.S. Pontryagin on optimal processes, which gave rise to *optimal resource allocation*, as the most general representation of the combination of means calculated to achieve a target, a desired result, in the course of irreversible time.[7]

The target function is expressed in irreversible time (t), for a period (O,T), as a combination of *allocation variables* (u) and *variables of state* (x). A functional expression of the variables (vectors) of state (the 'x's) and of the variables of allocation (the 'u's) for the period considered is processed. The problem is stated in 'Lagrangian' terms with $m + n$ unknown $(nx + mu)$.

This gives us:

Target function

$$J(\vec{x}, \vec{u}) = \int_0^n L(\vec{x}_{(t)}, \vec{u}_{(t)}) \, dt$$

These limiting conditions or equalities must be satisfied by the x (t) and the u (t):

$$\overset{\circ}{x}i - fi(\vec{x}(t), \vec{u}(t), t) = 0$$

Using these equalities with Lagrange's generalized multipliers and appropriate transformations the optimal allocation variables can be expressed as a function of:

1. variables of state

2.   multipliers
3.   time

$$u_i = \varphi i\,(\vec{x}_i, \lambda \vec{1}, t) \quad i = 1, 2 \ldots m$$

This results in a system of differential equations in x and in λ and, for the extreme conditions, determinate solutions.

This formalization provides a perfectly general expression of activity, namely the *linking*, in irreversible time, of the intentional operations of an agent or *actor* who sets himself a target and makes allowance for changes in the states he observes. The means are adapted by the agent to the modifications of his environment.

It would be hard to imagine a sharper contrast with the robot of the classical market which, in the midst of identical units like itself, is subject, in common with all the others, to the rule of prices, with no other possibility of reaction than adaptation through quantities.

The major company capable of modifying its environment is clearly of paramount importance when it comes to interpreting the development of the developing countries.

Such a company does not regard its environment – people and things – as parametric but indeed as malleable, ready to be shaped to its advantage by its own operations. It does not simply make use of the *selling costs* which concern the market but has an intervention budget which enables it to act upon its natural environment, upon its competitors. upon the trade unions and even upon the rules of the game laid down by the public authorities. It may thus be said to incur *environmental transformation costs*.

The target of the major company is expressed as the discounted value of the flow of profit it sets out to obtain during a period:

$$\Pi\,(to)$$

It is a function of:

the volume of the product (output), Q
the price of the product, P
strategic expenditure on transforming the environment, S
time, dt

This gives us:

$$\Pi\,(\text{to}) \;=\; f\,(Q,P,S)\; dt \tag{1}$$

And with the inclusion of the discount rate ρ:

$$\Pi\,(\text{to}) \;=\; \int_{o}^{n} \epsilon - \rho t\; f(Q,P,S)\; dt \tag{2}$$

This formula, attributable to A. Jacquemin, can be developed, applied to private units and to public units, and amplified by specification of the environmental transformation*s*. Through comparison of several mutually incompatible target functions, the conditions of conflict between major companies in a situation of oligopoly or of dominant positions can be analysed.

Like any model, that of the active major company is only a *guide* in seeking to understand the world of action. 'Logic enters into the world of action only through the will of the real decision-makers', according to Bertrand Saint Sernin, and there is always a considerable gap between the 'real decision-makers' and the 'abstract decision-makers'.

The Extension of Cost-benefit Analysis

Cost-benefit analysis was first used to shed light on decisions relating to a specific project. In the classic case of the construction of a dam to provide hydro-electric power and at the same time to allow of irrigation, three sorts of costs and benefits were distinguished: those of construction, those of the use by the people concerned of the electricity and water, and the more indirect items connected with improved sanitation in an area (recovery of lost man-days). Such evaluations, of course, are based on the discount rate. In the early stages it was often proposed that the third level, relating to better health conditions and the likely gains in hours worked, could be left out of account.

The analysis has since been extended to such areas as hygiene, health, education and transport. The object nowadays is to cover an entire developing country (*country specific project evaluation system*).[8]

One example among the most striking may give a clearer idea of such extensions.

Because the introduction of science and technology is decisive for the developing countries, let us take the example of Research &

Development, which will clearly show up the limitations of the method.

To apply cost-benefit analysis to R & D, it would be necessary to *define the operation*, and to *attribute specific costs* and *specific benefits* to it.

In the case considered, it is practically impossible to define research. The scientist carries his investigation into a field that he does not seal off *a priori*; he feels his way forward by a series of tentative efforts, each suggesting the next; he revises his plans as they proceed; and he sometimes finds something quite different from what he was seeking. In the case of a new method or a new product, it should be noted that the operations associated *ex ante* with this success are included in broader conditioning sets without which success would not have been possible. The frontiers of the operation therefore remain hazy.

The calculation of *costs* is, incidentally, barely possible, for the simple reason that we can never know *whether* and *when* research will lead to anything, or exactly how far the result obtained tallies with the result desired.

So far as *benefits* are concerned, it should be noted that private economic benefit differs in nature from social benefit, and that the devices recommended for evaluating the latter by means of *shadow prices* are derived from information somewhat arbitrarily carried over from private markets.

We may therefore legitimately doubt whether it is possible to follow the *subsequent* costs and benefits of a research operation and to valuate *beforehand*, with all the desirable exactitude, the comparative merits of several research projects.

These reservations also apply to the use of cost-benefit analysis in a variety of fields.

For our purposes, the extension of cost-benefit analysis for programmes *concerning the structure of an entire country* is the most significant (*country specific project evaluation system, modular country specific system*). In this area, extensive and remarkable work has been done by teams from OECD, the United Nations (UNIDO – United Nations Industrial Development Organization) and the World Bank.

A recent case study on Peru, by Daniel M. Schydlowsky, deserves attention.

The concentration of industrial and commercial resources in the conurbation of Lima and its port of Callao is such that the area accounts for over 60 per cent of all the country's labour and bank deposits. With the exception of mining, fish-meal production and processing industry *points*, the north and the south of the country are very underdeveloped. Most Indians speak neither Spanish nor any other vehicular language. Changes of government have been far-reaching, engendering a policy receptive to foreign capitalism, following on a socialist-inspired mixed economy policy.

In dealing with such an unevenly developed economy, any calculation presupposes the establishment and discipline of a macroeconomic framework for the global structure. Traditional optimization demands are inevitably abandoned in favour of those still conventional second-best solutions which are never in any case directed against the market economy and capital, from which they are in fact derived.

In these circumstances, the expert accepts the permanence of structures; he takes it that fundamental changes in structure are impossible 'in the foreseeable future' and that, since investment projects cannot be worked out by reference to savings, they should be left to the discretion of 'financial capital'. *Once these conditions are accepted*, 'calculations' of production and consumption functions can proceed apace.

A method of this kind, when compared with the demand for a new approach to development, has much to teach us.

It throws a harsh light on the dependence of the developing country and the weight of external constraints. It explains why populations rise up against the almost intolerable severities of the market-based and capital-based economy. It takes no account of autonomous structural reforms and the requirements of self-reliance.

The technical sophistication of these methods must not lead us to overlook the fact that it is decided in advance not to overstep certain limits; they are effective from the point of view of the profit economy and serve a specific policy, the very policy indeed against which the demand for a new approach to development is directed.

The frontier between the possible and the impossible has, however, often shifted in the course of history, irrespective of the most reliably grounded forecasts.

The Models 'of' the Club of Rome and Reports 'to' the Club of Rome

The Directions of Evolution

There can be no doubt that the most recent formalizations of exploratory econometrics are designed to lead to an understanding of structures and their linking in time (see Table A.1: 1(a, a')), seek to take account of human variables (see Table A.1: 3(c')) and describe structural interconnections (see Table A.1: 2(d)).

Those who come to mind here are J. Tinbergen, who introduced the causal chain system (1937, 1951), W. Leontief, who launched input–output analysis (1941) which has gradually been amplified and made more dynamic, T. Haavelmō, who introduced the idea of interdependent systems (1943), and Hermann Wold, who, from 1950 to the present day, has built up original contributions centred on forecasting; all specialists are familiar with his Janus factor, his fix point theorems and his recent NIPALS (non-linear iterative partial least squares approach) models which admit of indirectly observable latent variables and represent a move towards soft modelling.[9]

These achievements, even in the countries that are richest and best equipped with specialists and statistics, have by no means yet brought about any far-reaching practical change in economic policy. They needed mentioning for the attention they accord to multidisciplinary patterns and to the action and reaction of structures during the course of time, or in other words for the fact that they go beyond summary and far from clear views on *growth* and pay more heed to *development*.

Another sign of the times is to be found in the *World Reports of the Club of Rome*.

Their very existence is evidence of the fact that thoughtful people now appreciate that the fate of nations depends today on world conditions and that the 'planetary economy' and the 'economy of the world as a whole' – bringing in the cosmos since the conquests of outer space – are not notions devoid of meaning.

The earlier of these reports are significant as counter-demonstrations in regard to our subject; the later ones are good examples of the attention being devoted to the new conception of development.

The first report, produced by J.W. Forrester and his team, considers those natural resources which are, in the long run, becoming depleted (coal, oil), evaluated for the earth as a whole, together with four world flows: population, investment, investment for agriculture, and pollution. Each is accompanied by indicators of change, with rates qualified as 'normal' for the period 1960–70. Multipliers are applied to the flows, linking them with operations that increase them (e.g. for the population flow: food and living standards) and with others that reduce them (e.g. overpopulation and pollution). From a conventional 1970 base year, the computer plots *paths through to the year 2100*.

Hence a number of hypotheses and supposed results:

1. No change in 1970 – Exhaustion of natural resources.
2. Investment up by 20 per cent in 1970 – Disaster in the year 2000.
3. Drastic reductions in 1970 in investment, the birth rate and the use of natural resources – Stability of the world system round about the year 2000.

These grouped *projections* attracted scathing criticism. What is the *meaning on a world scale* of flows of investment, population and food? How are these drastic reductions, without which the world is apparently heading for disaster, to be distributed? What is the operational worth of the multipliers used? Is this an instance of *persuasive* econometrics? This seems to be the view of Denis Gabor (Nobel Prize for Physics, 1971) and it is also the conclusion reached in a detailed and far-reaching study by the University of Sussex.

Any reader can appreciate that these projections take no account of explicit changes in institutions and the rules of the game and that, for each nation, the margin of possibilities clearly does not depend solely on global conditions but on the strategy the nation *may* adopt towards its *principal partners*.

The second *Report for the Club of Rome* attempts to remedy the shortcomings of the first.

It arouses concerns when it suggests, right at the start, that traditional values are, ultimately, responsible for our misfortunes, and regrets that man imposes his own will on nature and intervenes in the course of natural selection. This passage may well be dedicated to the developing countries, which are so rightly concerned with the idea of self-reliance, served by institutions tending to make full and worthwhile use of human resources.

The second *Report* divides the world into ten major regions and puts forward scenarios accompanied by figures for the period 1975–2025.

As an example, let us take South–East Asia and the relationship between population and subsistence requirements.

Scenario 1, the 'standard run', points to a huge food deficit and concludes that the countries concerned will be quite unable to *pay* for their imports.

Scenario 2, building on the same general assumptions, adds strict rationing and points to *catastrophe* in the form of widespread famine.

Scenario 3, where agricultural investment is not accompanied by industrial investment, suggests *disastrous* results.

Scenario 4, with fertility balanced over 15 years, points to extensive malnutrition unless recourse to *paid* imports becomes possible.

Scenario 5, presupposes *stringent* birth control. Given this and with the collaboration of all countries (Eastern Europe included), South–East Asia makes good its food deficit and gets its balance of payments into equilibrium as a result of appropriate industry and competitive exports.

To the tragedy which has been unfolding in that region of the world since 1975, a rereading of the second *Report* perhaps adds another tragic observation, namely that some Westerners do not concede the possibility of organizing the market economy differently in the interests of saving vast numbers of people who stand in danger of death.

The most recent *Reports* 'to' the Club of Rome, since the RIO one (Reshaping the International Order), bear witness to a shift of emphasis conducive to a new approach to development on a worldwide scale.

Integration is now coming to be regarded as the interconnecting of the nations and 'regions of nations' which go to make up the community of the earth's inhabitants. Serious threats impose on the latter an obligation and a duty to learn, to think about others, and to regulate production and consumption in accordance with standards laid down for mankind as a whole.

The development recommended is *global*; it puts technology back among the intellectual, social and moral disciplines of human communities. The fact of the planet's becoming a whole, without an 'external' sector in the sense of the current theory of international trade, lends greater topicality than ever to Henri Bergson's views on societies which are starting to open up and on the surge of generous anticipation which is now already bearing the open society, in intention, to the very limits of humanity.

Here, backed by scientific surveys, we have the condemnation of the senseless waste of resources characteristic of the most industrialized societies; technological progress geared to the absorptive capacity of the less-developed societies; acknowledgement that the real limits to growth are 'political, social and administrative' rather than technological; and the rediscovery of 'morality' and 'ethics', after the eclipse they suffered under the influence of shortsighted scientism and blind trust in 'neutral' market forces.[10]

The exercise of the computer and the prescriptions of world ethics brings sharply to the fore self-reliant development policies involving direct contact with actual people, their land and their traditional mores.

Critical Analysis of Projections

All the foregoing studies rest on projections, and it is the *quality* of the projections that matters.

So far as we know, the properly *predictive* value of roughly quantified models in any country whatever is very slight. When the supervisory services compare the *ex post* results with the expected results, disappointments are the rule. The statistician, the social accountant and the economist try to work their way round the impossibility of a *forecast* in the strict sense of the term; they set out to procure mutually compatible items of information that may provide some guidance for the *trial and error* of action. To be quite precise, varied–object projections should be reasonably consistent with one another, but all the phenomena they are meant to cover proceed in irreversible time, and we have neither tested *dynamic laws* nor usable *probability* factors for any of them.

'Population' projections, 'economic' projections and 'social' projections, when these distinctions are taken in their usual acceptation, overlap with one another.

The distinction between them is consequently conventional and liable to be extremely misleading.

Another point resulting is that we have not the necessary well-tried material and preliminary studies to identify them scientifically and arrange them intelligibly with the appropriate weightings.

We aim at *anticipation* rather than at projections, the two being clearly distinct from one another. The prospect we outline should make us modest, even so far as the term 'significantly grouped projections' is concerned.

It is therefore worth while to consider the *overall* effort so as to gauge the limits of the present results and attempt to extend them by securing further documentation and working on it.[11]

This observation, while holding good for the countries long since developed, is very much more relevant in the case of the developing countries, considered in their own particular circumstances.

'Population' Projections.[12] Details of the methods recommended by United Nations experts can be obtained from basic documents. The analytical assessment of results drawn up by experienced demographers of continental Europe and recently published are no less worthy of attention.

So-called population forecasts are regarded as the object of the most soundly-based studies. When *direct*, they are based on fertility and mortality. When *derived*, they are founded on a great many other factors such as the labour force participation rate and head of household rate based on sex, age and marital prospects groupings.

At the outset, the basic components and quality of *censuses* are decisive and leave much to be desired everywhere. The United Nations takes the ten-year yardstick for distinguishing the short and the long term.

Beyond ten years, groupings and behaviour patterns cease to be stable. The population projections for Europe made in the 1960s proved wrong with regard to fertility. The 1976 world survey on fertility in the developing countries showed an appreciable (Peru) or very marked (Colombia) downward trend.

None of the classic methods is satisfactory. Linear projections, by its construction, fails to show fluctuations. Exponential projection depends on the choice of the exponent and suffers from the same shortcoming. Logistic projection would assume knowledge of the long-term trend, the inflexion point (or area) chosen, and the logistic point at which the population is situated at the time of an observation. The only remedy – and a makeshift one – is the *periodical revision* of *long-term projections* by calculations over shorter periods, taking account of fresh developments. This is in fact the method used by the United Nations, and it is significant that the revisions are now carried out every *two* years instead of every *five*.

The basis provided by 'population' projections is therefore

uncertain, and this uncertainty has repercussions on the subsequent operations attempted with these projections as the starting-point.

'Economic' Projections. These consist in ascribing to a growing population values for product, income, consumption and savings (investment). A choice has to be made between one or the other of these quantities, evaluated in average terms (which in the case of heterogeneous populations is misleading) or calculated by means of appropriate weightings (which, even for developed countries with an abundance of statistics, presents major difficulties). What was said above about the non-stability of behaviour patterns over time is still, quite obviously, no less relevant here.

In the field of production, major innovations (labelled strategic innovations) are imported into the developing countries as required for the purposes of the programmes of foreign corporations, without there being any possibility of establishing a clear-cut, univocal relationship between this policy and the specific features – either recorded in the past or anticipated – of the populations of the recipient countries. Examples that come to mind are the consequences of the introduction of nuclear energy and data-processing in the enclaves of transnational corporations and in urban environments.

Input–output matrices with fixed or approximately fixed coefficients represent no more than a tabulation of questions. In trying to answer those questions, we have no theory, nor any sound analysis of the notion of *propagation* in a given space of time, on which to work.

Wassily Leontief's matrices have the advantage of being simple. They do not yet take account of the most recent advances in analysis, as they are to be found, already formalized, in the remarkable studies of Leif Johansen.

It would, furthermore, be dangerous for the developing countries to base their economic policy on the projection of matrices which, on account of the coefficients fixed, reflect a situation of *technological stagnation*.

Special studies on the evolving structures of the leading sectors, even if not tied in with the whole system, represent desirable means of adjustment.

From the standpoint of the whole system considered and the operational consistency of evaluation, we can only regret the inadequacy of statistical multipliers. They are a convenience but nothing more. The underlying models derived from Keynes or the post-Keynesians scarcely provide a suitable basis for any meaningful guidance system.

For want of anything better, it will be worth while to try to rectify them by quantitative analysis – in special cases – of the propulsion effects exerted at the input and output stages (H.B. Chenery) by grouped and growth-inducing investments. The tactical idea is always to escape the limitations of mechanical projections by revealing their shortcomings at *particular points* and thereby paving the way for operation dynamization of the whole.

'Social' Projections. J. Bourgeois-Richat, by applying analysis to a flow table, has established that the relationships between demographic phenomena and economic phenomena are so complex that *no available census* provides a key to their comprehension. What, then, can be said about the projections made on the basis of censuses? The two functions of production and consumption are not strictly interrelated: 'There is a risk that a population will wish to consume (much of) what it cannot produce', whether or not there is any regulation by foreign trade and migrations.

J. Bourgeois-Richat goes further and asks for 'sub-populations' to be taken into account. Extending population analysis, he urges the desirability of statistics of the number of individuals who, during a given period – 'in the course of one year for example' – 'experience a major difficulty necessitating action by society'. Those concerned are handicapped children or those abandoned by their parents: orphans and those not fitting into the normal education system; and, among the economically active population, the sick, the victims of accidents and the undernourished.

A fresh population analysis is therefore required. It adds tragically to the burden of military expenditure and abates the unconscious optimism, based on statistical gaps, to which we are a prey when we calculate or project such quantities as output or productivity for a set or a sub-set.

The Lack of Clarity about how Projections are Inter-related. The distinction between the 'population', the 'economic' and the 'social' series is necessary for the purposes of analysis. For the time being there is a measure of *obscurity* about it which distorts projections and the interpretations offered of them.

Statistical gaps and imperfections make the underlying models even more unreliable. Drawn up under the impetus of Keynesian economics, by and for the developed countries, these models essentially take account of investment and multiplier mechanisms; they are quite unattuned to the concepts and linkages necessary for understanding and assessing the implications of development for the populations undergoing it.

National Plans and World Models

If it is to be effective, development policy must be able to count on sustained effort by the nation as a whole. Development planning, taken here, as previously, on its own, is, in contrast with totalitarian planning, 'indicative' or 'active' planning of the French type.[13]

Such a plan is, in brief, the quantified scheme of the *desired structure* (Jean Weiler) for the nation, at the end of a five-year period for example, put into effect by consistent measures designed to encourage or to curb specific activities or operations.

This type of plan presupposes correct quantitative description of the economy, combined projections of its probable evolution, a statement of mutually compatible objectives, the combination of which will provide the desired structure, choice of the corresponding means and monitoring of their interconnections.

The success of the plan thus hinges on interchange between the planner and the model-builder; its improvement depends on communication between the programmes for the parts and the preparation of the programme for the whole.

In France, for instance, after the establishment of a projection of economic activities for the nation as a whole, efforts were directed to the building of multisectoral models: the physical–financial model (FIFI, R. Courbis), the dynamic multisectoral model (DMS model, Fouquet) and regional models (REGINA, R. Courbis). In its rudimentary forms, the development plan enables 'blocks' of variables and means to be set up; in more sophisticated forms, it *would be* a supremely suitable instrument for promoting the new approach to development.

It would be so *if* the national authority were competent and vigorous enough to arbitrate between the interests of categories from the standpoint of the entire nation. In the developing countries, such authority is slowly emerging, with irregularities and regressions; it is groping towards effective exercise in the difficult dialogues of international organizations and through the formation of independent political elites capable of calling forth the solidarity of populations who are learning, not without difficulty, the disciplines of nationhood.

The development plan provides a means of assessing the obstacles to achievement of the new sort of development.

A plan for *global* development must theoretically cover the variables of health, hygiene and education – the very ones which, even in the developed countries, give rise to the greatest difficulties as regards their strict evaluation and their association with the variables relating to material goods.

A plan for *endogenous* development is based on the identification of potential human resources, divides responsibilities between self-reliance and international collaboration, seeks to grade regional projects and national objectives, and establishes permanent communication between a downward and an upward flow of information, representing not merely the transmission of orders and reactions to those orders but also a circuit of trust between governors and governed.

An *integral* development plan meshes together external trading and the internal system of production, trade and distribution. At best, by means of domestic and imported industry, it organizes propulsion effects on local agriculture. It distinguishes between products and techniques suited to the populations concerned and those imports which are held to be undesirable because they estrange and set apart from the bulk of the people a handful of indigenous beneficiaries.

It is an imposing programme, 'spelt out' as it were in the special studies of experts and independent researchers and properly appreciated by the most clear-sighted of the political leaders when they rise above personal or party bickering. It is salutary to present it in epitome, however remote it may be from the capacity of the 'soft states' (Gunnar Myrdal) at grips with the superpowers acting through intermediary nations and their own major companies.

The latter are indeed sometimes (as in the case of particular South-East Asian countries) invited to choose locations for their establishment which are consonant with the development plan of a developing country; on occasion they may have to accept the host country's capital participation – which, incidentally, in no way entails its control over subsequent operations.

Despite persistent efforts, alliances and coalitions among the developing countries, their dealings with the developed countries are governed by the balance of power.

If real national situations from the point of view of the new approach to development are to be properly understood, a decision must be made between the two general views given below, the choice of one or the other influencing the gathering of statistics and model-building.

Either economics involves nothing more than the *market* and comes down to the balancing of prices and quantities on perfectly communicating markets of goods and services – in which case the conclusion of the analysis *must* be that the nation is an accident of history tending to thwart the regular operation of the world market.

Or economics involves *organization* of the struggle against scarcity. It makes use of the organized market among other sorts of institutions such as the tax system, the monetary authorities and all the public services. Market operations are in this case inconceivable without *extra-market operations*.

The nation becomes an organized system of powers for the purpose of maintaining social cohesion and increasing the collective benefit to its members. Viewed in this light, the nation as an economic reality is:

(1) a *reservoir of social and economic externalities*;
(2) a form of *mixed economy*, by construction;
(3) a *cultural identity* and a *cultural heritage* which, through the motivations they arouse, contribute to personal fulfilment and may increase economic returns.

Being interested in the new type of development, the developing countries are inclined to adopt the second of the standpoints outlined above; they act as though the political order in the broadest sense possessed a *multidimensional* (and of course economic) efficacy.

Groupings of nations (e.g. common markets and economic communities) have been preceded and are guided by statistical studies of the short-term situation, by medium- and long-term forecasts and by operational models. The difficulties encountered in elaborating and using such devices stem from the unequal propensity of the parties to communicate information and from the inadequate international comparability of data. For the developing countries, the scarcity of statistical material, the extent of subsistence production and consumption, and the limited number of specialists, are handicaps which make national accounting and the technical handling of the relevant data particularly difficult.

Within a particular developed nation, regional accounting systems, though progressing, are so behindhand that their practical use is limited. Attention may be drawn at this juncture to a contradiction that is theoretically revealing, and insufficiently highlighted by statistical documentation, between the region taken as a territory and the region regarded as the area of influence of a leading centre, such as an industrial centre.

The field of the global 'world models' is that showing the clearest convergence between the demands of the new approach to development and the requirements of the scientifically controlled economy.

The term global refers to:

(1) all the variables which have to be taken into account in development and therefore those concerning the human being (health, hygiene and education), and all the ecological variables as well;
(2) all nations and regions of the world.

A programme on such a grand scale calls for sustained effort over several generations; it should be hailed as a landmark in the annals of mankind. For the first time in all human history, we command the economic resources to achieve those rational and religious ideals which have for so long been doomed to be no more than Utopias or wishful thinking. The huge industrial machine serving science and technology prompts the gathering of worldwide and, wherever possible, quantified documentation. At the same time, it throws into the effort the powerful resources of the computer and information science.

Several channels are already being opened up where use is being made of general–systems representation and simulation models. One method is to start from a nation and simulate the alternative international environments associated with a policy (cf. the METRIC model in France). Another is to take existing models of national economies and seek to express the international links between them (cf. the LINK Project – Linkage of National Economic Models – with which the name of Lawrence R. Klein is associated).

A more directly global approach, centred on development policy, underlies the remarkable work of A.K. Sundaram and J.G.

Krishnayya (Systems Research Institute, India), Vladislav Tikhonirov (UN Institute for Training and Research, New York) and N.N. Moiseev (Computer Centre of the USSR Academy of Sciences, Moscow), in conjunction with M. Medow (York University, Toronto).

Quite apart from their intrinsic merits, world models of this kind can be credited with broadening intellectual horizons by way of reaction against the 'narrow', pseudo-exact school of economics which does not *locate* its models. The models extend and refine the qualitative representations of the natural and human economic resources of the planet, which have haunted the imagination of all universalisms up to the time when they could be gradually formalized and subjected to machine calculations.

The approaches represented by mathematical formalization and modelling are in line with the requirements of the new form of development, which calls for a restructuring of the world 'whole', the 'world system'; it aims at the interconnection of parts, of structured sub-sets, and dialectical interchange between them; it is deliberately centred on man, whom it apprehends in his individual reality and in his relationship with the environment. These are the actual lines along which the latest statistics, projections and models have moved forward.

The legitimate enthusiasm generated by the models produced in such numbers throughout the world and in all international organizations cannot, it seems, yield lasting results unless care is taken not to nourish illusions.

Mention may be made in passing, without stressing it too much, of the monopoly-seeking, rigid compartmentalization and tendency to ostracism to be observed among some specialists. This attitude may be forgiven when the specialist field is truly erudite; it is less excusable when it involves would-be initiation and promotes a certain esoterism without being too sure of its tenets. 'Without models there can be no hope of salvation', that is, no reliable economic thinking!

But if theoretical and practical economics had to be based *solely* on tried and tested models, economic life would come to a halt. Its quantitative formulations are derived from observation of facts and from the observer's hypotheses. As the work proceeds, these hypotheses become crystallized and refined or are even transformed through judicious use of the tool provided by mathematics;[14] but scientifically-minded economics, because it is empirical as regards its object, seeks to start from reality and to lead back to it.

Something more elusive is the misuse of insufficiently reasoned modelling. The model-builders would, in this case, offer the developing countries a model based on the experience of the developed countries and designed to serve their interests, meaning in practice the interests of their ruling classes. The mere mathematical expression of economic concepts and the ways in which they are arranged does not automatically safeguard them against the danger of being implicitly normative; they tend to be in such a case regarded in fact as norms, which will be accepted uncritically by the less informed countries even though they are ill-suited to their economic and social structures.

Lastly, we may say that the more satisfactorily irreversible time is taken into account, the harder it is to incorporate in a model all the variables on which the functioning of an economy may depend, or to make an objective choice of the variables whose presence and effect are decisive.

These epistemological reservations are not directed against the use of mathematics or of models; they are merely intended to indicate some of the bounds beyond which the model-builder's approach would be under suspicison of unduly diminishing the scope and fruitfulness of scientific reasoning.

Notes

1. Morgenstern, Oskar and Neumann, J. Von. *Theory of games and economic behaviour*, 3rd ed., New York, NY, John Wiley & Sons, 1967. Burger, Ewald. *Einführung in die Theorie der Spiele*, Berlin, Walter de Gruyter, 1959. Duncan Luce, R. *Howard Raïffa, games and decisions*, London, John Wiley, 1957. Schotter, Andrew and Schwodianer, Gerhard. 'Economics and game theory. A Survey', *Economic Literature*, June 1980.

2. Nash, F.J. 'The bargaining problem', *Econometrica*, 1950. 'Two-person cooperative games', *Econometrica*, January 1953.

3. Makinson, David C. *Topics in modern logic*, London, Methuen, 1973. Lions, J.L Inaugural lecture at the Collège de France, Chair of Mathematical Systems Analysis and Systems Control, 1973 (booklet). For an excellent introduction, see Vallee, R., 'La théorie des systèmes', *Pour la Science*, No. 19, Pay 1979. Delattre, P. *Système, structure, fonction, évolution*, Paris, Doin, 1971. Kornai, J. *Anti-Equilibrium*, Amsterdam, North Holland Publising Co., 1971. Lesourne, J. *Les systèmes du destin*, Paris, Dalloz, 1976. Walliser, B. *Systèmes et Structures*, Paris, Editions du Seuil, 1977. Lemoigne, J.L. *La théorie du système*

général, Paris, Presses Universitaires de France, 1977.Kramer, Nic J.T.A. and De Smit, Jacob. *Systems Thinking*, Leiden, Martinus Nijhoff, Social Sciences Division, 1977. Simon, Herbert A. 'La science des systèmes, science de l'artificiel', *EPI*, Paris, 1974. Nordmann, Ramiro Campos. *Cibernética y planificación económica*, Ediciones Pirámide, Madrid, 1975. Mesarovic, M.D., Macko, D., Takahara, Y. *Théorie des systèmes heiérarchiques à niveaux multiples*, Paris, Economica. French translation by Jacques Eugène, with a foreword by Jacques Lesourne.

4. Guilbaud, G. Th. *La cybernétique*, Paris, Presses Universitaires de France, 1954. From the same publishers, Couffignal, Louis. *La Cybernétique*.

5. Glansdorf, P. and Prigogine, I. *Structure, stabilité et fluctuations*, Paris, Masson et Cie, 1971. Prigogine, Ilya and Stengers, Isabelle. *La nouvelle Alliance. Métamorphose de la science*, Paris, Gallimard, 1979.

6. Perroux, François. *La rénovation de la théorie de l'équilibre économique général*, *Recherches interdisciplinaires*, Paris, Maloine, 1977. Palomba, Guiseppe. *L'espansione capitalistica*, 2nd ed., Naples, Giannini, 1968. *Lezioni di economica matematica*, Rome, Liguori, 1973. *Tra Marx e Pareto*, Naples, De Simone, 1980.

7. For further details see Perroux, François, 'La notion de "dépense stratégique" et l'unité "active"', *Cahiers de l'AFEDE*, April 1979. Jacquemin, Alexis. 'La firme et son environnement industriel. Une relation dynamique' In *Hommage à François Perroux*, Grenoble, Presses Universitaires de Grenoble, 1978. Perroux, François. *Les entreprises transnationales et le nouvel ordre économique du monde*, with an introduction by G. Blardone, Director of the Institut de sciences sociales appliquées, and D. Dufourt, Professor at the University of Lyons II, Centre Croissance des Jeunes Nations, Lyons, 1980.

8. Schydlowsky, Daniel M. 'The design of benefit-cost analysis of investment projects in Peru', *Industry and Development*, No. 2, United Nations, New York, NY, 1978. 'Plans et projets spécifiques du développement', *MED*, No. 16, 1976. Sterpi, Severino. *Lo sviluppo dell'analisi costi-benefici e la crisi dei valeri del libero mercato*, Milan, A. Giuffré, 1974.

9. Wold, Hermann. *Open-path models with latent variables, the NIPALS approach. Soft modelling: intermediate between traditional model building and data analysis*, University of Uppsala, Department of Statistics, 1977–8. 'Mathématiques d'interprétation générale. Mathématiques d'exploration empirique. Mathematiques pour la politique économique', *Economie appliquée*, special issue, Nos. 2, 3 and 4, 1973. Dagum, Camilo and Dagum, Estella. 'Construction de modèles et analyse économétrique', *CISMEA*, E.M. Series, No. 5, 1974.

10. Cole, H., Freeman, C., Jahoda, M, Pavitt, K. *Thinking about the future. A critique of the limits to growth*, London, Sussex University Press, 1973. Gabor, Dennis and Colombo, Umberto. *Beyond the age of waste. Fourth Report for the Club of Rome*, 1976 (French edition translated by M.A. Revelet, Paris, Dunod, 1978). Meadows, D.L., Behrens III, W.W., Meadows, D.H., Naill, R.F., Randers, J., Zahn, E.K.O. *Dynamics of growth in a finite world* (French edition prefaced by Joseph Fontanet, former Minister, Chairman of the Club of Paris, Paris, Economica, 1977). Also useful is *Le défi économique du tiers monde*, Paris, La Documentation Française, 1978 (2 volumes).

11. Tinbergen, Jan (co-ordinator). *The Rio Report. Reshaping the International Order: a Report to the Club of Rome*, French edition, SNED, Paris, Dunod, 1978. Brandt Commission. *North–South: A Program for Survival. The Report of the Independent Commission on International Development Issues under the Chairmanship of Willy Brandt*, Cambridge, Mass., MIT Press, 1980. *A new world employment plan*. A Proposal by J.M. Tinbergen, J.M. den Vyl, J.P. Pronk and W. Kok, mimeographed papers, The Hague, 29 October 1980.

12. This critical analysis of projections is among the latest works by M.

Bourgeois Pichat of the Institut National des Etudes Démographiques, Paris.

13.   Ullmo, Y. *La planification en France*, Paris, Dalloz, 1974. Perroux, François. *Les techniques quantitatives de la planification*, Paris, Presses Universitaires de France, 1965.

14.   Hadamard, Jacques. 'An essay on the psychology of invention in the mathematical field' (French edition translated from the English by Jacqueline Hadamard, Paris, Albert Blanchard, 1959), Princeton University Press, 1948.

INDEX

212   *Index*